Indian Secularism

T0341926

Indian Secularism

A Social and Intellectual History
1890–1950

SHABNUM TEJANI

Indiana University Press
Bloomington & Indianapolis

This book is a publication of

Indiana University Press
601 North Morton Street
Bloomington, Indiana 47404-3797 USA

http://iupress.indiana.edu

Telephone orders   800-842-6796
Fax orders   812-855-7931
Orders by e-mail   iuporder@indiana.edu

The paper used in this publication meets the minimum requirements of
American National Standard for Information Sciences—Permanence of Paper
for Printed Library Materials, ANSI Z39.48-1984.

Manufactured in the United States of America

Cataloging information is available from the Library of Congress.

ISBN 978-0-253-35256-9 (cl.)
ISBN 978-0-253-22044-8 (pbk.)

1 2 3 4 5   13 12 11 10 09 08

Contents

II: COMMUNALISM

III: SECULARISM

MAPS

Acknowledgements

The debts I have incurred in the years it has taken me to bring this book to completion are many. The book grows out of my doctoral work at Columbia University and so my first debt is to my supervisor, Ayesha Jalal. Ayesha has been friend and mentor over many years. The intensity of her intellectual engagement as well as the affection underlying her belief in this work is a lesson I aim to take forward. Ayesha has engaged with this project at all stages. I hope she sees her imprint on it. Thanks also go to David Armitage, Talal Asad, Dennis Dalton, and Nicholas Dirks, with whom I had the privilege of working for some time. Each of their contributions enabled me move the project forward.

I am grateful to the staff at libraries in India and Britain from which I drew the material for this study: the National Archives of India and the Nehru Memorial Museum and Library in New Delhi; the Maharashtra State Archives, the Deputy Inspector General's Office, Bombay University Library and the Asiatic Library in Mumbai; the Oriental and India Office Collections in London; and the library of the Centre for South Asian Studies in Cambridge. Conversations with scholars in India in the initial stages of research helped formulate my methodological approach: Mushirul Hasan, Asghar Ali Engineer, the late Ravinder Kumar, Y.D. Phadke, Asiya Siddiqi, and the late Rafiq Zakaria.

I received support from a number of different sources to pursue this project. I would like to acknowledge, in order of receipt, a multi-year fellowship from the History Department at Columbia University, a junior research fellowship from the American Institute of Indian Studies, an alumni grant from Oberlin College, a travel grant from the Old Bancroftian's Association, a Whiting dissertation writing fellowship from Columbia University, and a fellowship from the Arts and Humanities Research Council in Britain which my employing institution, the School of Oriental and African Studies (SOAS), very generously agreed to match.

The research time in India was perhaps the most enjoyable part of this process. But it would not have been as productive or rewarding had it not been for the many people who generously took me into their homes. In Delhi, my cousin Anis Raza and her family took care of me in the way that only family can. I also befriended Kavita Misra. I am especially grateful to her parents, Soumendra and Chandramohini Misra, who have taken me in and treated me like a daughter on many occasions. I was equally fortunate in Bombay. Despite many other pressing demands, Indubhushan, Indira and Mona Doctor welcomed me into their home for several months and on many subsequent visits.

I am lucky to have colleagues and friends with whom I have been able to talk through many of my ideas and from whom I have learned immensely. Daud Ali, Chetan Bhatt, Durba Ghosh, Sangeeta Kamat, Biju Mathew, Rajit Mazumder, Ali Mir, Sanghamitra Misra, Anu Needham, Rochelle Pinto, Subir Sinha, Deborah Sutton, Mridu Rai, Siddharth Varadarajan, and Rashmi Varma among others have provided an engaging intellectual environment over the years. Peter Robb and Tom Tomlinson at SOAS read the dissertation and provided invaluable advice on how to find the book that was buried in there. Many thanks go to Rukun Advani for believing in this book and for going above and beyond the call of duty to ensure its production was as rapid and wrinkle-free as one could ever hope.

In the solitary endeavour of writing, one becomes acutely aware of the importance of friendship. In this, my acknowledgements go to Aaron Agnee, Naomi Burns, Valerie De Cruz, Anene Ejikeme, Nelida Fuccaro, Shaalan Farouk, Amy Hsi, Sangeeta Kamat, Emanuelle Kihm, Biju Mathew, Rachel Mattson, Carol Miles, Kavita Misra, Joey Mogul, Renu Nahata, Sonali Sathaye, Sam Shinn, Mohan Sikka, and Vinay Swamy for their unswerving affection and for providing welcome distraction from my work. Thank you to Mike Spencer for teaching me the importance of non-intellectual work. My debt to John Parker is of a different order. Without his encouragement, advice, and critical editorial interventions, the book would have been far less than it is.

My greatest acknowledgement, however, is to my family, for without them this would not have been possible. In particular, my thanks go to my two aunts, Malika Amin and Gulbanu Mavany; my mother Sakkar Tejani; and my brother, Abbas, who have always provided a loving environment and a sane perspective. It is to my mother that I dedicate this book.

Glossary

Adivasi	term for India's tribals
Anjuman	an association, usually of Muslims
Arya	here refers to Indo-European tribes who are meant to have invaded the Indian subcontinent around the second millennium BC
Bahujan Samaj	Marathi phrase, loosely meaning 'the society of the majority', commonly used to denote Dalits in the Hindi belt
Bania	term used for members of castes associated with commerce, trade, or moneylending
Bhadralok	'decent folk' (Bengali); educated high-caste Bengali Hindus
Bhatia	Bania trading caste from Gujarat
Chaturvarna	the system of the four varnas (see varna)
Chitpavan	a subcaste of Brahmans from the Konkan; the caste of the peshwas, who played an important role in Maharashtra as governors and administrators
Dalit	Marathi/Hindi term meaning 'the oppressed'; term for untouchable groups, now used in preference to the Gandhian appellation 'harijan'
Dar-ul-harb	Arabic term meaning 'land of war'; a territory in which the sharia is not

	observed and in which, according to classical Muslim jurisprudence, believers should choose between jihad and hijrat
Dar-ul-Islam	Arabic term meaning 'abode of Islam'; a territory in which the sharia is observed
Deshastha	Brahman caste of Maharashtra
Deshmukh	Marathi term for the head of an armed elite family vested by Maratha rulers with authority over a grouping of villages; a revenue official under the British
Gaorakshini Sabha/ Gorakshak Mandali	association for cow protection
Harijan	term coined by M.K. Gandhi for the untouchable castes, usually translated as 'child of God'
Hartal	work stoppage or strike
Hindutva	a right-wing ideology of 'Hinduness' advocated by Hindu nationalist organizations; term coined by V.D. Savarkar in 1923
Inam	heritable emolument granted by the state; usually tax-free land
Jagir	land grant; the right to collect state revenues from a specified area which was often given in Mughal times in lieu of a salary
Jagirdar	one who has been given a jagir
Jazirat al-Arab	lit. 'land of Arabia'; during the Khilafat movement this reference was to the holy places of Islam
Jnati/Jati	an endogamous caste or subcaste generally
Julaha	see *Momin*

Karkun	member of the police constabulary
Karsevak	activist of a Hindu nationalist organization
Khaddar	homespun cloth; an important symbol during the Swadeshi movement and later
Khalifa	'Caliph'; successor to the Prophet Muhammad as head of the Muslim community, and up to 1924 the sultan of Turkey
Khilafat	institutionalized spiritual and temporal authority over the Muslim community
Konkanasth	'one from the Konkan coast'; Konkanasth Brahman is used interchangeably with Chitpavan
Kshatriya	the second of the four varna divisions of Hinduism. In theory, Kshatriyas are rulers and warriors
Kunbi	general Marathi term for a common peasant farmer
Lohana	a bania caste of Gujarat
Madrasa	a secondary school or college for Muslims
Mahajan	lit. 'great man'; in Maharashtra, a hereditary officer in a village; a Gujarat trade guild
Mahar	a caste of untouchables; Maharashtra's largest such caste
Mali	a caste of fruit and vegetable growers to which many members of the Satyashodhak Samaj belonged
Mamlatdar	government official, responsible for collecting the revenues of a district
Maratha	the dominant peasant caste of Maharashtra; also used as 'Maratha-kunbi' to denote an individual of lowlier status than the *assal* or genuine Maratha

Marwari	native of Marwar in Rajasthan; Marwaris settled throughout India as merchants and bankers
Maulana	title usually applied to an alim, but, during the Khilafat movement, also assumed by, or given to, leading Western-educated Muslim politicians
Maulvi	term used for Muslim religious teacher versed in Arabic and Islamic law
Mofussil	term here for the rural hinterland of Bombay; also generally for that of any large city
Mleccha	derogatory term used for foreigners or non-Aryans
Mohulla	division or quarter of a town
Momin	weaving caste from the United Provinces that migrated to several parts of India after the revolt of 1857, derogatorily referred to as julaha
Muharram	the first month of the Muslim year; during the first ten days of this month Shias mourn the deaths of the sons of Ali
Murid	disciple; follower of a Sufi pir
Padamsali	weaving caste from Hyderabad
Peshwa	term for Chitpavan Brahman ministers who served Shivaji's descendants, eventually exercising power in their own right
Pir	spiritual guide, religious preceptor, a Sufi or descendant of a Sufi saint; in Sind, powerful landholding religious figures associated with Sufi shrines
Ryot	peasant cultivator

Sabha/Samaj	Marathi terms for an association or society; also common in the Hindi belt
Sanatan Dharm	orthodox Hindu observance; also denotes the average person's everyday practice of Hinduism
Sangathan	Hindu unity
Sangh Parivar	the 'family' of Hindu nationalist organizations
Sardar	man of consequence; 'chief' (used as honorific)
Satyagraha	lit. 'the way of truth'; form of political agitation based on moral pressure pioneered by Gandhi
Sayyid/Saiyid	descendant of the Prophet Muhammad; more generally denotes Islamic nobleman
Shastra	general term for the Hindu institutes of religion, law, or letters
Shastri	one versed in the shastras
Shet	merchant, banker, trader; often used as honorific; in nineteenth-century Bombay a shet was the head or leading member of a trading body or caste, exercising authority over them in matters of business and caste
Shetia	the head of a caste or trading body, distinguished by great wealth; also, in nineteenth-century Maharashtra, the official who regulated the traffic of a market town
Shuddhi	'purification'; reconversion to Hinduism of those who embraced other faiths
Shudra	the fourth of the four varna divisions of the caste system, which provides in theory servants and labourers to the other three varnas

Swadeshi	lit. 'own country'; home industry; early-twentieth-century nationalist campaigns featuring the boycott of British goods
Taluka	subdivision of a district
Tanzim	consolidation; Muslim efforts to resist the Shuddhi movement
Twice-born	denoting upper caste, usually Brahmans, whose male members are ritually invested with the sacred thread, signifying their second birth
Ulema	(sing. *alim*) scholars of Islamic jurisprudence; learned men
Vaishya	the third of the four varna divisions, whose members in theory supply the material wants of Hindu society as merchants and traders
Vaniya	members of a high-status caste grouping traditionally associated with commerce
Varna	one of the four hierarchically arranged categories into which all Hindus, with the exception of untouchables, are in theory divided
Zamindar	loosely used term for landowner, large or small

Abbreviations

Bo Judl Procd Confdl	Bombay Judicial Department Proceedings, Confidential Branch
BPCP	Bombay Presidency Confidential Proceedings
CAD	*Constituent Assembly Debates*
CSAS	Centre for South Asian Studies, Cambridge
CSSH	*Comparative Studies in Society and History*
CWMG	*Collected Works of Mahatma Gandhi*
EPW	*Economic and Political Weekly*
IESHR	*Indian Economic and Social History Review*
JAS	*Journal of Asian Studies*
JD	Judicial Department
MAS	*Modern Asian Studies*
MSA	Maharashtra State Archives
NAI	National Archives of India, New Delhi
NMML	Nehru Memorial Museum and Library, New Delhi
OIOC	Oriental and India Office Collections, London
SAPI	Secret Abstracts of Police Intelligence for the Bombay Presidency
SRB	Selections from Records for the Bombay Presidency

Introduction

'Secularism is dead', the eminent Indian public intellectual Ashis Nandy announced at a conference in 2002.[1] The proliferation of fundamentalisms—Christian, Muslim, and Hindu—across the globe would appear to prove him right. The idea of secularism emerged in early modern Europe as an ethics of behaviour and a prescription for political organization that promised to supersede the violence and irrationality that seemed inherent in collective forms of religious expression. It prescribed a separation between the institutions of church and state—between religion and politics—and signified 'toleration' for societies that had been riven by religious conflict. For the individual, it delineated the world into private and public arenas with activities appropriate to each.[2] That the point at which individuals consigned religion to the realm of private faith and became secular citizens in a rational world would mark the pinnacle of human history was an idea that had become almost common sense. But the so-called resurgence of religion in many parts of the contemporary world has profoundly challenged this certainty. Flying in the face of the secularization thesis, increasingly widespread technological sophistication and democratization have been accompanied by religious movements—Hindu nationalism and political Islam in particular—and have served

[1] 'Siting Secularism' conference, Oberlin, Ohio, 2002; published as 'Closing the Debate on Secularism: A Personal Statement', in Anuradha Dingwaney Needham and Rajeswari Sunder Rajan (eds), *The Crisis of Secularism in India* (Durham, NC 2007).

[2] See Talal Asad, *Formations of the Secular: Christianity, Islam, Modernity* (Stanford, 2003), pp. 1–15; J.R. Jakobsen with A. Pellegrini, 'World Secularisms at the Millennium', *Social Text*, 64, 18, 3, Fall 2000; Peter van der Veer, *Imperial Encounters: Religion and Modernity in India and Britain* (Princeton, 2001).

them well.[3] That religion has not receded from the public sphere should give us pause. Not because of the 'failure' of societies to modernize, but for what it might say about the very categories of modernity—secularism and religion—and the historical processes they are supposed to encompass.

This book is a study of the historical emergence of the idea of secularism in India. Secularism in the subcontinent was an inextricable part of the nationalist self-conception at Independence, and has remained central to subsequent debates about citizenship and belonging in the postcolonial state. It signified all that was enlightened and integrative within a modern society. The Indian constitution enshrined freedom of religion as one of its core principles, but the practise of religion was to be personal and private. The public presence of religion, 'communalism', it was adamantly stated, would not be entertained any further. There was no place in the new democracy for the ascriptive identities of sect and caste that had dictated the outlook and aspirations of so many for so long. Closely tied to definitions of nationalism, communalism was secularism's opposite—regressive, atavistic, fragmentary—and was thus seen as the antithesis of Indian nationhood.

As a postgraduate student looking to write a paper on modern India, I was struck by how ubiquitous and vehement was the insistence, in the journalistic and scholarly literature as well as amongst my friends, that India was a secular nation. This was barely three years after the 1989 Mandal Commission recommended a dramatic increase in reservations in education and employment for people from 'backward' classes, a move that prompted the self-immolation of protesting Brahman students in Delhi. Four years earlier, in 1985, the Supreme Court

---

[3] See Birgit Schaebler and Leif Stenberg (eds), *Globalization and the Muslim World: Culture, Religion and Modernity* (Syracuse, 2004); and Chetan Bhatt, 'Democracy and Hindu Nationalism', *Democratization*, 11, 4, August 2004. On the secularization theory, see Steve Bruce (ed.), *Religion and Modernization: Sociologists and Historians Debate the Secularization Thesis* (Oxford, 1992); and André Béteille, 'Secularism and Intellectuals', *EPW*, 29, 10, 1994. The theory has been largely discredited for its teleological assumptions. For critiques, see Jose Casanova, *Public Religions in the Modern World* (Chicago, 1994); and Talal Asad, 'Religion, Nation-State, Secularism', in Peter van der Veer and Hartmut Lehmann (eds), *Nation and Religion: Perspectives on Europe and Asia* (Princeton, 1999).

ruled that Shah Bano, an aged Muslim woman who had been divorced by her husband, was entitled to maintenance payments to prevent her from becoming destitute. The ruling challenged the practice of Muslim customary law, provoking a furore among a conservative leadership that saw this as a threat to the integrity of the community. Prime Minister Rajiv Gandhi overturned the ruling for his own political ends, but in doing so also acknowledged the right of a religious community to a public presence, and for its self-appointed representatives to speak on behalf of all its members.

On the heels of Mandal came the rise of the Bharatiya Janata Party (BJP), the political wing of the Sangh Parivar or the 'family' of organizations propagating an ideology of Hindu nationalism (Hindutva). In the run-up to the 1989 elections, L.K. Advani, president of the BJP, dressed as the Hindu god Ram, led a garish rath yatra around the country in a Toyota converted to look like the deity's chariot. Advani was collecting bricks to build a new temple on the site of the Babri Masjid in Ayodhya (built in 1528) that the BJP claimed was the site of an earlier temple and the birthplace of Ram. The 1989 elections saw the BJP win enough seats in the Lok Sabha (lower house of parliament) to become part of a ruling coalition. Two years after Advani's chariot voyage, the largest Sangh organization, the Vishwa Hindu Parishad (VHP) or World Hindu Council, together with the BJP, escalated the campaign in Ayodhya. On 6 December 1992 some 300,000 VHP karsevaks (activists) dismantled the mosque, brick by brick, in the space of five hours. In the weeks that followed Bombay experienced some of the most devastating violence between Hindus and Muslims that the country had seen since Independence. From where I was standing in February 1993, India looked anything but secular.

The events at Babri Masjid and the riots that followed shocked the world. Postcolonial India had long been held up as a political success story. The world's largest democracy, whose citizens enjoyed freedom of speech and religious tolerance, was seen to have escaped the military dictatorships and sectarian conflicts that had been the fate of so many ex-colonial states. The violence of 1992 appeared to many in the Western media as the resurgence of internecine rivalries, evidence that Indians had failed in the task of overwriting their sectarian affiliations with a national identity. The electoral successes of the Sangh Parivar caused great alarm in India in liberal circles. How could such religious hatred take root? The state of secularism in India became a subject of vigorous debate. These debates turned on the binary ideas of secularism and communalism, modernity and religion. Liberal scholars and social commentators argued that communalism had brought about a crisis of secularism, and needed to be opposed in all its forms. In a reflection of a broader debate, many in India maintained that the persistence of communalism represented the failure of Indians to modernize adequately and of religion to take its proper place in the private sphere.[4] Others, in contrast, argued that secularism had a history rooted in the West and represented a mode of social relations unsuited to the particular traditions of India.[5]

There is something unsatisfyingly circular about such arguments and the simple binaries on which they are founded. Both positions employ secularism and communalism as analytical tools with which to understand religious identity, sectarian conflict, and the problems of 'integration' in a liberal democratic state. Yet each reifies these categories: they share the premise that 'secular' and 'communal' have a meaning in themselves, one that transcends historical context. As a result, events as distinct as the Partition of India, the opposition to a Uniform Civil Code in 1985, and the destruction of the Babri Masjid have been brought together under the rubric of communalism and understood as the problem of religion in a modern society. But as this category is universalized, it is simultaneously depleted of analytical value. The circularity of much of the contemporary debate has to do with the way in which secularism and communalism have been treated as hermetically sealed, universal categories. It is this that has allowed them to be locked in binary opposition.

I argue that a consideration of the historical dynamics that shaped the meaning of secularism allows us to approach this problem anew. Secularism is not a stable, predetermined, universal category, but one

[4] See Asghar Ali Engineer, *Communal Challenge and Secular Response* (Delhi, 2003), and Amartya Sen, 'Secularism and its Discontents', in K. Basu and S. Subrahmanyam (eds), *Unravelling the Nation: Sectarian Conflict in India* (Delhi, 1996).

[5] See T.N. Madan, 'Secularism in its Place', *JAS*, 46, 4, 1987; and Ashis Nandy, 'The Politics of Secularism and the Recovery of Religious Tolerance', *Alternatives*, XII, 1988, both reprinted in Rajeev Bhargava (ed.), *Secularism and its Critics* (Delhi, 1998).

whose meaning is particular to its historical context. This book shows how secularism came to be bound up with what it meant to legitimately call oneself 'Indian', and why this genealogy of nationalist belonging was so imbued with a language of religion. Through narratives of six historical moments, beginning in the late nineteenth century, I examine how an ideology of secularism emerged in the midst of changing ideas of nationalism and communalism in the sixty years that preceded the ratification of the Indian constitution in 1950.

It was not until well into the 1940s, when India was on the cusp of Independence and Partition seemed a foregone conclusion, that the term secularism began to be used in Indian political discourse. Given how imbricated it was with Indian nationalist ideology, that it emerged so late in the day should give us pause. What explains its apparently sudden appearance? Or perhaps one should approach the question from the opposite direction: given how embedded religion and the 'religious community' have appeared to be in Indian social and political life, why was it considered appropriate and even desirable for India to be a secular society? These are two separate questions. The first has to do with the emergence of secularism as a political doctrine. The second refers to secularization—a process whereby those activities deemed religious become differentiated from political, economic, and social activity and are confined to their own sphere. This process is seen to mark a change in the self-conception of individuals as well as a new ethics of social interaction. Both, however, indicate the *historicity* of the idea.

Secularism—the idea that was supposed to secure social integration and reflect the universal character of human enlightenment—*is* dead, in India and elsewhere. Not because religion has run rampant in the world, but because the prescriptive and explanatory value that secularism was believed to possess is no longer tenable. Historical research on Europe and North America has shown how differently each society negotiated the question of religion. No single trajectory is visible for how public and private spheres were differentiated, nor is there a uniform understanding of what this meant.[6] There is also increasing

---

[6] See E. Waterhouse, 'Secularism', in J. Hastings (ed.), *Encyclopaedia of Religion and Ethics* (Edinburgh, 1959), vol. 11; Owen Chadwick, *The Secularization of the European Mind in the Nineteenth Century* (Cambridge, 1975); Susan

evidence that people in South Asia, the Middle East, and Africa appropriated the categories of modernity—public and private, religion and
politics, secularism and democracy—in ways that rendered these
meanings particular.[7] This brings us to the current problem: if a universal meaning for secularism cannot be assumed, what did it represent
at the moment of its emergence in India? And what relevance does it
have in contemporary India's political climate?

Debates on secularism in India have largely been conducted in
the predictable forums of elite universities and the English-language
media. But a number of events since the destruction of the Babri Masjid indicate that these are not questions of merely academic or liberal
concern. Reports that began in 1998 of the systematic targeting of
Christian communities—firebombing churches, sexual violence against
nuns, the murder of clerics, the forcible 'reconversions' of Christians
to Hinduism in Gujarat, Rajasthan, Madhya Pradesh, and Orissa—
continue. In February and March 2002 some 2,500 Muslims were
murdered and 200,000 driven from their homes in a premeditated
pogrom in Gujarat. The killings were justified as a response to the
burning of a train carrying Hindus returning from Ayodhya after
placing foundation stones there for a new Ram temple on the site of
the Babri Masjid. Reports from Gujarat well into 2007 indicate that

---

Mendus, *Justifying Toleration: Conceptual and Historical Perspectives* (Cambridge,
1988); Casanova, *Public Religions*; Darrin McMahon, *Enemies of the Enlightenment:
The French Counter-Enlightenment and the Making of Modernity, 1778–1830*
(Oxford, 2001); David Martin, *On Secularization: Towards a Revised General
Theory* (Aldershot, 2005).

[7] See Partha Chatterjee, 'Two Poets and Death: On Civil and Political Society
in the Non-Christian World', in Timothy Mitchell (ed.), *Questions of Modernity*
(Minneapolis, 2000); Aditya Nigam, 'Secularism, Modernity, Nation: Epistemology of the Dalit Critique', *EPW*, 35, 48, 2000; Ayesha Jalal, *Self and Sovereignty:
Individual and Community in South Asian Islam since 1850* (London, 2000);
Mridu Rai, *Hindu Rulers, Muslim Subjects: Islam, Rights, and the History of Kashmir* (London, 2003); T.C. McCaskie, *Asante Identities: History and Modernity in
an African Village, 1850–1950* (Edinburgh, 2000); Yael Navaro-Yashin, *Faces of
the State: Secularism and Public Life in Turkey* (Princeton, 2002); Asad, *Formations
of the Secular*.

Muslims continue to experience fear and intimidation: many are unable to return to their homes, their jobs, and their lives.

A number of factors allow the targeting of social minorities. One is when the idea takes hold that a certain community does not properly belong. Proponents of Hindutva have sought to disseminate the idea that Muslims and, to a lesser extent, Christians are interlopers in Indian society. Muslims, the argument goes, took their place in India illegitimately through conquest. They were never truly loyal Indians—the creation of Pakistan is seen as testimony of this notion. The image of the conspiratorial Muslim, always ready to commit a random act of violence, has fed easily into the current discourse of the 'war on terror'. No longer are Muslims in India Indian; they are seen by Hindu chauvinists as members of a global community of potential terrorists. At no point since Independence and Partition, with the possible exception of 1984 when the Sikh community was targeted in the aftermath of Indira Gandhi's assassination, has the meaning of being properly Indian been so contested. And secularism—so intimately tied to the genealogy of nationalist belonging in India—has been central to this series of contestations. By examining the historical emergence of secularism, this book pries apart the binary oppositions that have framed the debate so far. In so doing it shows the ways in which Indians negotiated and contested ideas of belonging before they were finally distilled in the constitution in 1950. And, in light of contemporary crises, it allows us to reimagine how a just and truly plural society may take form.

The Contemporary Debate

There are four distinct strands to the debate on secularism in India.[8] First, the 'liberal left' position holds that religion and politics belong in different realms. This position saw the rise of Hindutva in the 1980s as a failure of the secular state and of modernization. Religion had not taken its rightful place in the private lives of individuals, and it was the excessive attachment of Indians to their primordial and ascriptive

---

[8] See especially Bhargava, *Secularism and its Critics*; also Prakash Chandra Upadhyaya, 'The Politics of Indian Secularism', *MAS*, 26, 4, 1992.

identities that had prevented the emergence of a civic ideal. For the proponents of this position, secularism represented progress, liberty, and the 'operation of scientific temper and rationality'.[9] However, not all defenders of secularism have embraced the modernization model. Some have argued that secularism is not a Western concept but has a long history in India. This is the secularism-as-tolerance argument which asserts that the ancient history of India demonstrates the inherent secularity of its culture. India, the argument goes, has since ancient times accommodated many different peoples: Aryans, Huns, Turks, Bactrians, Scythians, Persians, and all the rest. Hindu dharma, with its loose, accommodative structure, was able to draw into its ambit the mores of these different people, for it held within it an indigenous concept of secularism, *sarva dharma samabhava*, the idea that all religions are true. Gandhi, most famously, argued that tolerance and the accommodation of difference was a core characteristic of Indian culture.

The second strand is the argument that secularism was never indigenous to India and is therefore inappropriate. This view is perhaps best articulated by T.N. Madan and Ashis Nandy. Madan maintains that Indian religions, specifically Hinduism and Islam, have no history of a Reformation, and have therefore never delineated separate spheres for secular and sacred activities. Any attempt to make them create these discrete spaces would involve an erosion of the uniqueness of Indian culture: 'models of modernization . . . prescribe the transfer of secularism to non-Western societies without regard for the character of their religious traditions or for the gifts these might have to offer. . . . [I]n traditional . . . societies they can only mean conversion and the loss of one's culture, and . . . the loss of one's soul.'[10] What Madan

[9] H.S. Verma, 'Secularism: Reflections on Meaning, Substance and Contemporary Practice', in B. Chakrabarty (ed.), *Secularism and Indian Polity* (Delhi, 1990). There is a vast literature on the subject of Indian secularism that champions this view. See, for example, V.R. Krishna Iyer, *India's Wobbling Voyage to Secularism* (Ahmedabad, 1976); K.C. Chaudhry, *Role of Religion in Indian Politics* (Delhi, 1978); P.C. Chatterji, *Secular Values for Secular India* (Delhi, 1984); Saroj Prasad, *Nehru's Concept of Freedom* (Allahabad, 1989); Sarto Esteves, *Nationalism, Secularism and Communalism* (Delhi, 1996); Sen, 'Secularism and its Discontents'; Engineer, *Communal Challenge*.

[10] Madan, 'Secularism in its Place', in Bhargava, *Secularism and its Critics*, p. 308.

calls the 'recrudescence' of religion in the late twentieth century shows that religion was never going to reside happily in the private lives of Indians, and nor should it. Advocates of secularism in India 'ignored the fact that religion itself could be a powerful resource in the struggle against religious extremism.'[11] Similarly, Nandy sees the project of secularism in India as an attempt to impose from above a model of social behaviour incompatible with the particularities of a 'traditional' society such as India. The attempt represents, he argues, an 'imperialism of categories'.[12] Madan and Nandy both maintain that Indians have practices of tolerance that they can draw on from their own religions. However, in their search for indigenous answers to the problems of sectarianism, they see Indian traditions of tolerance as stemming from what can broadly be called Hindu civilization. In this sense, as Sumit Sarkar argues, this view shares discursive ground with the Hindu Right.[13]

The third position is the one represented by the proponents of a Hindu nation. This holds that any recognition of minorities, specifically Muslims, is 'pseudo-secularism'.[14] This was the charge that members of the Sangh Parivar brought against the Congress Party, arguing that this so-called secular party was pandering to religious forces and bringing religion into politics. Reservations for minorities in civil and educational institutions and concessions to Muslim opinion in the case of Shah Bano were seen as evidence of such pseudo-secularism. This position maintains that a genuinely secular state would not recognize any difference amongst its citizens and that it would treat each as equal before the law. Its position stems from the claim that the norm of Indian civic culture is Hindu. The perspective draws on a history of reformist thought dating back to the nineteenth century that sought to erase claims to difference by appropriating all Indians as basically Hindu. This position shares the secularism-as-tolerance idea that, over thousands of years, migrants, traders, and warriors came to India and became Indian. However, where it diverges is that the accommodative

[11] Ibid., p. 316.

[12] Nandy, 'The Politics of Secularism', in ibid., p. 321.

[13] Sumit Sarkar, 'The Anti-Secularist Critique of Hindutva: Problems of a Shared Discursive Space', *Germinal*, vol. 1, 1994.

[14] See Kajnayalal M. Talreja, *Pseudo-secularism in India* (Mumbai, 1996).

nature of Hindu dharma is seen as a weakness rather than a strength. The tolerance of Indian civilization is represented as naïve innocence; it resulted in Indians falling prey to the proselytizing religions of Islam and Christianity. At the same time, the argument goes that Hinduism retained its qualities of dharmic universalism. Converts to other religions remained in essence Hindu because it was from the same racial and cultural stock that all Indians had emerged.

The fourth position is represented by the political philosopher Rajeev Bhargava, who argues that the discussion of secularism in India has to move beyond the opposition with religion in which it is mired. He reflects that 'the divide between the "secular" and the "religious" is somewhat of an institution in our country' and asks if it is not possible to take the spiritual and ethical elements common to all religions and transpose them into a secular, non-doctrinal framework for behaviour. More specifically, Bhargava asks if there cannot be a 'spiritualised, humanist secularism'.[15] He clearly hopes to be able to incorporate values shared by many religions into the public life of India in a way that could be embraced by all—a sort of secular religion. Interestingly, this suggestion is not very different from that of George Jacob Holyoake who first coined the term secularism in England in 1851. Holyoake also wanted to create an ethic for everyday life that was not irreligious or hostile to religion but was not bound by any particular religious tradition. In this sense, it was a secular, namely *worldly*, ethic.

The apparent anti-modernism of Madan and Nandy, the dharmic universalism of the Hindu right, and the spiritual humanism of Bhargava are all primarily responses to the failure of the liberal ideal that posed secularism as an answer to the problem of communalism. The incongruence between a normative model of secularism and the reality of Indian society prompted either a wholesale rejection of the idea, as with Madan and Nandy, or an adoption of the term by qualifying its meanings. The latter approach has been more common. As the normative model did not appear to correspond with Indian society, India developed *its own* version of the idea: 'Indian secularism'. According to the Hindu right, by pandering to minorities liberals had not properly applied the institutional rules required of a secular state and were

[15] R. Bhargava, 'Religious and Secular Identities', in U. Baxi and B. Parekh (eds), *Crisis and Change in Contemporary India* (Delhi, 1995), p. 341.

therefore 'pseudo-secularists'. For Bhargava the doctrinal intransigence towards religion implied by the term should be forsaken in favour of an ethics of tolerance.

Each employs the term, but, motivated by divergent political agendas, finds three separate meanings for it. The first is a culturalist argument, the second advances a Hindu majority position, and the third finds its place firmly within a liberal framework. That the meaning of secularism can no longer be held to be universal is borne out by these multiple positions. However, the moves to reject secularism or infuse the category with new meaning are inadequate, for even in their critique of the normative category they still reinscribe an idea that there can (and should) be a stable, containable meaning for the term, however defined. Furthermore, the 'many meanings' approach allows wildly contradictory political positions to exist on a level with each other and dissolves into an uncritical relativism: as an 'empty' category devoid of inherent meaning it has been open to appropriation in sometimes cynical ways.

Partha Chatterjee, Neera Chandhoke, and Aditya Nigam are three social scientists who have addressed this ambivalence.[16] Each recognizes the profound intolerances in the normative approach as well as the many blind alleys that the debate has spawned. However, rather than trying to evolve new meanings for it, each examines what secularism has meant in the different circumstances of its contestation. In their own ways, each argues that secularism in India has not had to do simply with the legal contours of separating political and religious institutions, or with the relative degree of religiosity of Indians. Rather, it is closely related to what the recognition of difference—of minority (religious) communities—means for the formulation of a national community within the framework of liberalism. Moreover, by turning the gaze away from the accepted focus on religion, these writers are able to bypass the urge to stabilize and normalize meanings for religion and secularism, and not spiral down the path of relativism. In his argument for a public recognition of religious plurality ('toleration'), Chatterjee

---

[16] Partha Chatterjee, 'Secularism and Toleration', *EPW,* 29, 28, July 1994; Neera Chandhoke, *Beyond Secularism: The Rights of Religious Minorities* (New Delhi, 1999); Aditya Nigam, *The Insurrection of Little Selves: The Crisis of Secular-Nationalism in India* (New Delhi, 2006), chapter 3.

advocates the formation of an autonomous forum that could represent minority religious opinion. In this way, such affiliations would be written into the self-definition of the body politic rather than being subsumed under the rubric of a unitary democracy.

Similarly, Chandhoke contends that secularism in India represented a democratic ethos, albeit one expressing itself in a language of religion. Thus, it was not about finding the right place for religion per se, but ensuring equality for religious communities and defending the rights of minorities. And Nigam, in examining the Dalit critique of secular nationalism, argues passionately against the totalizing nature of normative secularism and the homogeneous empty time in which it exists. The 'immense historical burden' on secularism to create the abstract citizen should be lifted, he argues.[17] In common with Chatterjee, he implies that the nation and its 'little selves' must be seen as inhabiting 'heterogeneous' time.[18]

In arguing that secularism in India can be understood only when situated in the particularities of its historical context, I am not defending simply one more meaning for it, nor do I want to recover a lost or unrealized meaning. Rather, I seek to place myself alongside what I see as these more productive 'critical modernist' approaches. Where I distinguish myself from them is in the need for a longer historical analysis.

The Proposition Encapsulated

What is striking about the growing volume of writing on Indian secularism is its presentism. In part, this is a problem of disciplinary boundaries: in India, 1947 remains the point at which 'history' becomes 'politics'. So, while there has been substantial historical research on nationalism and communalism, this has not been the case with the category of secularism.[19] The debate on secularism has been dominated

---

[17] Nigam, *Insurrection*, p. 172.

[18] Partha Chatterjee, 'The Nation in Heterogeneous Time', *IESHR*, 38, 4, 2001. Talal Asad makes a similar point in *Formations of the Secular*, p. 15.

[19] The number of studies on Indian nationalism is enormous. Some influential works include: John Gallagher, Gordon Johnson, and Anil Seal (eds), *Locality, Province and Nation* (Cambridge, 1973); Bipan Chandra, *Nationalism and*

by sociologists and political theorists who have seen it as a question for the postcolonial state. The absence of a systematic historical examination of Indian secularism can be partly explained by the relatively late appearance of the term itself. However, I suggest here that by the time it became current it was already imbued with the meanings that would come to define it in the following decades. Thus, the emergence of Indian secularism as an idea marked not only the beginning but also the end of a historical process.

Independence can be seen to mark a crucial slippage in terminology: in short, nationalism before 1947 became secularism after. In the two decades before 1947—the period of late or 'mature' nationalism—communalism was the term that stood in for the politics of religious minorities, specifically that of the Muslim minority. Increasingly after 1935, communalism was deemed by those at the centre of mainstream nationalism to be inward looking, anti-national, and, above all, illegitimate. Communalism had become the despised stepchild of nationalism. Most importantly, the latter came to be defined around and through the former; in this sense, as Gyanendra Pandey has argued, they were defined *together*.[20] And these meanings carried over into the postcolonial period. After 1947 the charge of 'communalism' continued to refer to any corporate challenge to the nationalism of the state, but now extended to offensives from regional, linguistic, and caste groupings. But significantly, this nationalism was now explicitly secular nationalism, or secularism. For the leaders of newly independent India, still reeling from the shock of Partition, Pakistan represented the most extreme manifestation of the politics of communalism. It was in

---

Colonialism in Modern India (Delhi, 1979); Partha Chatterjee, *The Nation and its Fragments: Colonial and Postcolonial Histories* (Princeton, 1993). On communalism, see Sandria Freitag, *Collective Action and Community: Public Arenas and the Emergence of Communalism in North India* (Berkeley, 1989); Gyanendra Pandey, *The Construction of Communalism in Colonial North India* (Delhi, 1992); Tanika Sarkar, *Hindu Wife, Hindu Nation: Community, Religion, and Cultural Nationalism* (London, 2001). For a critique, see Ayesha Jalal, 'Exploding Communalism: The Politics of Muslim Identity in South Asia', in S. Bose and A. Jalal (eds), *Nationalism, Democracy and Development: State and Politics in India* (Delhi, 1997).

[20] Pandey, *Construction of Communalism*.

this context that secularism was posed as a truer form of nationalism, the answer to the problem of national integration. In a speech to the Constituent Assembly in 1948, Nehru spoke of how destructive the combination of religion and politics was to such a project:

> The combination of politics and religion in the narrowest sense of the word, resulting in communal politics is . . . a most dangerous combination and must be put an end to. It is clear . . . that this combination is harmful to the country as a whole; it is harmful to the majority, but probably it is most harmful to any minority that seeks to have some advantage from it. . . . [A] minority in an independent State which seeks to isolate and separate itself does some injury to the cause of the country.[21]

This was a clear warning that the communal politics of a minority would never be pandered to. Indians would never again accept such a 'balkanization' of the country, as Nehru called it, as was witnessed in the creation of Pakistan.

Two fundamental contentions lie at the heart of the present book. First, to understand the emergence of the idea of secularism in India, one must move beyond the established concern with religion to a consideration of caste. The ideal of secularism was at the centre of the formulation of the independent state as a liberal democracy. As such it was shaped by the imperative of creating a democratic majority— which in turn relied on the appropriation of 'Untouchables' (Dalits) into an upper-caste Hindu identity.[22] Indian secularism was not simply about a separation of political from religious institutions, or creating a peculiarly Indian ethics of tolerance, *sarva dharma sama-bhava*—the idea that all religions are true. Rather, it represented a formulation of nationalism that involved dovetailing liberal discourses around individual representation with definitions of the democratic majority as broadly Hindu. Moreover, secularism became one of the

[21] Jawaharlal Nehru, *Jawaharlal Nehru's Speeches, Volume One, September 1946–May 1949* (Calcutta, 1949), p. 74.

[22] See Sumit Sarkar, *Writing Social History* (Delhi, 1997), chapter 9; Kancha Ilaiah, 'Towards the Dalitization of the Nation', in Partha Chatterjee (ed.), *Wages of Freedom: Fifty Years of the Indian Nation-State* (Delhi, 1998); Nigam, 'Secularism, Modernity, Nation'; Dilip Menon, *The Blindness of Insight: Essays on Caste in Modern India* (Chennai, 2006).

pillars of Indian nationalist thought because the architects of the new nation-state—overwhelmingly middle-class, upper-caste Hindu men— saw it as providing a counterpoint to challenges posed from the margins by Muslim and Dalit communities.

Second, the idea of secularism took on quite specific historical meanings in the context of Indian politics. Rather than being distinct from community and caste, nationalism and communalism, liberalism and democracy, Indian secularism was a relational category that emerged at the nexus of all of these. The term had meanings that were broadly modern, in the sense that they were contemporaneous with such negotiations elsewhere in the colonial world. Far from being universal, however, those meanings were closely tied to the particular historical contexts from which they emerged and did not replicate the narrative of history as staged in the West.[23]

On Methodology

The term secularism only became current in India in the period of late nationalism. Yet, by the time it entered public discourse it was imbued with the meanings that would come to define it in the postcolonial era. I reconstruct the history of the category of secularism before the point of its emergence. In this sense, it can be seen as a genealogy. Such a project poses a central methodological problem: if a thing does not exist, what does one look for? My contention is that secularism in India, as it existed by 1950, had conceptual preconditions that were situated in earlier histories and on which its meanings relied. These included a transregional notion of Hindu community, ideas of patriotism and who the patriot was, a definition of what constituted communalism, a classification of minority and majority populations, and a notion of citizenship. A genealogy of Indian secularism involves an understanding of these ideas and shows how they evolved according to a particular historical trajectory.

Central to my approach is the idea that political concepts are grounded in, and emerge from, social, political, and intellectual histories. My study is none of these entirely, but draws on the methodologies

[23] Timothy Mitchell, 'The Stage of Modernity', in Mitchell (ed.), *Questions of Modernity*.

of each. Various scholars have elaborated the social, political, legal/ constitutional, and philosophical aspects of secularism in India, but few have sought to understand the relationship between them. For instance, we know very little about mass anti-colonial mobilization and its relation to how India emerged as a democracy.[24] Yet, to fully grasp the breadth and depth of this question, one cannot simply pursue the social, political, or constitutional questions; they have to be understood as bearing on each other. To focus on the social and cultural expressions of religion and the ways in which such collective identities became politicized is a necessary component of my book, but not sufficient to address the question fully. A reconstruction of certain political events and debates, sometimes with the most traditional of methodological approaches, forms an integral part of my project because negotiations over the place that religious and caste minorities could legitimately occupy within the formulation of 'Indian' often took place at the highest levels of politics. But this cannot solely be a history of political machinations. Similarly, it is not an intellectual history in a conventional sense, for, while the writings of nationalist intellectuals are central, it is the ways in which their ideas were read into and out of popular social and political arenas that makes them significant.

My approach takes much from the methodology developed by the theorist of French democracy Pierre Rosanvallon, who writes what he calls histories of 'the political'. As part of this approach, Rosanvallon incorporates materialist and social histories as well as the study of the texts of political philosophy and constitutionalism as objects of historical analysis, but he has a philosophical aim that extends beyond their individual methodologies.[25] 'The political', he argues, is both a field and a project:

> As a field it designates the site where the multiple threads of the lives of men and women come together, what allows all of their activities and discourses to be understood in an overall framework. It exists in virtue of the fact that there exists a 'society' acknowledged by its members as a

[24] Sumit Sarkar makes this point in 'Indian Democracy: The Historical Inheritance', in Atul Kohli (ed.), *The Success of India's Democracy* (Cambridge, 2001).

[25] Pierre Rosanvallon, *Democracy, Past and Future,* edited by Samuel Moyn (New York, 2006), p. 12.

whole that affords meaningfulness to its constituent parts. As a project the political means the process whereby a human collectivity, which is never to be understood as a simple 'population', progressively takes on the face of an actual community. It is, rather, constituted by an always contentious process whereby the explicit or implicit rules of what they can share and accomplish in common—rules which give a form to the life of the polity—are elaborated.[26]

Rosanvallon distinguishes 'the political' from 'politics'. The former refers to the totality of what constitutes political life—'power and law, state and nation, equality and justice, identity and difference, citizenship and civility'—beyond simply political debate, rivalry for position, or the functioning of state institutions; the latter does not compete with the former but is a constituent part of it.[27]

The aspect of the political that Rosanvallon elaborates is that of the history and experience of democracy. His approach is useful in thinking about secularism in India. Secularism represents a nodal point around which the collective rules of postcolonial Indian polity have been articulated. But these articulations are constantly shifting and remain unsettled. Indeed, Rosanvallon maintains that for such concepts this must necessarily be the case. Secularism in India held out the promise of freedom to practise one's religion, of individual justice and representation, of the protection of minority cultures. However, these freedoms were embedded in a regime of power—democracy—and thus the promise was simultaneously conflicted and permanently deferred. This deferral was not the same as an unrealized ideal. The indeterminacy of such concepts as democracy and secularism is, in Rosanvallon's words, 'due fundamentally to their essence'.[28] It is not that secularism is an inappropriate, failed, distorted, or not-yet-realized project, or one in need of redefinition. Rather, the ambiguity is precisely because the promise of freedom and its betrayal are contained within the category itself. In the Indian context, what it meant to be a patriot, how this was conceived of by different individuals and ethico-political communities, how citizenship and the place of minorities were to be defined, are all part of the history of nationalism and

---

[26] Ibid., p. 34.

[27] Ibid., p. 36.

[28] Ibid., p. 37.

were all implied in what came to be called secularism. All these elements were contested and reach much further back than when the term became part of a broader political language. Historical analysis must therefore be at the heart of any attempt to understand what secularism signified at the point of its emergence, how its meanings have since shifted, and why it continues to be so deeply inflected with aspects of both religious identity and national belonging.

The object of histories of the political is to trace what Rosanvallon calls the 'long genealogies' that make such questions intelligible: 'to follow the thread of trial and error, conflict and controversy, through which the polity sought to achieve legitimate form. It consists, in a metaphor, in the publication of the script of the play in which different acts of the attempt to live together have been performed.'[29] It involves the empirical reconstruction of these 'acts', not with the teleological aim of arriving at a stable definition, but to see how riven through with conflict and possibility they were, and to examine why certain definitions came to the fore while others receded and were lost. A history of secularism in India is a history of a pressing contemporary question with profound implications for the contours of the polity, but without an identifiable destination.

This book reconstructs such a history as a series of acts, focusing on six historical moments from 1890 to 1950. I argue that each moment represents both possibility and closure, marking a point when the meaning of a certain political concept crystallized. These concepts include Hindu community, patriotism, communal, communalism, the democratic majority, and secular citizenship. While the chapters take narrative form with regard to the individual historical moments and follow a temporal arc, the book does not trace a single question or follow an obvious narrative progression. Moreover, the historical moments vary quite widely in scope. They focus on popular movements: cow protection, Swadeshi, and Khilafat, as well as key constitutional debates in 1909, 1932, and 1950. Those addressing popular politics have a regional focus (the western regions of Maharashtra and Sind) and draw upon source material that includes pamphlets and newspapers, reports of public demonstrations and riots, and the writings of self-styled leaders and intellectuals. These chapters address the emergence

[29] Ibid., p. 38.

of broad-based patriotisms, and the ways in which nationalism and communalism were defined together through such movements. The chapters that address constitutional questions have no regional dimension and focus more narrowly on the debates themselves. They reconstruct moments in which the concepts of communal, majority and minority, and secularism and citizenship were defined.

Although not limited by regional focus or source material, the chapters are linked conceptually. I argue that the concepts defined in each moment relied on those that had emerged earlier. Thus, the patriotism of the early twentieth century relied on ideas of Hindu community that had emerged at the end of the nineteenth. The use of the term 'communalism' by the late 1920s relied on a meaning for 'communal' that had emerged after 1909. This would seem to imply a causal link between the political categories emerging in successive moments, but this is not my position. For instance, while I argue that the term 'communal' came to refer to the politics of a Muslim minority in 1909 during the debates around Council Reform, and 'communalism' emerged in the aftermath of the mass mobilizations around Non-cooperation and Khilafat after 1924, these are markedly different political arenas separated by more than a decade, and an argument that linked them causally would be tenuous at best. A more productive approach would be to see the concepts defined in each moment as being part of overlapping and intersecting discourses that were not bound by the politics of the region or the personalities involved. Although these political concepts were closely tied to the historical contexts from which they emerged, once their meanings became established people at other historical junctures appropriated these ideas into new contexts where they had the potential to frame, describe, and determine new experiences of social reality.[30]

An evolving terminology and shifts in language are thus an important part of this study, and each chapter pays attention to words and their meanings and how these meanings change. In this, Quentin Skinner's contribution has been instructive. Skinner argues that words are not 'unit ideas', they do not have a 'normal structure', but are bound by an

---

[30] William Gould has suggested something similar in his study of political languages in the United Provinces in the 1930s and 1940s: *Hindu Nationalism and the Language of Politics in Late Colonial India* (Cambridge, 2004), p. 11.

entire network of meanings born of historical experience—social, philosophical, and political. So, when the meaning of a word changes, it changes its whole relationship to this conceptual framework; and where there are disagreements over meaning, these are as much disagreements about our social world itself.[31] Where Raymond Williams argued that language mirrors social reality and social change is reflected in a change in our social vocabularies, Skinner maintains that disputes over the meaning of a term or whether a term properly reflects a particular kind of social behaviour do not give rise to new meanings. Rather, new social perceptions may be generated but the meanings are unchanged. It is only when these arguments fail that new meanings are established and can go on to frame social behaviour and historical experience.[32] Moreover, terms such as nationalism, communalism, and secularism have an evaluative and moral aspect. While they are always disputed, they nevertheless continue to legitimate certain social, political, or ideological practices and also have a profound bearing on how such practices are constituted.[33]

The argument that as a concept crystallizes it not only frames but also delimits the field of possible politics is borne out in many instances through this study. However, when I argue that political concepts are established in a particular historical moment, even at points where such concepts were gaining currency, I do not suggest that these meanings were hegemonic or unchanging. My contention is that the moments examined in each chapter are best understood as creating a political space, a historical possibility. The ideas were more often than not defined in quite narrow contexts: they did not necessarily change the way people lived every day, nor were they acknowledged or embraced by all. But the emergence of these ideas made possible new categories of identity and new understandings of society. As Rosanvallon has argued, such moments represent 'historical nodes around which new political and social rationalities organized themselves.'[34] To begin with

[31] Quentin Skinner, *Visions of Politics, Volume I: Regarding Method* (Cambridge, 2002), chapter 9, esp. pp. 162–5.

[32] Ibid., pp. 166–7. Partha Chatterjee has explored this idea for secularism: 'Secularism and Toleration', p. 1769.

[33] Skinner, *Visions of Politics, Volume 1*, p. 174.

[34] Pierre Rosanvallon, 'Toward a Philosophical History of the Political', in *Democracy*, p. 62.

the answer and to seek the elements that will return one to that same answer might be seen as a teleological project. But my concerns are anti-teleological, for the end of the story was neither obvious nor inevitable, and several of the moments I examine point to other possibilities.[35] The subject of each chapter revisits a much studied period in the career of Indian nationalism and employs many of the same sources. However, I have sought to read these moments and sources differently. Each provides new examples as well as a re-reading of existing evidence to reconstruct genealogies of secularism and of communalism.

The Architecture of the Argument

The book is organized chronologically and divided into three thematic parts, each with two chapters. Part One, 'Nationalism', considers the beginnings of an urban, upper-caste, self-consciously Hindu cultural politics that successfully claimed the mantle of 'nationalism' in western India in the period 1893–1911. The cultural and political idioms of this period became integral to formulations of Indian nationalism in later years. Part Two, 'Communalism', looks at the years 1906–9 when the term emerged with its peculiarly Indian meanings, and then at 1919–32 when, during the Khilafat movement and its aftermath, other possibilities were sidelined and meanings for nationalism and communalism hardened. Part Three, 'Secularism', takes the study from 1932 through Independence and on to 1950. It shows how a democratic imperative appropriated 'communities' into minority and majority populations. Significantly, this process involved distinguishing between caste and religious minorities. It was by this differentiation that secularism and the secular citizen were defined.

Chapter 1 explores the cow protection movements, Ganpati festivals, and conflicts around Hindu processional music in front of mosques that took place across Maharashtra from the 1890s. It was out of such events that the potential for a regional, cross-caste Hindu community, deeply inflected with an upper-caste idiom, emerged at the turn of the century. In the context of colonialism, these events represented an avenue by which local change and particular grievances could be articulated in ways that were translocal, and in a language that was both

[35] On this point, see Talal Asad, *Genealogies of Religion: Discipline and Reasons of Power in Christianity and Islam* (Baltimore, 1993), pp. 17–18.

anti-colonial and anti-Muslim. Their replication from one district to another created political spaces that allowed people of different caste and occupational backgrounds to appropriate, however sporadically or strategically, the vocabulary that emerged.

Chapter 2 argues that between 1905 and 1911 a new kind of patriotism emerged in Maharashtra. In 1905 Bal Gangadhar Tilak launched the Swadeshi movement as a parallel to a similar movement begun in Bengal. Swadeshi was the first self-consciously nationalist movement in India and urged a boycott of colonial institutions. In western India, the movement spoke in a language of Maharashtrian regionalism, but it served to articulate a patriotism that was 'Indian' in its formulation. It was a formulation that was high caste in its inflections and subsumed social difference within definitions that conflated 'Hindu' with 'Indian'. Non-Brahmans challenged these ideas, but what they offered were competing public spheres, not a competing language of nationalism. Consequently, at the end of this period, the language of nationalism was largely owned by upper-caste men.

The political threat posed by the Swadeshi movement to British rule prompted the first concerted move towards constitutional reform in India. Chapter 3 is a study of the debates that prefigured these reforms. It argues that it was during the course of these debates that the term 'communal' first became attributable to the politics of a Muslim minority. The reforms are best known for their institution of a separate or communal electorate for Muslims, which formulated a corporate Muslim identity in Indian politics. At the outset of the discussions in 1906, the term 'communalism' was not pejorative, nor was it used solely in reference to confessional communities. Yet by 1909 it was taken to mean the political mobilization of a minority religious community to the furtherance of its own ends, contrary to the interests of a greater national good. It was this shift—from the idea that communal bodies were a foundational part of Indian society to one where their interests were considered 'particular' and contrary to the priorities of nationalism—that was to have profound implications for how future debates around the representation of communities and the nature of what it meant to be 'Indian' would be framed.

Chapter 4 turns to the Khilafat movement and its aftermath in Sind in the period 1919–32. By 1910 the categories 'national' and 'communal' had been formulated as the opposing interests of majority and minority populations. The Khilafat and Non-cooperation movements ten years later (1919–22) marked the possibility of envisioning an India where Muslims and Hindus were equal partners in nationalism. I argue that it was in the post-Khilafat period that the meanings of nationalism and communalism crystallized. After 1924 Muslims like Mohamed Ali, who had been central to the movements, became increasingly alienated from Congress nationalism, arguing that the interests of Muslims had been sacrificed for a totalizing idea of unity. Such criticisms were branded as communal and quickly sidelined. Debates around the question of the separation of Sind also broke down along lines of community. The idea of parity that had held sway in the early 1920s and the calls for the creation of autonomous Muslim provinces by 1928 represented the possibilities of imagining a way for Muslims to be Muslims within India. It was through the process of constitution-making in the late 1920s that such possibilities of a federated nationalism were lost.

Chapter 5 looks at the communal question as articulated by Ambedkar during the Round Table conferences of 1931–2. This moment is of particular significance because it reflects competing ideas about the legitimate place—the *citizenship*—of the 'community' and the 'minority' within India at a time when such ideas were still largely malleable. It was during the course of these conferences that Gandhi went on his famous 'fast unto death' in protest at Ambedkar's attempt to have untouchables recognized as a minority community. Gandhi argued that separate electorates for untouchables would fragment the unity of Hinduism and of the nation, reiterating the idea of the democratic majority as effectively Hindu. This process was intimately tied to the Muslim question. But the Muslim question was a communal one, and the same could not be true for untouchables. The upshot of this episode was that while untouchables wanted to be recognized as a minority, they were appropriated into a majority. Muslims who had fought against minority status were confirmed as exactly that.

Mass anti-colonial mobilization in the 1920s had failed to achieve Hindu–Muslim unity and subsequent efforts to formulate a constitution to reflect a consensus on national identity had been similarly unsuccessful. Both sets of historical experiences represented attempts to resolve what had been called the communal or the minority question. These terms were used interchangeably and referred to a range of religious and backward caste communities. One of the imperatives for the constituent assembly, whose task it was to finalize a constitution for India, was to resolve, once and for all, the position of minorities in the emergent democracy, and thus, the nature of citizenship.

The final chapter examines the arguments in the constituent assembly around instituting political safeguards—reservations in legislatures and public bodies—for minorities, and the implications of this for a secular state. Much of the discussion turned on what the purpose of such representation would be. Many argued that reservations undermined national unity and the values of a secular state. Others maintained that such opposition reflected not a defence of secularism but the communalism of the majority. Nationalism had always foundered on the communal/minority question. This was resolved in the transition to a secular democracy. The consensus that was ultimately forced retained safeguards for the 'backward classes and castes' alone, on the grounds of their economic and political inequality. The provisions for freedom of religion that were guaranteed by a secular state were deemed adequate protection for religious minorities. The minority question was thus differentiated into class and religion. Indian nationalism had had to grapple with both. Indian secularism could afford to address only the latter. It was in this transition that an ideology of secularism emerged in India.

PART I

Nationalism

1

A Hindu Community in Maharashtra?
Cow Protection, Ganpati Festivals, and Music before Mosques 1893–1894

Between April and August 1893 a series of riots took place between Hindus and Muslims in the United Provinces, in Rangoon, and in Bombay city and its surrounding areas around the issue of cow protection. The riots in Bombay were linked to an increasingly hostile cow protection movement that was part of a wider series of cultural innovations in the late nineteenth century led by upper-caste Hindu reformers. Among these innovations was the Ganpati festival. Traditionally a small-scale family affair, in 1894 it became very much a public festival for high- and low-caste Hindus, and was accompanied in towns and cities across the region by violent conflict between Hindu and Muslim communities. Cultural innovation and conflict went hand in hand in nineteenth-century Maharashtra. Since the 1850s, the issue of music before mosques had been one around which self-styled Hindu and Muslim leaders focused competing claims, arguing before the adjudicating powers of the colonial state that the religious rights of their respective communities were being violated. Hindus claimed it was time-honoured tradition to play processional music as they passed before mosques, Muslims asserted it was their religious right to pray in silence. With the new cow protection movements and the reconfigured Ganpati festivals, music before mosques once again became the locus of such claims.

There has been significant scholarly interest in the conflicts of the last decade of the nineteenth century, particularly around the issue of cow protection. This can be accounted for largely by the proliferation of studies on communalism.[1] This scholarship has been driven by a fundamental question: when can an event, such as a local sectarian conflict, be seen as evidence of a universal category—communalism? At what point can a local experience be understood as a manifestation of the translocal?[2] Scholars of communalism have associated broad-based identity formation with the emergence of conflict between Hindu and Muslim communities and have identified the conflicts and cultural innovations of the late nineteenth century as lying at the root of this process. Sandria Freitag, for example, focusing on cow protection movements in the United Provinces, has argued that the cow provided a popularly revered symbol that could be mobilized in the name of a putative Hindu community.[3] In her view, the various ways in which this symbol was shared allowed for the emergence of a public arena where community identity could be expressed. The festivals, public meetings, and pamphlets that proliferated around this issue provided meanings as well as common ground between elite and popular culture. Cow protection was a central pillar of Hindu reform movements in Punjab, Maharashtra, and the United Provinces in the nineteenth century, and was heavily imbued with an upper-caste idiom. However, Freitag is unable to offer an explanation of why lower castes (Shudras) and untouchables—the latter often ate beef—may have participated: it is simply enough that they did. Freitag sees behaviour as the 'text' of popular politics.[4] So, participation in community activities implied an acceptance of the meaningfulness of the signifiers of that community. Moreover, she also understands participation as reflecting a shift in self-understanding. Thus, low-caste and untouchable participation in an essentially upper-caste affair should be seen as an ideological 'joining up', marking a shift in their self-conception as Hindus.[5]

---

[1] For studies on communalism, see Introduction, fn. 19.

[2] Paul R. Brass has attempted to answer this question for a more contemporary period in *Theft of an Idol: Text and Context in the Representation of Collective Violence* (Princeton, 1997).

[3] Freitag, *Collective Action*, pp. 148–76.

[4] Ibid., p. 13.

[5] I use 'caste' both in terms of varna and in terms of jati. Varna can be understood as one of the four hierarchically arranged categories into which all Hindus, with the exception of untouchables, are in theory divided. Jati is the term for

Another scholar who has looked to the cow protection riots in the United Provinces as a means to chart the emergence of 'Hindu' and 'Muslim' communities has argued that these categories bore little reality to events on the ground. Rather, they were created by virtue of a colonial archive that classified such conflicts as sectarian and as taking place between Hindus and Muslims.[6] Emphasizing the autonomy of peasant politics, Gyanendra Pandey demonstrates that many low-caste communities were indifferent to the clarion call of cow protection and notes the many reconciliation meetings held between Hindus and Muslims in the post-riot period. Pandey's conclusions detract from the idea that participation in these riots necessarily implied alignment with an upper-caste reformist programme, or that such conflicts reflected an irreversible development in inter-community antagonism. He argues that community differences were neither permanent nor irreconcilable.

A further contribution to the debate on communalism comes from research on an earlier period in Indian history. C.A. Bayly takes examples of sectarian conflict from the eighteenth century that look quite similar to those from the late nineteenth, arguing that, far from being a modern phenomenon, communalism existed much earlier.[7] However, this argument for continuity of form holds within it the analytical weakness of treating local and communal conflict as one and the same. Bayly's approach is unable to answer the core question of communalism: when and how does a sectarian conflict that is local and particular become a communal conflict that is translocal and universal?

This chapter revisits the conflicts and cultural innovations of the late-nineteenth-century Bombay Presidency, focusing on the region of Maharashtra to see how far such innovations marked the emergence of a Hindu community. It opens with a brief background to reform

---

endogamous castes and subcastes. I use 'non-Brahman' to refer to jatis that fall within the Shudra varna, the lowest of the four, and 'upper caste' to refer to the so-called 'twice-born' castes, the Vaishyas, Kshatriyas, and Brahmans. The term untouchables or Depressed Classes (the official term) refers to occupational groups outside the four-varna system.

[6] Gyanendra Pandey, 'Rallying Around the Cow: Sectarian Strife in the Bhojpuri Region, *c.* 1888–1917', in R. Guha (ed.), *Subaltern Studies II* (Delhi, 1983).

[7] C.A. Bayly, 'A Pre-history of Communalism? Religious Conflict in India, 1700–1860', *MAS*, 19, 2, 1985.

movements in nineteenth-century Maharashtra. Subsequent sections examine the cow protection movement in 1893 and the Ganpati festival of 1894.

Mobilization around cow protection and the reworked Ganpati festivals took place in towns and cities across Maharashtra. They were defined not only by conflict and public festivity, but also by the kind of information that was produced and circulated alongside them. Through petitions and memorials, songs, pamphlets, posters, and speeches a vocabulary emerged across the presidency that was strikingly similar in its political and cultural symbols. It was a language that was weighted around the tenets of high-caste Hinduism, including vegetarianism, temperance, and ideas of purity and pollution. Central to this formulation was the idea of true Hindus as warriors battling the illegitimate rule of foreigners. The forms these activities took were propagated by upper castes. Their replication across the region through cow protection societies and during the Ganpati festivals was significant because of the way ordinary people—however briefly or even tangentially—chose to appropriate these positions. The momentous changes wrought in the nineteenth century, in both urban and rural communities, were experienced locally and in particular ways. Historians of Maharashtra have shown that the articulation of a regional Hindu identity inflected with an upper-caste idiom in the late nineteenth century was enormously contested and existed alongside a range of interpretations of Maratha history and social identity.[8] I argue below that the reasons for participation in Bombay's cow protection riots and in the Ganpati festivals were not uniform across high- and low-caste communities, or indeed within them. In this sense, these events cannot be understood as the coming together of Hindus or as the beginnings of communalism. At the same time, they cannot be understood as simply local events. The fact that many chose to appropriate the vocabulary of this high-caste Hinduism requires some attention.

---

[8] See Rosalind O'Hanlon, *Caste, Conflict and Ideology: Mahatma Jotirao Phule and Low Caste Protest in Nineteenth-Century Western India* (Cambridge, 1985); Raminder Kaur, *Performative Politics and the Cultures of Hinduism: Public Uses of Religion in Western India* (Delhi, 2003); Janaki Bakhle, *Two Men and Music: Nationalism in the Making of an Indian Classical Tradition* (New York, 2005); and Prachi Deshpande, *Creative Pasts: Historical Memory and Identity in Western India, 1700–1960* (Delhi, 2007).

The final section examines a series of conflicts that took place in 1894 in Yeola, a weaving town in eastern Maharashtra, around the issue of whether Hindu processional music should be played in front of mosques during the time of prayer. In September 1893 people calling themselves Hindus began deliberately to route religious processions past mosques, claiming this to be an ancient custom. Those claiming to represent Muslims alleged, in response, that it was their custom to be able to pray in silence. Queen Victoria's proclamation of 1858 had stated the policy of crown rule to be one of 'non-interference' in the customs and traditions of Indians. This assurance also contained the promise that the state would protect such traditions from interference. By enshrining a way for communities to legitimize their claims against others in their localities, the proclamation had the effect of ensuring that the language of protest was articulated in the categories of community. In light of the conflicts in Yeola, the central problem for colonial officials was how to uphold the state's pledge of non-interference while determining whether a particular practice was integral to the traditions of one community or another. An examination of the way this process coincided with local events is important in understanding how the categories of Hindu and Muslim were brought into and made meaningful in such situations, and reciprocally how events in a locality were read out of and beyond the particular.

Social Reform in Nineteenth-Century Maharashtra

Maratha Brahmans and Gujarati trading castes from urban centres in the Bombay Presidency were central to upper-caste reform movements in nineteenth-century Maharashtra. Maratha Brahmans had enjoyed an unrivalled position of religious, intellectual, administrative, and economic dominance under peshwa rule and experienced a keen sense of loss following the transfer of power to the British in 1818.[9] The first

[9] Peshwas were Chitpavan Brahman ministers who served the descendants of the seventeenth-century Maratha warrior-king Shivaji, eventually exercising power in their own right. For the social history of pre-colonial Maharashtra, see H. Fukazawa, *The Medieval Deccan: Peasants, Social Systems and States* (Delhi, 1991); and B.G. Gokhale, *Poona in the Eighteenth Century: An Urban History* (Delhi, 1988).

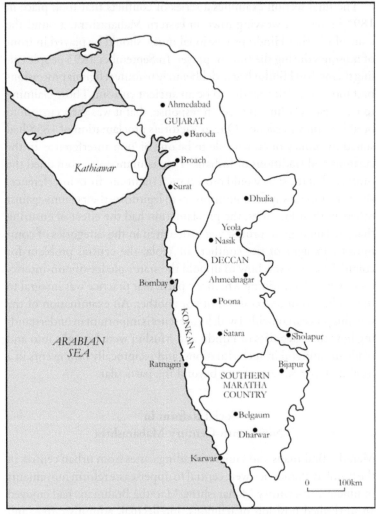

Map 1. Bombay Presidency

commissioner of the Deccan, Mountstuart Elphinstone, had sought
to implement the concepts of efficient and responsible government
into a society that had given free rein to corrupt practices under the rule
of the last peshwa.[10] Elphinstone resolved to reform the administration

[10] For social histories of western India in the nineteenth century, see Kenneth
Ballhatchet, *Social Policy and Social Change in Western India, 1817–1830*

of land revenue, believing it to be weighted against the interests of the peasants. Attempting to circumvent the need for intermediaries, he established a direct revenue relationship between state and peasant, and consequently a number of traditional rural offices went into decline. The office of the mamlatdar, for example, was totally transformed after 1818. A revenue official formerly in charge of a taluka (subdivision of a district), the mamlatdar had previously enjoyed considerable freedom. Under the British, his powers were restricted, his accounts audited and his functions regulated by the collector. Likewise, deshmukhs (largely landed aristocrats), who had played a key role in the collection of land revenue under the peshwas, were now considered superfluous and were eclipsed.[11] The new administration's reforms were also directed at the authority of religious elites and traditional forms of learning.[12] Elphinstone sought to introduce Indians to the 'scientific' knowledge of the West, which he felt would undermine what he saw as the superstitions and hierarchies of Hinduism. However, government policies seemed to reinforce rather than check the position of upper castes. The majority of applicants to government schools, for instance, were Brahmans. Poor Brahmans, especially, were ready to alter their line of study if their education was paid for and they were guaranteed a secure position in government service. By the 1840s they made up the vast majority of graduates and dominated administrative positions at all levels, as well as the professions of law, teaching, and journalism.[13]

After the revolt of 1857 the British adopted an anti-Maratha Brahman policy for college admission and administrative positions in an attempt to stem the latter's growing monopoly of government

---

(London, 1957); Ravinder Kumar, *Western India in the Nineteenth Century: A Study in the Social History of Maharashtra* (London, 1968); and Sumit Guha, *The Agrarian Economy of the Bombay Deccan, 1818–1941* (New Delhi, 1985).

[11] Kumar, *Western India,* pp. 58 and 128; Guha, *Agrarian Economy,* chapter 2.

[12] On the challenge to the shastris (Brahman priests), see R. Tucker, 'From Dharmashastra to Politics: Aspects of Social Authority in Nineteenth Century Maharashtra', *IESHR,* 7, 3, 1970.

[13] See Kumar, *Western India,* pp. 49–50; Ballhatchet, *Social Policy,* pp. 266–9; and M.L.P. Patterson, 'Changing Patterns of Occupations among Chitpavan Brahmans', *IESHR,* 7, 3, 1970.

institutions. However, Brahmans had already secured the majority of studentships to government high schools, so it proved difficult to draw the necessary numbers from other communities. By the 1870s they comprised almost 90 per cent of students at Deccan College, the foremost arts college of the presidency, a pattern repeated in institutions across the region. With the extension of local self-government in 1882, Brahmans returned a majority of representatives to the partially elected boards, and by 1886 held two-thirds of administrative positions in the presidency.[14] So, informed by the principle of creating a fair representation of various 'interests', the Bombay government ruled in 1881 that they should work 'to secure a due admixture of the various races and castes' in the administration.[15]

The first attempt was made in 1885, when officials in the education department proposed that half of all studentships be reserved for Muslims and the 'backward' (i.e. Shudra) Hindu castes. The response from Poona, the heartland of Maratha Brahmans, was hostile: they alleged that the policy violated the state's 1858 pledge of neutrality between all religions and classes since reservations made caste and religion a basis for exclusion. In 1892 the governor of Bombay, Lord Harris, introduced elections to the provincial legislative councils. He maintained that a balanced reflection of the different interests in the presidency had been impossible to achieve through open election, and devised a scheme of representation to rectify this. The proposal involved creating eight electoral bodies that would each elect one representative on the council. These included the Bombay and Karachi chambers of commerce, the landed elites of Sind and the Deccan, and the municipalities of the different divisions of the presidency. Efforts to implement these policies proved largely futile. Nevertheless, attempts to reduce the influence of Maratha Brahmans meant that their sense of diminished status, damaged pride, and being at the receiving end of exclusionary policies continued.

While the administration of Maharashtrian society underwent change, a small section of the new, largely Western-educated, elite

---

[14] Cashman, *Myth of the Lokamanya,* pp. 19–20.

[15] L. Robertson, Secretary to the Bombay Government, 17 September 1910, Home/Special file nos 283–1, 'Employment of Brahmins in Government Service', Maharashtra State Archives, quoted in ibid., p. 37.

began to formulate responses to the profound criticisms of Hinduism put forward by Christian missionaries. Rosalind O'Hanlon, in her study of the Non-Brahman movement in Maharashtra, has argued that it was missionary critiques in combination with radical ideas taken from the European Enlightenment—ideas that included a rejection of traditional religious hierarchies and a concern for the natural rights of the individual—that gave rise to the movement for the reform of Hinduism.[16] Poona, even more than Bombay, became the centre of upper-caste reform in the nineteenth century. Unlike Bombay, Poona did not have a strong history of missionary activity, but had been the seat of peshwa power and, in contrast to Bombay's plurality, was an almost totally Maharashtrian city.

While there was a wide spectrum of opinion as to what forms social and religious change should take, upper-caste reformers shared the opinion that Hindu society had undergone a gradual decline since the time of the Vedas, resulting in the economic, moral, and spiritual poverty of the present.[17] They launched a public attack on practices of traditional Hinduism such as caste, idol worship, sati, and the prohibition against widow remarriage. Caste came under particular scrutiny. In the late 1840s the prominent reformer Gopal Hari Deshmukh ('Lokahitavadi'), argued that caste stifled individuality and held Brahmanism responsible for bringing about the degradation of Hindu society.[18] At the same time, the English-language Student's Literary and Scientific Society and the Marathi- and Gujarati-language societies for the propagation of knowledge (Dnyanprasarak Mandali) advanced secular education over knowledge of the puranas. The second half of the nineteenth century saw a series of reformers who developed ideas in this

[16] O'Hanlon, *Caste, Conflict and Ideology*, p. 50.

[17] On these strands of social reform in Maharashtra, see M.L. Apte, 'Lokahitavadi and V.K. Chiplunkar: Spokesmen of Change in Nineteenth-Century Maharashtra, *MAS*, 7, 2, 1973; R. Tucker, 'Hindu Traditionalism and Nationalist Ideologies in Nineteenth-Century Maharashtra,' *MAS*, 10, 3, 1976; F. Conlon, 'Vishnubawa Brahmachari: A Champion of Hinduism in Nineteenth Century Maharashtra,' in A.R. Kulkarni and N.K. Wagle (eds), *Region, Nationality and Religion* (Mumbai, 1999). On Hindu social reform more generally, see J.N. Farquar, *Modern Religious Movements in India* (New York, 1919); Charles Heimsath, *Indian Nationalism and Hindu Social Reform* (Princeton, 1964).

[18] O'Hanlon, *Caste, Conflict and Ideology*, chapter 4.

vein. Vishnubawa Brahmachari, for example, argued that Hinduism, like Christianity, was a revealed and essentially monistic religion, the various deities being reflections of the same cosmic whole. Although upholding the value of caste as a perfect social order, he emphasized that one's caste should be by merit and not by birth. Thus, individuals by their virtuous acts could ascend the caste hierarchy. Vishnubawa emphasized moral and spiritual qualities as the essence of Hinduism rather than its specific practices. In so doing, his message resonated with reformist as well as orthodox Hindus. [19]

However, religious debate lost its urgency by the mid 1860s as reformers began to address the political and economic consequences of crown rule. In 1870 a group of young Brahmans from Poona founded a new association, the Poona Sarvajanik Sabha, whose members debated issues of local government, taxation, rural poverty, and public health.[20] Mahadev Govind Ranade and Gopal Krishna Gokhale were prominent both in the sabha and in the Indian National Congress, founded in 1885.[21] Early Congress demands, such as that for the Indianization of the civil service, reflected a concern for racial equality. Economic issues were concerned with the poverty of India and focused on the 'drain of wealth' theory later elaborated by the Bengali economist R.C. Dutt.[22] However, the politics of these years rested on the understanding that civil rights would be gradually extended, eventually resulting in 'self-government'. It was an approach that drew criticism from others as a politics of 'mendicancy' and as too easily accepting of the values of the West. Vishnu Krishna Chiplunkar was among those in Maharashtra who argued that freedom would come only when

[19] Ibid., pp. 327–9; and Conlon, 'Vishnubawa Brahmachari'.

[20] 'Sarvajanik', lit. 'of all the people'. See S.R. Mehrotra, 'The Poona Sarvajanik Sabha: The Early Phase (1870–1880), *IESHR*, VI, 3, 1969. For scholarship on public associations in western India, see Christine Dobbin, *Urban Leadership in Western India: Politics and Communities in Bombay City, 1840–1885* (Oxford, 1972); and J.C. Masselos, *Towards Nationalism: Group Affiliations and the Politics of Public Associations in Nineteenth Century Western India* (Bombay, 1974).

[21] See John R. McLane, *Indian Nationalism and the Early Congress* (Princeton, 1977).

[22] Romesh Chandra Dutt, *Economic History of India in the Victorian Age* (London, 1904).

Indians looked to their own indigenous—what he called 'national'—traditions and values.

Chiplunkar (1850–82) graduated from Deccan College in 1866 and began teaching in a government school in 1873. Starting in 1874 he published a series of essays on the condition of India in his journal *Nibandhamala*, where he berated earlier reformers such as Lokahitavadi Deshmukh for focusing on the corruptions of Hinduism. Chiplunkar argued that the degradation of Hindu society was not the result of the inherent bankruptcy of Hinduism, but of India's subjection to foreigners. He maintained that Brahmans had only become corrupt in the last years of peshwa rule and that they should once again become leaders of their society. Colonialism had deprived Indians of their self-regard, something that could only be revived with swaraj, self-rule, and it was Brahmans who should come forth and re-instil in Hindus an understanding of their worth and the glories of their history. Like others, Chiplunkar criticized Hindu practices such as caste. Yet he argued that caste distinctions should be dissolved not because they violated the rights of the individual but because they hindered national unity.[23] He asserted that Indians should no longer be taught in government schools but should be given a 'national education'. He resigned his post in 1879 and, with Bal Gangadhar Tilak and Gopal Ganesh Agarkar, two young nationalists, founded the New English School in Poona. In 1881 they started two newspapers, *Kesari* in Marathi and *Mahratta* in English, which became the most widely circulating papers in the Bombay Presidency. Chiplunkar died in 1882 and Tilak, having split with Agarkar over divergent political agendas, stepped in to fill the gap.

From a defence of past glories, through a criticism of the policies of the colonial state, to an assertion of the inherent superiority of indigenous Hindu values over those of the West, Brahmans in nineteenth-century Maharashtra evolved a set of anti-colonial discourses that were regional in idiom and upper caste in inflection. Towards the end of the nineteenth century, relative prosperity rather than an acute sense of loss brought a number of other communities to associate with these reform movements. Members of Gujarati Hindu and Jain trading

[23] Apte, 'Lokahitavadi and V.K. Chiplunkar', p. 202; Tucker, 'Hindu Traditionalism', p. 346.

castes (Banias) were prominent among these. Over the course of the century, Banias had come to dominate commercial life in western India, particularly in urban centres such as Bombay and Surat. In the 1870s the vast majority of bankers and moneylenders in Bombay were Jains and, by the 1880s, many Parsis and Banias who had dominated trade in cotton, tea, silk, and opium had become industrial capitalists.[24] Writing on Surat, Douglas Haynes has shown that Banias were part of a complex of upper castes—'Brahman-Vaniya'—that included Brahmans, Vaishnava Banias, Jains, Bhatias, Lohanas, and others associated with either commerce or government service.[25] Haynes argues that while each caste maintained its own rules of conduct, these were often flexible in relation to others in the same caste complex. Thus, it was not unusual for members of different commercial castes to intermarry, for a Bania to enter administrative service, or for a Brahman to become a merchant. It was imperative, however, to maintain social standing since, for commercial communities in particular, social reputation and creditworthiness were inextricably linked.[26] Communities whose fortunes were relatively recent endeavoured to mark their respectability in society. Shastric texts depicted handlers of money as little better than Shudras; thus, the new Bania elite sought to distance itself from activities considered unclean and came increasingly to associate with the practices of Brahmanical Hinduism. This entailed abstention from meat eating and alcohol consumption, avoidance of contact with low castes and untouchables, sexual restraint, the pursuit of appropriate

[24] See T.A. Timberg, *The Marwaris: From Traders to Industrialists* (Delhi, 1978); Dwijendra Tripathi and M.J. Mehta, 'Class Character of the Gujarati Business Community', in D. Tripathi (ed.), *Business Communities of India: A Historical Perspective* (Delhi, 1984); Rajnarayan Chandavarkar, *The Origins of Industrial Capitalism in India: Business Strategies and the Working Classes in Bombay, 1900–1940* (Cambridge, 1994); A. Siddiqi, 'The Business World of Jamsetjee Jejeebhoy', in A. Siddiqi (ed.), *Trade and Finance in Colonial India, 1750–1860* (Delhi, 1995); Dobbin, *Urban Leadership*, p. 154.

[25] Douglas Haynes, *Rhetoric and Ritual in Colonial India: The Shaping of a Public Culture in Surat City, 1852–1928* (Berkeley, 1991), p. 55. 'Vaniya' was the term in Gujarat for people of Bania caste groupings.

[26] For a similar argument on North India, see C.A. Bayly, *Rulers, Townsmen and Bazaars: North Indian Society in the Age of British Expansion, 1770–1870* (Cambridge, 1983), chapter 10.

marriage alliances, sponsoring hospices for cows, and religious gift giving. Gift giving—the sponsoring of festivals, temples, and donations to particular deities—as a means of establishing social reputation is a practice visible at least since the seventeenth century, and continued by leaders of these newly prosperous communities for whom commercial success and religious piety went hand in hand. As Susan Bayly has argued, Bania elites at the end of the nineteenth century 'sought to establish themselves as leaders of a self-consciously "Hindu" social order, giving their own favourable meaning to the conventions of the textual varna tradition.'[27] And the ways in which this social order was defined was often exclusive of Muslims and lower castes.

Shudras had shown little interest in upper-caste reform movements and the issues that they raised. Non-Brahman movements in the nineteenth century focused not on critiques of colonialism, but of caste. Jotirao Phule's centrality to the formulation of a non-Brahman identity in Maharashtra has been well documented.[28] Phule (1827–90) was from a gardening caste (Mali). He attended a Scottish missionary school in the 1840s where he was introduced to the religious radicalism of nineteenth-century Europe. In 1849 he founded a school in Poona for Shudra girls and began promoting the education of low-caste, untouchable, and Muslim communities, establishing a society for Mahar and Mang education in 1852.[29] Phule developed a scathing critique of Brahmanism during the 1850s and 1860s, arguing that it was a form of slavery responsible for the social and mental degradation

[27] Susan Bayly, *Caste, Society and Politics in India from the Eighteenth Century to the Modern Age* (Cambridge, 1999), pp. 216–20; see also Haynes, *Rhetoric and Ritual*, pp. 55–9. On the Jains, see James Laidlaw, *Riches and Renunciation: Religion, Economy and Society among the Jains* (Oxford, 1995).

[28] On Jotirao Phule, see O'Hanlon, *Caste, Conflict and Ideology*, chapters 11–17. On the Non-Brahman movement in Maharashtra, see Gail Omvedt, *Cultural Revolt in a Colonial Society: The Non Brahman Movement in Western India, 1873–1930* (Bombay, 1976); Eleanor Zelliot, *From Untouchable to Dalit: Essays on the Ambedkar Movement* (Delhi, 1992), chapter 2; M. Naito, 'Anti-Untouchability Ideologies and Movements in Maharashtra from the Late Nineteenth Century to the 1930s', in H. Kotani (ed.), *Caste System, Untouchability and the Depressed* (Delhi, 1997).

[29] Mahars and Mangs were the two largest untouchable communities in Maharashtra.

of non-Brahmans and untouchables. In 1873 he was one of the founders of the Satyashodhak Samaj (Truth-seeking Society). The Samaj's
stated mission was to 'free Shudras from subjugation to Brahmans'.[30]
It focused primarily on educational issues: night school for farmers,
assistance with school fees, tuition exemption for poor students, and
so on. The emphasis on education was one of the key themes in low-
caste politics in this period. Education was seen to be both enlightening
and a potential equalizer against caste hierarchy. Non-Brahmans
appealed to the liberal values espoused by the colonial state, expressing
their loyalty and requesting that greater state resources be made available for their education. By 1877 the samaj also had a publication,
Din Bandhu (Friend of the Poor). In the early 1880s the Satyashodhak Samaj extended its activities into the rural areas around Poona,
supporting small farmers and tenants in their boycotts of Brahman
landlords.

There were many aside from Phule who began schools, published
newspapers, formed labour organizations, and submitted memorials
on education and employment.[31] Narayan Rao Meghaji Lokhande,
for instance, took the circulation of *Din Bandhu* to 1,650 in 1884,
which made it the most widely read Anglo-Marathi newspaper of the
time after Chiplunkar's *Kesari*. Lokhande also campaigned for some
measure of positive discrimination for backward castes in educational
policies, arguing that 5 per cent of places in government high schools
should be in the form of free studentships for Maratha boys. When
Lee-Warner, director of public instruction for the Bombay Presidency,
ruled in 1885 that half of the 5 per cent of studentships should go to
non-Brahman boys, editorials in *Kesari* vehemently protested the
decision, clashing bitterly with *Din Bandhu* over the issue. The concerns of low-caste movements were thus at odds with those led by the
upper castes. Phule eschewed organizations such as the Poona Sarvajanik
Sabha, arguing that they were under the corrupt leadership of Brahmans
and had little to offer other communities.[32] In contrast to those such

[30] J.G. Phule, *Pune Satyashodhak Samajacha Report* (1877), quoted in Naito,
'Anti-Untouchability Ideologies', p. 180

[31] O'Hanlon, *Caste, Conflict and Ideology*, pp. 281–301; Zelliot, *From Untouchable to Dalit*, chapter 2; Naito, 'Anti-Untouchability Ideologies', pp. 182–3.

[32] Zelliot, *From Untouchable to Dalit*, p. 44.

as Chiplunkar, Phule, and the Satyashodhak Samaj expressed their loyalty to the state and pursued issues of expanded opportunities for non-Brahmans.

The second half of the nineteenth century also saw a reconfiguration of identity amongst the Muslims of western India. The main Muslim communities were the Konkanis, Momins, Kutchi Memons, Daudi Bohras, and Ismaili Khojas. There were also gentry families once associated with the top ranks of Mughal administration.[33] The Konkani Muslims were Sunnis claiming descent from Arab traders who landed on the Konkan coast around CE 700. In Bombay and surrounding areas they tended to be employed in the powerloom industry, dairy farming, and rice cultivation. The Momins were a weaving caste from the United Provinces and Bihar that had migrated to the region after 1857.[34] The Memons, Bohras, and Khojas were originally Hindu castes that had converted to Islam between the eleventh and fifteenth centuries. All three were commercial communities that became prosperous in the early nineteenth century. They were known for being close knit and highly organized, with a strong sense of corporate identity. Muslims had generally avoided Western education and the sorts of associational and reformist politics that had begun to characterize various Hindu communities of the region. Moreover, there was no unified body of ulema to which the Muslims of western India looked. The organization of their communities closely resembled that of the castes from which they had converted. In addition, each had its own spiritual leader. Partly for this reason, they had not experienced the kinds of movements for reform as had their co-religionists in North India.[35]

---

[33] See Gregory Kozlowski, *Muslim Endowments and Society in British India* (Cambridge, 1985); Haynes, *Rhetoric and Ritual*; Jonah Blank, *Mullahs on the Mainframe: Islam and Modernity Among the Daudi Bohras* (Chicago, 2001); and Amrita Shodhan, *A Question of Community: Religious Groups and Colonial Law* (Calcutta, 2001).

[34] A.R. Momin, 'Muslim Caste in an Industrial Township of Maharashtra', in I. Ahmad (ed.), *Caste and Social Stratification Among Muslims in India* (Delhi, 1978),

[35] On Muslim reform movements in North India, see Aziz Ahmad, *Islamic Modernism in India and Pakistan* (Lahore, 1974); David Lelyveld, *Aligarh's First Generation: Muslim Solidarity in British India* (Princeton, 1978); Barbara Metcalf, *Islamic Revival in British India: Deoband, 1860–1900* (Princeton, 1982); Usha

There were, of course, some exceptions. The few who showed concern with reform were influenced by Sir Syed Ahmad Khan of the Mahomedan Anglo-Oriental College in Aligarh via their focus on the relative 'backwardness' of their co-religionists in government colleges and the civil service.[36] Some prominent commercial families in Bombay had begun to send their sons to government colleges around the 1850s. Kamruddin and Badruddin Tyabji became Bombay's first Muslim solicitor and barrister, respectively. Influenced by the anjumans (community associations) of North India, the Tyabjis founded the Anjuman-i-Islam in Bombay in 1876, the aim of which was to improve the educational and social status of Muslims of the presidency and foster a sense of belonging to a broader Muslim community. Badruddin Tyabji stressed the use of Urdu rather than Gujarati as the language of Muslims, and expressed a wish to 'cement these discordant elements into one compact mass whose watchword will be "Islam" without any of the later differences'.[37] Such associations promoted the value of Western education, encouraged colonial officials to make provisions for the employment of Muslims in public services, and in doing so sought to identify a specifically Muslim corporate identity.

The purview of such forms of politics was limited, however, as most Muslims shunned higher education and government employment. Philanthropy was a more acceptable way for prosperous Muslims to demonstrate social position. In the 1860s and 1870s the Sunni gentry in Surat, who had contributed to charities for health, education, and the construction of public buildings, began to direct funds to more obviously Muslim causes such as Muslim education, mosques, and religious festivals.[38] All this served to develop new ideas of their place in a broader Muslim community. At the same time, the various Muslim communities were involved in their own processes of self-identification. Kutchi Memons had been submitting memorials to the state

---

Sanyal, *Devotional Islam and Politics in British India: Ahmad Riza Khan Barelwi and his Movement, 1870–1920* (Delhi, 1996).

[36] Lelyveld, *Aligarh's First Generation*.

[37] Letter from Tyabji to Muhammad Ali Roghay, a liberal Muslim and another founder of the Anjuman-i-Islam, quoted in Dobbin, *Urban Leadership*, p. 233.

[38] Haynes, *Rhetoric and Ritual*, pp. 121–37.

since the 1870s that their inheritance laws must be brought in line with those of the Sunnis.[39] A controversy over the issue of whether they should follow Shia or Sunni practices split the Khoja community in the 1860s.[40] During this same period the Bohras were beginning to rethink their relationship with the wider Muslim umma.[41] Central to the reformulation of these various identities was the role of the colonial state, and specifically colonial law. Muslim communities increasingly turned to the state to resolve disputes, the rulings on which further reshaped community identities. In this sense, as Douglas Haynes argues, 'appeals for justice went hand in hand with the process of defining self.'[42]

Cow Protection

On 11 August 1893 the acting commissioner of police, R.H. Vincent, reported that a 'terrible riot' had broken out in Bombay city.[43] At about 1:45 p.m. the 'Mahomedans . . . issued forth from the Jumma Masjid and . . . in spite of the endeavours of the respectable members of their community, began to shout "Deen," "Deen," and made a rush for the Hanuman Lane, whereabouts there [was] a Hindu temple. . . . The tumult was enormous; fighting, and especially stone throwing, was going on in half a dozen different directions'.[44] The destruction of the Hanuman temple was prevented, but violence quickly spread to several other parts of the city, often involving several hundred people and sometimes over a thousand: 'Not only did the Musalmans attack all Hindus they met, but the latter also retaliated and both turned on

[39] See, for example, a memorial to Lord Lansdowne, Viceroy and Governor General, by the Cuchi Memon Mahomedan Community of the City of Bombay, 27 August 1892, JD, vol. 202, 1894, MSA.

[40] J.C. Masselos, 'The Khojas of Bombay: The Defining of Formal Membership Criteria during the Nineteenth Century', in Ahmad, *Caste and Social Stratification*; and Shodhan, *Question of Community*.

[41] Blank, *Mullahs on the Mainframe*.

[42] Haynes, *Rhetoric and Ritual*, p. 141.

[43] R.H. Vincent, Preliminary report of the Bombay riots addressed to G.C. Whitworth, Secretary to Government, Judicial Department, Poona, 12 August 1893, JD, vol. 94, compilation no. 948, 1893, 'Riots between Hindus and Muhammadans', MSA.

[44] Ibid.

the police.'[45] Beginning in the evening of 11 August, and continuing into the following day, several shops were broken into and looted and a number of temples and dargahs (Sufi shrines) were damaged or destroyed.[46]

Vincent reported that there were 'not less than' 25,000 who took part in the riots, of whom one-third were Muslim and two-thirds Hindu, a proportion that broadly reflected the population of the city. However, there were a greater number of Muslims arrested (858) than Hindus (647), something that Vincent explained by a delay in the military and police reaching outlying parts of the city—where most Hindus resided—in time to make arrests.[47] He noted that it was working class rather than middle class ('respectable') Hindus and Muslims who had participated in the conflict. Prominent on the Muslim side were Pathans, who were mostly dockworkers; Momins who were *Julahas* or weavers originally from the United Provinces and Bihar; and Kathiawari Muslims, who were labourers often employed in driving bullock carts. Among Hindus, most prominent were Ghatis and Kamatis, migrants from the Deccan who worked in the mills around the city. But there were others, both Muslim and Hindu, from a range of occupational backgrounds: barbers, gardeners, plumbers, servants, cooks, mendicants, tailors, milk sellers, and toilet cleaners, as well as well-to-do Maratha castes such as Sonars (goldsmiths).[48]

Police and military reports indicated that the riots had a large organized element to them, a point seemingly borne out when interviews were held with spokespersons of different communities. Muslim leaders alleged that they had headed for the Hanuman temple, which was opposite the Jumma Masjid, in response to the beating of a drum during afternoon prayers. However, Vincent maintained that this was false, noting that there were a thousand more worshippers at the Juma

[45] Ibid.

[46] R.H. Vincent, full report of 11 August 1893 riot in Bombay, 9 September 1893, Proceedings of the Bombay Presidency, 1894, P/4665, OIOC.

[47] Ibid.

[48] Statement showing numbers of deaths due to the Bombay Riots as registered in the Registration Branch, Health Department, L/P&J/6/362, file no. 2243, OIOC.

Masjid that day than was usual, and when they emerged they were already armed with sticks.[49] The initial confrontation, Vincent believed, was premeditated and encouraged by Muslim leaders. Yet he identified a simultaneous mobilization among prominent Hindus. The acting commissioner of police was convinced that the causes of the Bombay riots were, first, a conflict the previous month in Prabhas Pattan, a town in the princely state of Junagadh in northern Gujarat, where it was reported that Muslims killed eleven Hindus and destroyed a temple; and second, the recent militancy of the movement around cow protection. Vincent stated that, after the events at Prabhas Pattan, some Gujarati merchants of Bombay held meetings under the auspices of two cow protection societies, demanding justice. One, the Gaupalan Upadeshak Mandali (Society for the Propagation of Cow Protection), was headed by Lakhmidas Khimji, a prominent Gujarati millowner and ardent reformer of his caste. Those attending the meetings were told they should prepare themselves, since it was rumoured that Muslims were planning to create a disturbance on 11 August. Many of those involved were employed in Lakhmidas Khimji's mills, where work was suspended from 12 August. However, despite evidence of preparation on both sides, Vincent saw fit to conclude that '[o]nly the lower and lowest classes of the Musalmans took part in the riots and today's doings are clearly due to them, but in a measure the cow-protecting societies of the Hindus goaded them into their evil doings by their senseless preachings, from which . . . they would not desist.' Of the Hindus, it was the 'Bhattias, Lohanas and Gujaratis'—Gujarati merchants and traders—who sustained the agitation, and 'chiefly the Bhattias under Lakhmidas Khimji'.[50]

Cow Protection Societies in
Late-nineteenth-century Maharashtra

Cow protection societies were originally started under the auspices of the Arya Samaj in 1882, and colonial officials held the influence of

[49] From Vincent's full report, 9 September 1893, P/4665, OIOC.

[50] Vincent's preliminary report, 12 August 1893, JD, vol. 94, compilation no. 948, 1893, MSA.

the samaj responsible for the cow protection riots in northern and western India.[51] The Arya Samaj, founded in 1875 in the Punjab by Swami Dayanand Saraswati, advocated a radically reformed Hinduism reminiscent of Chiplunkar's.[52] Dayanand, it is well documented, advocated a revival of Hinduism as he believed it existed in Vedic times. He sought to dispose of what he called the 'accretions' of Hinduism— idolatry, caste hierarchy, child marriage, pilgrimages, horoscopes, prohibitions against widow remarriage, restrictions on foreign travel— which comprised the vast bulk of Hindu practice.[53] These cleared, he argued, the kernel of religious purity reminiscent of the ancient heights of Hinduism would remain.

The Aryas developed a new set of practices, such as shuddhi (purification), which readmitted converts to Christianity or Islam back into the Hindu fold. Among these practices, Dayanand included cow protection. In a lecture in Bombay in 1882 he said that if India was to rise again in the scale of nations a common language, Hindi, was needed to promote unity, and foreign travel and commercial ventures to encourage prosperity. Most importantly, there was a pressing need to combat malnutrition and physical degeneration brought about by a scarcity of milk. For this he blamed cow slaughter and called for its immediate end.[54] Cow protection had initially come to the notice of officials in the Bombay Presidency with the Society for the Preservation of Horned Cattle, begun in Bombay in 1887.[55] It was a society with moderate goals, engaging in the building of goshalas (cow refuges) and occasionally taking a procession of animals through the city streets. The president of the society was the wealthy Parsi millowner Dinshaw Petit, and most of its members were Gujarati Hindus.[56] By 1892 cow

[51] 'Note on the Agitation Against Cow Killing', 24 January 1894, L/P&J/3/ 96, file 257, OIOC.

[52] On the Arya Samaj, see Kenneth Jones, *Arya Dharm: Hindu Consciousness in 19th Century Punjab* (Berkeley, 1976).

[53] Ibid., p. 32.

[54] On Dayanand's visit to Bombay in 1874, see Dobbin, *Urban Leadership*, pp. 254–9.

[55] See S. Krishnaswamy, 'A Riot in Bombay, August 11, 1893: A Study in Hindu–Muslim Relations', unpublished PhD dissertation, University of Chicago, 1966, p. 8.

[56] Bombay CID, SAPI, 14 November 1891 and 5 November 1892, noted in Cashman, *Myth of the Lokamanya*, p. 67.

protection societies existed in many Deccan towns. However, their activities seem to have passed without much notice until, in June 1893, they took a more militant turn under Lakhmidas Khimji.

The societies produced and circulated petitions and memorials, songs, pamphlets, posters, and newspapers. Petitions addressed to local officials argued that cow slaughter be prohibited on grounds of public health. One petitioner wrote that in earlier times 'cows maintained the people of the land in comfort and their agriculture in good condition. These animals furnish bullocks for agriculture, manure for enriching the soil, and give milk to drink and feed the owner.'[57] There came a change when 'the promiscuous slaughter of the cow led to the loss of the advantages set forth above. . . . The price of the agricultural products having risen, the nation is underfed and the health of the [people] is greatly affected.'[58] Many argued that cow slaughter had devastated India's economy and resulted in the undernourishment of its vegetarian population. And the culling of cattle, particularly since the advent of Muslim (Mughal) and Christian (British) rule, represented a grievous attack on the Hindu religion. Petitioners strove to present the societies as 'purely philanthropical and in no way political' for fear of their being deemed seditious and banned.[59] These were social welfare organizations, petitioners claimed, that existed to 'benefit . . . the community without regard to race or creed.' Protecting cattle from slaughter had 'increased the resources of the country and protected and improved agriculture.' The milk drawn from cows that had been given shelter was sent 'to railway stations and dharamsalas for distribution amongst the infants of travellers whose mothers were not able to suckle them, and the dung collected from them was every fortnight divided into three shares, one being sent to the musjids, another to the temples, and a third to the dharamsalas in the town of Dharwar.'[60] Gaurakshini sabhas (cow protection societies) also highlighted the importance of milk 'to eradicate the growing taste for spirituous liquors'.[61]

Saffron-clad lecturers at public meetings exhorted listeners to prevent the sale of cows altogether, urging them to pay an extra rupee to

[57] SAPI, Poona, 28 September 1893.
[58] Ibid.
[59] SAPI, Dharwar, 16 October 1893.
[60] Ibid.
[61] Ibid.

prevent cows from falling into the hands of butchers. Indeed, officials observed that cattle would be 'occasionally purchased to keep them out of the hands of butchers', and that 'the better class of Hindus have been noticed buying cattle that [were] being driven . . . to Poona and Bombay for slaughter.'[62] Cow protection, audiences were told, was an auspicious act, a religious duty which, if ignored, would result in a failure to attain eternal happiness.[63] Leaders were quick to insist that cow protection was 'not due to our religious sentimentality or any racial prejudice'.[64] Whatever their protestations, an anti-Muslim sentiment appeared integral to the movement: Muslims were identified as a force to be countered and resisted.[65] One poster depicted a cow, on which were inscribed the names of Hindu deities being milked by a matronly woman in the dress of a Chitpavan Brahman. A plump, milk-fed child stood by and in the background was a reverential Brahman worshipping the cow. Nearby a Muslim butcher with a villainous expression brandished a long knife and eyed the cow with murderous intent.[66] This representation of the villainous Muslim stalking the god-fearing Brahman and his gentle cow was repeated in picture after picture, and reports of variations on the theme circulated throughout the presidency. One pamphlet circulating after the riots lauded 'the brave deeds of the Ghatis and Kamatis' and asked them 'to fight again for cow and country'.[67] By 1893 cow protection societies existed in all districts of the presidency and conflicts similar to that of 11 August in Bombay had occurred in several urban centres in Maharashtra.

Responses

Indigenous responses to the Bombay riot overwhelmingly interpreted it as evidence of a fundamental antagonism between Hindus and Muslims. A letter to the editor of the *Times of India* signed 'A Hindoo' maintained that official understanding of the event was that 'the

[62] SAPI, Ahmednagar, 2 October 1893.

[63] SAPI, Satara, 16 August and 11 October 1893.

[64] SAPI, Poona, 28 September 1893.

[65] Conversation with a Maulvi, JD, vol. 194, compilation no. 948, 1893, 'Riots between Hindus and Muhammadans', MSA.

[66] JD, vol. 194, compilation no. 948, 1893, MSA.

[67] SAPI, Bombay, 4 September 1893.

unwise activity of the Cow-Protection Society set the ball rolling; that the Hindoo demonstration of sympathy for the Hindoo sufferers in the Prabhas-Patan riots made matters worse; and that finally, the counter-demonstration of the Mahomedans put a strain on the relations between the two communities which finally resulted in open rupture.' But the 'real origin', the author maintained, was 'the unfortunate ignorance and fanaticism of the uneducated members of the Mahomedan community.'[68] Opinion on the other side was equally stark. An appeal to raise money for the trials of Muslims arrested in the aftermath of the riot had been found making the rounds of Muslim neighbourhoods in Bombay. Muslims, it claimed, were being persecuted: 'the ship on which we are embarked . . . gyrating in the whirlpool of adversity, clouds of oppression . . . rising on all sides . . . Lo! The downpour has set in. It has already rained destruction in Azamgarh, Ballia, Mhow and Rangoon and Hilsa'—these being other districts where cow protection riots had taken place.[69] Hindus had 'begun rebellion and [had] without rhyme or reason become enemies of our life and property, honour and reputation. . . . We are forbidden to make sacrifices—Hindus interfere in our legitimate luxury.' A ban on cow sacrifice would simply be the beginning, for Muslims would be 'prevented . . . tomorrow from their even proclaiming the hour of prayer and the day after from praying altogether.'[70]

Officials feared that mobilization around cow slaughter was part of an agenda to build a Hindu bloc, the ultimate goal of which was to dislodge the British from power: 'the cow protection question furnishes a common platform on which all Hindus of whatever sect, however much at variance in other questions, can and do unite. . . . The aspiration at the root . . . being directed to the formation of an Indian nation. . . . Though the movement is ostensibly directed against the Muhammadans, it is . . . a form of disloyalty towards the British Government.'[71] However, the results of a government questionnaire

[68] *The Bombay Riots of August 1893,* reprinted from the *Times of India* (Bombay, 1894), p. 52.

[69] Pamphlet submitted by Babu Ramdhari Sahai to the District Magistrate, Muzaffarpur, Bengal, SAPI, Bengal, week ending 23 September 1893.

[70] Ibid.

[71] 'Note on the Agitation Against Cow Killing', L/P&J/3/96, OIOC.

demonstrated how much variation there was in this supposed community of Hindus. The membership of the Society for the Preservation of Horned Cattle, for instance, comprised those who were zealous advocates of the movement, but also, as one respondent put it, the 'old Hindu Shetias [who] know very little of its inner workings but pay handsomely when asked for the Go-Mata, Mother-Cow.'[72] Moreover, many who took part in the riots seemed little moved by gaurakshini sabhas or cow slaughter: 'The Ghatis know very little about the Gorakshak Sabha and are as indifferent now as they were before to the eating of beef. Even our high class Maratha Hindus with a few exceptions (like Dr Deshmukh, Dr Balchandra and Anna Martand who are well known agitators) were and even now *are* indifferent to the eating of beef by the Mahomedans. The agitation is carried on mainly by the Gujarati Vaishnavas and Jains.'[73]

A maulvi justice of the peace stated that the riot was organized by Western-educated Hindus as a means to oppose the British: 'Many of the educated young Hindus who visit Europe imbibe their hatred for the British from the foreigners they meet with. . . . Their vanity is equal to their political cheek and they look upon the British as aliens who feed upon and keep them from their birthright.'[74] He scoffed: '[t]he Cow, sacred in their eyes? Not more than the pig! I know one of their C.P. Sabba Leader eating beef and pork with as great gusto as his ancestors ever relished their Puranpoli!'[75] Cow protection, he argued, was a recent phenomenon, and entirely political. How else could one explain the fact that 'during the late riots many of those who formed the Hindu mobs were not only cow-eating, but cow-carrion eating Telegu Chamars and Mahars'?[76]

---

[72] Untitled questionnaire, 20 August 1893, JD, vol. 194, compilation no. 948, 1893, MSA.

[73] Questionnaire. The question asked: 'How far were the Ghatis and Kamatis indifferent to the eating of beef by Musalmans till they were stirred to rage by the English speaking Gujarati Brahmin, Bania, Bhatia and Jain?' Ibid.

[74] Conversation with a Maulvi, ibid.

[75] Ibid. *Puranpoli*, or *puran puri*, a roti filled with a sweet stuffing, is a delicacy in Maharashtra and Gujarat.

[76] Ibid.

That some rioters were beef-eaters appears to qualify the role of cow protection in the conflict. Similarly, the questionnaire reflected a spectrum of positions within the movement itself. Gyanendra Pandey, in his study of a similar riot in 1893 in the United Provinces, argues against easy conclusions of ideological uniformity among those who participated. Pandey also questions whether they embraced an idea of themselves as Hindus in the long term. He concludes that it was the way officials recorded these events that forged an understanding of them—albeit in the colonial rather than indigenous imagination—as riots between Hindus and Muslims. Evidence from the Bombay riot suggests that this argument can be taken a stage further. Beyond colonial classification, it was also the ways in which Indians themselves engaged with and negotiated in the language of these categories that gave them form.

In the weeks following the riots, subscriptions were raised to rebuild mosques that had been derelict for many years in several parts of the presidency. In Ahmednagar district, for example, it was reported that 'Muhammadan subscriptions . . . are being raised ostensibly with a view to repairing the Jumma Masjid here but they probably have some connection with the riots in Bombay, as they were only started a month ago and there have been no subscriptions of the kind raised before, while the Jumma Masjid and other mosques have been in their present condition for years.'[77] In addition, in towns across the presidency—Wai, Yeola, Poona, and Belgaum—Hindus began to take processions past mosques during the time of prayer, claiming this to be their ancient and therefore rightful religious custom. Muslims claimed that it was their time-honoured tradition to pray in silence. Officials had first legislated on the 'music before mosques' issue in 1859. Conflict around this took place sporadically in various districts in Maharashtra after this point, but it was during the post-riot period in late 1893 that the question once again became a pressing concern. Colonial officials discussed how to respond to petitions from self-styled representatives of Hindu and Muslim communities to legislate in their favour, in ways that would uphold and not alter the 'established customary practice'

[77] SAPI, Ahmednagar, 19 September 1893.

of either.[78] Thus, while people from a range of occupational and caste backgrounds participated in cow protection movements and the August riot, and had their own reasons for doing so, the language in which this was negotiated was in terms of a broad Hindu community.

It was also in the ways that the conflicts were sought to be resolved that this became apparent. That the riots themselves did not create an irreconcilable rift between people in towns and districts that had been affected by conflict was apparent when, as early as October 1893, despite rumours of distrust between Hindus and Muslims, it was noted that trade and general interaction in market centres across the presidency had recommenced.[79] Moreover, the organization of reconciliation fetes to demonstrate this reborn unity was widespread.[80] A key feature of the attempts at reconciliation was the role of 'natural leaders'—Hindu and Muslim religious men, as well as Western-educated professionals— who took on the task of brokering good will between communities.[81] Thus, representatives came together in Dharwar district to draw up regulations on the music question.[82] The possibility of presidency-wide conciliation boards to address such problems was also raised. In their attempt to resolve local conflicts, reconciliation committees appointed Hindus and Muslims who would address their constituencies as such, and not as members of a particular sect or caste. This process was significant because it reproduced the idea that Hindu and Muslim communities existed as recognizable wholes, and implied a parity between them. So, in Nasik, as in many other places, community leaders held meetings where they passed resolutions demonstrating 'great sympathy for the Hindu and Muslim sufferers in the recent Bombay riots . . . [and] a standing committee consisting of 12 Hindus and 12 Muslims was appointed to decide amicably the disputes arising from religious differences between both parties.'[83] That conciliation boards

---

[78] SAPI, Dharwar, 26 October, 1893; JD, vol. 284, compilation no. 545, pt III, 1894, 'Riots between Hindus and Muhammadans in Yeola of the Nasik District', MSA. See the final section in this chapter.

[79] SAPI, Bombay, 11 September 1893.

[80] SAPI, Bombay, 9 October 1893.

[81] On the question of 'natural leaders', see Freitag, *Collective Action*, chapter 2.

[82] SAPI, Dharwar, 26 October 1893.

[83] SAPI, Nasik, 30 September 1893.

were made up of Muslims and Hindus reflected the longstanding colonial idea that Indian society comprised sects and communities rather than individuals.[84] And Indians themselves took on these categories in their dealings with the state, as well as in the ways in which they addressed their own communities.

There was little especially new about the conflicts of August 1893: these were violent riots understood to have taken place between Muslims and Hindus, and after they were over people returned to living as neighbours and trading with each other as they had before.[85] The conflicts had not altered the nature of social relations in any permanent way; nor was there a cross-caste ideological coherence. Nevertheless, societies now existed across the presidency that expressed a common set of ideas about cow protection as a duty of Hindus, the plight of the country, and the demonic character of the Muslim butcher. It was these ideas that would be mobilized in the decades to come.

The Ganpati Festivals

A significant innovation in the articulation of a Hindu community in western India occurred the year after the Bombay cow protection riot with the modification of the Ganpati festival. Ganpati festivals became public events around the same time as the cow protection movements became more militant. Ganpati or Ganesh—the elephant-headed god and favourite deity of western India, the overcomer of obstacles—is also seen to bring peace and embody wisdom, and Ganesh Chaturthi features prominently in the ritual calendar of the region. Raminder Kaur has argued that the festival had been celebrated in a 'quasi-public' way since the time of the peshwas: the image of the god, the murti, would be installed in a room, and celebrations would be confined

[84] On this idea, see David Washbrook, 'Law, State and Agrarian Society in Colonial India', *MAS*, 15, 3, 1981; Bernard Cohn, 'The Census, Social Structure and Objectification in South Asia', in *An Anthropologist Among the Historians and Other Essays* (Delhi, 1987); Arjun Appadurai, 'Number in the Colonial Imagination', in Carol Breckenridge and Peter van der Veer (eds), *Orientalism and the Post-Colonial Predicament: Perspectives on South Asia* (Philadelphia, 1993).

[85] Katherine Prior also makes this point. See 'Making History: The State's Intervention in Urban Religious Disputes in the North-Western Provinces in the Early Nineteenth Century', *MAS*, 27, 1, 1993.

essentially to the kinship group.[86] After 1818, Kaur argues, widespread observance of the festival declined due to lack of patronage, although it continued to be held throughout the nineteenth century in a limited way: a group of three or four families would celebrate it over a three- to five-day period, at the end of which the Ganesh murti would be immersed in a river or the sea or in a well. The end of the nineteenth century saw a shift in the way Ganpati was celebrated, for the festival moved back into the public realm. By the 1890s, moreover, the cele- bration began to be politicized. This development is usually attributed to the efforts of Bal Gangadhar Tilak, although Kaur argues persuasively that there was an 'organic public growth' of the festival in 1892 that Tilak helped propagate but did not pioneer.[87] The revived Ganpati festivals, she maintains, captured the imagination of many Brahmans who had already been involved in cow protection societies in Poona and Bombay, and Tilak was simply their most avid publicist.

There is little doubt, however, that Tilak was at the forefront of re- working the Ganpati festival. By 1893 the festival had re-emerged as a very public event, one in which all Hindu castes participated to- gether. The 1893 festival was a ten-day affair, celebrated in the main avenues of cities and towns across Maharashtra and northern Karnataka. Images of Ganesh were displayed in mandaps—tents where religious ceremonies are conducted. On the tenth day the figures were taken in procession through the streets, on floats or by hand, and immersed in the sea or a river. This new Ganpati festival was consciously modelled as a mirror image of the Shia festival of Muharram in which Hindus had customarily participated. By publicly mobilizing western India's favourite deity, Tilak sought to bring low- and high-caste Marathas into the same political as well as physical space, and to have them iden- tify as Maratha Hindus.[88] The following year, 1894, witnessed a head- on collision between the two festivals, when they fell on the same days.

---

[86] Kaur, *Performative Politics*, p. 31.

[87] Ibid., chapter 2.

[88] The category 'Maratha' was one whose meaning was fluid and complex, shifting over the course of several centuries. It was a category that high and low castes in western India fought to appropriate and that colonial officials sought to categorize: see Prachi Deshpande, 'Caste as Maratha: Social Categories, Colo- nial Policy and Identity in Early Twentieth Century Maharashtra', *IESHR*, 41, 1, 2004.

In remaking Ganpati in the image of Muharram, Tilak sought to define it as a festival for Hindus and ensure that Muharram became a solely Muslim preserve.

Bal Gangadhar Tilak

Bal Gangadhar Tilak was born into an orthodox Konkanasth Brahman family in 1856.[89] His great-grandfather had been a district revenue collector (mamlatdar) under the last peshwas, his grandfather worked in the colonial survey department, and his father in the education department. Tilak studied for his BA and LLM at Deccan College, during which time he befriended fellow student Gopal Ganesh Agarkar. The two began talking about the importance of free or low-cost private educational institutions for Indians, run along the lines of missionary schools. A generation of young Western-educated Brahmans had been greatly influenced by the reform movements of the nineteenth century. Some, such as Gokhale, favoured reform framed in the terms of liberal humanism. Others, such as Chiplunkar, emphasized the importance of reform from within the traditions of Hinduism. When Tilak and Agarkar heard that Chiplunkar intended to start a school in Poona, they asked him to head their project, opening the New English School in 1880. The school proved a great success. By 1885 it had 1,200 students, 15 per cent of whom were free and half-free scholars. Its founders aimed to establish a network of schools around the presidency, to which end they founded the Deccan Education Society in 1884.

In 1881 Tilak and Agarkar, as we saw, became editors of *Mahratta* and *Kesari*. Both newspapers soon became vehicles for social and political commentary. Increasingly critical of the government, they urged people not to accept unpopular policies and to speak out against the drain of wealth from India. By 1891 *Kesari* had become the most widely read publication in Maharashtra, reaching a weekly circulation of 4,000. But Agarkar and Tilak's approaches diverged sharply. Agarkar, a student of logic and moral philosophy, had lost faith in religion and wanted to overhaul Hindu religious customs—something Tilak was

[89] See Ram Gopal, *Lokamanya Tilak: A Biography* (Bombay, 1956); Theodore L. Shay, *The Legacy of the Lokamanya: The Political Philosophy of Bal Gangadhar Tilak* (Bombay, 1956); Stanley Wolpert, *Tilak and Gokhale: Revolution and Reform in the Making of Modern India* (Berkeley, 1962).

deeply opposed to. After an acrimonious battle Tilak resigned from the Deccan Education Society in 1890, leaving it to Agarkar and taking control of the two newspapers. The event that catapulted Tilak into the public eye was the Age of Consent Bill in 1891, which proposed that the marriageable age for girls should be raised from ten to twelve. Tilak led a vigorous campaign against the bill in both newspapers, attracting particular support from orthodox sections of Hindu society. While he agreed with the notion of a later age of marriage for girls, he opposed what he saw as illegitimate interference by the state in religious practice. The Age of Consent Bill was hotly debated around the country. While much of Poona's English-educated elite supported it, many young Brahmans, as well as the orthodox rank and file, defended Tilak's position. A meeting of shastris in February 1891 resolved that the bill would 'interfere with social practice ordained by religious authorities.'[90] Although passed, the controversial campaign pushed Tilak to the forefront of politics in Poona, serving to politicize the discontent felt by three generations of Maratha Brahmans.

Muharram and the Ganpati Festivals

Muharram, the Shia commemoration of the martyrdom of the Prophet's grandsons, was traditionally a cross-community festival in Poona. Although it was an occasion marked only in the Shia ritual calendar, it was popular among many communities. Hindu musicians would be hired to play, dancing (nautch) girls performed, Hindu labourers' bullock carts were hired to carry the symbolic biers (tazias) of the Imams Hasan and Hussain. Indeed, sections of the Hindu population regularly made their own tazias, which would be paraded and then immersed along with those of Muslims. It was a festival that in Poona usually passed without disturbance.

July 1894 was different. A petition sent by inamdar Abdulla Khan Mokasi and 370 other inhabitants of Poona complained that that year 'the Brahmans . . . prevent[ed] the Hindu musicians from playing music before the *tabuts*, and the Hindu dancing girls . . . from singing *marsias* . . . they . . . prevent[ed] any labourers or bullock carts from being made available for carrying the *tabuts* even in the case of

[90] Cashman, *Myth of the Lokamanya*, p. 57.

those Hindus who had made *tabuts*.'[91] The district superintendent of police, MacPherson, noted in his report to the district magistrate that in previous years it was commonplace for there to be more Hindu than Muslim tazias and 'on the last day, the day of immersion, by far the greater part of the procession was entirely Hindu.'[92] That year, however, gangs of young men visited Hindu neighbourhoods and told people they should not participate in the Muharram preparations. They did the same in Muslim neighbourhoods, but MacPherson noted that their behaviour here was more aggressive: 'The greater portion of the Poona City is entirely Hindu and in those parts these noisy "melas" might have been quite unobjectionable. . . . [H]owever . . . they selected in preference the parts of the city where they would come in contact with the Muhammadans, and . . . in passing the mosques of the latter they would, on being prevented from playing music, become unnecessarily boisterous and noisy.'[93]

Numerous songs and pamphlets, published at local presses, were produced especially for the festival and circulated through the city. All shared similar elements: they chastised Hindus for their 'infatuation' with Islam, for dancing at the Muharram festival, and for disgracing the Hindu religion by forgetting who they were. They urged Hindus to be 'warriors and not women' in memory of Shivaji their liberator, to honour their duties of safeguarding the worship of the cow, and to have pride in their religion through reverence towards Shiva, Krishna, Ram, and Ganpati. One pamphlet instructed Hindus not to abandon their gods or the path of their ancestors by prostrating themselves before pirs (Muslim religious guides). They should honour the cow, break the tabuts, and 'put down the haughtiness of the Yavans' to celebrate Ganpati on a grand scale.[94] The verses narrated a golden age of Hinduism and the glories of Maratha history, lost because Indians had

[91] Petition from 370 inhabitants of Poona, 1894, JD, vol. 287, compilation no. 967, pt I, 1894, 'Riots in Poona between Hindus and Muhammadans', MSA.

[92] T.R.M. MacPherson, District Superintendent of Police, Poona, to District Magistrate, Poona, 21 September 1894, JD, vol. 288, compilation no. 967, pt II, 1894, 'Riots in Poona between Hindus and Muhammadans', MSA.

[93] Ibid.

[94] Untitled pamphlet in Marathi received at the Oriental Translator's Department, Bombay, 13 December 1894, ibid.

forgotten their way and surrendered to an alien religion. The notion of the precipitous decline of Hindu society in the face of alien assault was central to the ways in which reformers such as Chiplunkar and Dayanand retold a story of Indian history. This narrative of decline and humiliation in turn underpinned the politics of upper-caste activists and publicists at the turn of the twentieth century.

Most Hindus heeded the call to stay away from Muharram. Few tazias were made, no Hindu musicians could be persuaded to play, and very few—even with the offer of increased remuneration—agreed to carry tazias on the day of immersion. On the evening prior to the final day it was reported that 'most of the Hindu shops were closed and no lamps or illuminations put up'.[95] Simultaneous plans were being made for a festival in honour of Ganpati; the same gangs of young Brahmans who were organizing the boycott of Muharram were planning something unusually grand. A Marathi pamphlet entitled 'Do not make the Dolas [tazias]' outlined plans for the Ganpati festival:

> It is proposed to have processions in the Ganesh Chaturthi day this year in honour of Shri Ganpati . . . 'Melas' (gangs of fakirs &c.) such as are seen to be going about of late during the Mohurrum will go about at the time of the Ganpati procession and excellent songs have been prepared for the occasion. In this way by celebrating the Ganesh Chaturthi festival with more and more pomp and by entertaining a pride for his own religion and gods, every Hindu should give up his fondness for an alien religion.[96]

Local residents, Hindu and Muslim, noted that these preparations were in sharp contrast to previous years.[97] They prompted a slew of anxious and irate petitions from Muslim residents. One drew attention to 'the aggressive attitude of the Brahmins of Poona, in connection with the approaching Ganpati festival', maintaining that secret preparations were being made to give a 'needlessly mischievous aspect to the said Hindu festival'.[98] Petitioners held what they identified as the

[95] MacPherson to District Magistrate, Poona, 21 September 1894, ibid.

[96] Poona, 26 August 1894, Oriental Translator's Dept, JD, vol. 287, compilation no. 967, pt I, 1894, MSA.

[97] See, for example, the statement of Mr Coopuswamy Visairangam Mudllar, Rastias Peit, aged 48, taken 29 August 1894, ibid.

[98] Memorial to Governor Harris, ibid.

'Hindu press', with its circulation of 'inflammatory leaflets and pamphlets wherein the Moharram is ridiculed', responsible.[99] Significantly, Muslim petitioners argued that the Ganpati festival that year, with its recitation of verses, public procession, and immersion of effigies was being structured deliberately to mimic Muharram—an observation that the district superintendent of police of Poona confirmed: 'The gangs of youths parading the streets and reciting verses is in imitation of the "Alla-wa-mela" of the Mohurum and the erection by public subscription of Ganpatis in "mandwas" in various parts of the city, their subsequent removal on carts accompanied by a public procession with music etc, and final immersion in the river corresponds in every detail with the procession and immersion of the Taboots [tazias] on the last day of the Mohurum.'[100]

The transformation of the Ganpati festival in 1894 was an attempt to reinvent and politicize an established ritual. As a concerted bid to prevent Hindus from participating in Muharram, however, it was only temporarily successful. Many Hindus who deserted Muharram in favour of the Ganpati festival returned the following year. Yet official concern about public order and suspicion of the motives of Maharashtrian Brahmans meant that Muharram would no longer be an occasion for all communities. R.H. Vincent issued a public order that year indicating how Muharram was to be celebrated in the future. Henceforth, licences would be required to build tabuts and would be issued only to Muslims.[101] At the same time, a much larger number of people from Shia sects, such as the Khojas and the Borahs, were observed to have joined the festival that year. Also observed was 'the attendance in much larger numbers than before of . . . Hindustani Musalmans (Sunis), who in parties of several hundreds formed part of the Suni procession, though they did not belong to any of the licensed Tabuts.'[102] That year, through legislative intervention, Muharram in Poona had lost many of its Hindu participants, and gained a new contingent of Muslims. Concurrently, in an attempt to influence the final legislation, self-styled

[99] Ibid.

[100] District Superintendent of Police, Poona, to the District Magistrate, Poona, 29 August 1894, ibid.

[101] JD, vol. 154, compilation no. 1022, 1895, MSA.

[102] Ibid. Parentheses in original.

representatives of Hindu opinion began submitting petitions on which festivals should be exempt from the new rules relating to music before mosques.[103]

The remade Ganpati festivals had taken place in towns and cities across Bombay Presidency that year. However, official insistence that 'all the Hindus sympathised with the movement' was not accurate.[104] Without doubt, large numbers participated in the 1894 festival and communities that had previously joined the Muharram were conspicuously absent. But the success of the organizers in making it a cross-caste event was limited. Raminder Kaur and Richard Cashman have both argued that participation meant different things to different people.[105] The floats, for example, tended to be drawn from different sections of the city. Brahmans and non-Brahmans were segregated by residence; thus, floats were formed on a caste or occupational basis. In some neighbourhoods they were exclusively Brahman, in others non-Brahman—comprising separately, tailors, weavers, goldsmiths, traders, and sometimes millhands. The character of each was different, depending on the particular community organizing it: Brahman melas, for example, were much more openly militant, singing verses specifically written for the occasion. Non-Brahman melas, according to Cashman, 'were almost exclusively religious in orientation.'[106] Thus, there was little that tied them together ideologically. The new festivals continued for some years, but participation became increasingly sporadic. They had not succeeded in sustaining the participation of non-Brahmans. Nor had the semiticized upper-caste Hinduism that the new hymns and poems reflected, and that Tilak was trying to build, materialized.

However, the political, cultural, and linguistic innovations of the Ganpati festival had, like the cow protection movements, served to create an ideological space that proved more enduring. The boycott of Muharram and celebration of the Ganpati festivals had employed a language identifying who the oppressors were—the Muslims and the

[103] JD, vol. 173, compilation no. 838, 1895, MSA.

[104] H.T. Ommanney, District Magistrate of Poona, to Government of Bombay, 24 September 1894, MSA.

[105] See Kaur, *Performative Politics*, pp. 59–63; Cashman, *Myth of the Lokamanya*, p. 85.

[106] Ibid., p. 86.

British—and urged Hindus to resist the illegitimate rule of foreigners. As with cow protection, this was replicated in urban centres across the presidency. Although participation in the Ganpati festivals fell away quite quickly after 1895, it would become important again in later years. Ganpati festivals and cow protection were revived regularly throughout the twentieth century as a way to display opposition to the state or to Muslims through a militant upper-caste Hinduism. But what significance did this emerging political language have in localities in this period? The events in Yeola provide some insight into this question.

Music before Mosques

On 6 February 1894 in Yeola, a small weaving centre in Nasik district in the easternmost part of Bombay Presidency, conflict erupted over a report that a pig's head had been thrown into a local mosque. On receiving the news, the mamlatdar went to the mosque to verify the facts and found 'two portions of a dead pig, cut in half, lying in the mosque and its enclosure'.[107] He urged the crowd that had gathered 'not to attempt any reprisals', but news soon arrived that 'the Musalmans had retaliated by slaughtering a cow in the Hindu temple . . . known by the name of Muralidhar or Gopal-Krishna'. The mamlatdar found a cow 'slaughtered by *halalkhoring* in the Musalman fashion, lying inside the temple.'[108] Rioting broke out and military assistance was sent for. Later in the day the mamlatdar heard that 'the Hindus were making arrangements to burn the Juma mosque', but, while preparing for police protection to be sent, news came that Muslims 'had set fire to the Muralidhar temple'. Elsewhere, mosques and temples were damaged or destroyed and four people were reported killed.

The collector and district magistrate, H.E. Winter, wrote on 10 February that the riot was 'altogether unexpected'. And if one is to go by the commissioner's remarks, it was also somewhat unremarkable.

[107] From the report of the Commissioner-in-Charge in Poona, 16 February 1894. One of a series of enclosures sent by G.C. Whitworth, Acting Secretary to Government, Judicial Department, 15 March 1894, JD, vol. 284, compilation no. 545, pt III, 1894, MSA.

[108] Ibid.

What is striking, however, is that it prompted an official correspondence involving a detailed retrospective examination of a series of conflicts between 'Musalmans' and 'Hindus' that began as early as September 1893. At issue was whether Hindu processional music could be played in front of mosques during the hours of prayer. The commissioner pointed to 'a similar disturbance, but not originating in the same way . . . [that] took place at Yeola in October last.' It was a conflict that was followed by 'a systematic boycotting of the Musalman traders and artisans by the Hindus which resulted in great injury to the local trade and in many of the Musalmans being driven away from the town altogether'.[109] However, by January 1894 'friendly feeling' was reported in the town, the boycott had eased, and people were once again resuming trade. The conflict in February, then, took officials by surprise. Since they had no warning of it, they concluded that it was part of a number of disturbances whose roots they traced to the processions for the Ganpati festivals, which began in Yeola on 14 September the previous year.

The conflicts in Yeola had a profound effect on the social life of the town. At the end of the nineteenth century it had a population of about 20,000, of which 55 per cent were defined as Hindus, 26 per cent as Muslims, and 19 per cent from other communities.[110] The second half of the century had witnessed important social, economic, and ecological changes in Yeola. Natural disasters in eastern Nasik, from drought and famine in the 1870s, through locust plagues and cattle disease in the 1880s, and on to bubonic plague in the 1890s, had hit the region hard. Some of the worst ravages were in Yeola.[111] Unstable climatic conditions, the consequence of which was a dramatic rise in the price of foodstuffs, had made the position of the peasant cultivator of eastern Nasik highly insecure. Yeola was the most important market town in the collectorate. It was the only town that possessed any specialized manufacturing industry, with only 15 per cent of its population involved in agricultural

---

[109] Ibid.

[110] Papers relating to the revenue survey settlement of the Yeola Taluka of the Nasik Collectorate (1876–95), SRB, V/23/288, Index no. 1086, OIOC.

[111] *Gazetteer of the Bombay Presidency, Vol. XVI Nasik* (Bombay, 1885), pp. 300–3.

work.[112] Yeola had long been famed for its manufacture of silk cloth and gold thread for the embroidery of pagris, or turbans.[113] The town had been founded at the beginning of the eighteenth century when an ancestor of the village headman (patil) at the time had promised a Gujarati merchant by the name of Shamdas Valji a trade monopoly if he brought silk weavers to settle at Yeola. The monopoly was continued by the peshwa's government and newcomers could not start silk looms in Yeola except by paying the original settlers the sum of £35 (Rs 350), the majority of which went to the Gujarati silk weavers for a caste dinner. The British initially respected the monopoly, but then overturned it in 1864. By the 1880s the demographic profile of the weavers had changed significantly to include several hundred Khatris, Koshtis, Salis, and Muslims. Likewise, the profile of dealers had broadened considerably from Gujaratis to include members of several other castes: Pathis, Thakurs, Bhrama Kshatris, Shimpis, and Muslims. The seven silk-spinning establishments of Yeola were all Maratha-owned and control of much of the trade, despite the termination of the monopoly, remained in the hands of Gujarati banias and high-caste Marathas.[114]

In 1856–7 many of Nasik district's villages had become khalsa, or government-controlled land, and were 'settled' by the revenue survey.[115] Until August 1892, however, Yeola had been a 'Vinchur Saranjami' town, that is, one still not controlled by the government.[116] The nearby town of Vinchur was in the neighbouring Niphad taluka and was the residence of the chief of Vinchur, the 'Vinchurkar', a first class sardar.[117] Vinchur had been granted as a military or saranjam jagir to Vithal Shivdev, an ancestor of the chief in pre-colonial times. The Vinchurkar, a Deshastha Brahman, held forty-five villages in Nasik, as

[112] Papers relating to the original survey settlement of eight villages in the Yeola Taluka of the Nasik Collectorate (1898–9), SRB, V/23/291, Index no. 1131, OIOC.

[113] SRB, V/23/288, Index no. 1086.

[114] *Gazetteer, Nasik*, pp. 662–3.

[115] Ibid., p. 355.

[116] H.M. Gibbs, District Superintendent of Police, Nasik, to Commissioner, Poona, 12 February 1894, JD, vol. 284, no. 545, pt III of 1894, MSA.

[117] *Gazetteer, Nasik*, p. 662.

well as elsewhere in Maratha country, of which Yeola was one.[118] Yeola's Sardeshmukh (revenue superintendent) in 1892, at the time of the Vinchurkar's death, was one Ramchandra Ganesh Barve. Barve, a Chitpavan Brahmin, was a watandar (holder of a hereditary land right) who, along with his brother Trimbak Ganesh Barve, enjoyed shares of the tax-free pension attached to the watan. On the passing of the Vinchurkar in August 1892, Yeola, being without an owner or ruler, lapsed to the colonial government, and all the attached lands came under the revenue survey settlement.

Ramchandra was known to the police as a 'well known agitator' in the cause of cow protection and had launched a boycott of Muslim tradesmen and artisans in Yeola in late 1893. It is unclear how long-standing his commitment to the cause had been, but there can be little doubt of the links between his particular brand of militant, anti-imperial, anti-Muslim politics and the potentially devastating changes taking place through government appropriation of land, immigration of large numbers of pardeshis (outsiders), and the diminishing worth of traditional positions of power such as those of the deshmukh. Ramchandra Ganesh Barve, probably from a long line of village elites, had seen many of his castemen before him lose their status with the coming of the British, as they went from being prominent village revenue officials to audited bureaucrats. This was now the fate that appeared to be awaiting him.

A court order passed in 1859 by the sadr faujdari adalat had outlined the conditions under which Hindu processional music would be allowed in front of mosques. It determined that music in temples that formed part of religious worship had to be respected. However, since processional street music formed no part of religious ceremonies or prayer, it should only be conceded when it did not interfere with the liberty of others. Thus, the court ruled that 'The right of praying in their mosque must be secured to the Muhammadans so long as their prayers are not a nuisance to others, and the Hindus may be allowed to accompany their processions with music so long as their music is not a nuisance to others; but whenever it becomes a nuisance, it ought, the Judges think, to be prohibited.'[119] The 1859 order had set a precedent

[118] Ibid.
[119] Whitworth, Acting Secretary to Government, 16 February, 1894 detailing the riots in Yeola, JD, vol. 284, no. 545, pt III, 1894, MSA.

and was referred to again after the events of early 1894. Officials saw the February riot as linked to a series of conflicts that had taken place between Hindus and Muslims the previous year around the issue of music before mosques.

Conflicts first arose in Yeola during the Ganpati festival in September 1893, and again during Dassera in October. The Ganpati festival began on 14 September with a procession led by the Salis, a weaving caste, many of whom had migrated from the western part of Hyderabad to the Deccan after the 1840s, and who would thus have been in Yeola only a couple of generations.[120] It was intended that the procession would pass the Patel's mosque, one of the central mosques in the town, but that, as was usual, all music other than cymbals (tals) would be stopped within ten paces either side. Several hundred Muslims assembled at the mosque, many armed with sticks, but the procession passed quietly. On the final day of the festival, 24 September, Winter ordered that the Patel's mosque be closed between 3 and 4 p.m. while the procession passed and that only cymbals and small drums (tabors) should be played at fifteen paces on either side. It was noted that in the ten days of the festival 'the ground of dispute appears to have widened'. By the end of the week 'the Hindus demanded the right to pass the mosque playing all kinds of music, and the use of tabors as well as cymbals in front of the mosque was declared to be customary by several of the persons questioned by Mr Winter.'[121] As it happened, the order was carried out and the procession again passed off peacefully.

The next series of disputes around processional music took place about a month later, on 19 October, with the Balaji procession during the Dassera festival. There were to be minor processions held during the nine preceding days, and this time the district magistrate issued an order regulating the processions from the outset. This stated that from 10 to 17 October no procession of Balaji was to pass any mosque at all. On 18 October the procession could pass the Juma Masjid between 2 and 4 p.m. The following day it could pass the Patel's mosque during the same hours, and on 20 October the Banarasi, Kharekari, and Aina mosques between 5 and 6 p.m. There was to be no music other than

[120] Douglas Haynes and Tirthankar Roy, 'Conceiving Mobility: Weavers' Migrations in Pre-colonial and Colonial India', *IESHR*, 36, 1, 1999.

[121] Whitworth's Letter, 16 February 1894, JD, vol. 284, compilation no. 545, pt III, 1894, MSA.

a cymbal within fifteen paces on each side of any of the mosques. However, no processions were taken out until the first day on which they were allowed to pass mosques, 18 October. The procession was rushed down a side street, past the front of the Juma Masjid instead of by the west door of the compound, as had been decided in advance. Some present at the mosque confronted the processionists, resulting in a fight. For the following day's procession it was agreed that music would be continuous but that no instrument would be played immediately in front of the mosque. However, when the procession reached the mosque, the processionists refused to adhere to the compromise. Although there was no open confrontation on 19 October, the hostilities had clearly not dissipated: three days later, in response to a rumour that Muslims intended to slaughter a cow in public, a crowd of about 2,000 Hindus armed with sticks gathered at one of the gates of the town. Though the rumour proved to be false, the majority entered the town, and Assistant Collector Hayward heard that Hindus intended to take out a Balaji with 9,000 men collected from neighbouring villages, and to pass the town's mosques playing all kinds of music on 3 November.[122]

The conflicts prompted a slew of appeals to colonial officials. Petitioners from both sides maintained that the conflicts had arisen from the wrongful interference in the longstanding customs, religious practices, and legal rights of their community. These assertions were legitimized with reference to the queen's proclamation of 1858. In order to justify their claims, petitioners had to make the argument that what they defended was a tradition integral to the practise of their religion. Thus, one petition, signed by 'the Hindoos of Yeola', claimed that 'Since the late Mahomedan Riots in Bombay, the Mahomedans of Yeola as other Mahomedans in the Mofussil, are convinced that they can now interfere, with impunity, with the religious rights of the Hindoos.'[123] They argued that during Ganesh Chaturthi 'Hindoos of every caste [would] . . . carry God Ganpati in procession.' The custom, they maintained, was for the procession to pass along the main public

[122] Ibid.

[123] Petition from 'the Hindoos of Yeola', lead signatory: Ramchandra Ganesh Barve, dated Yeola, 20 September 1893 to J.F. Fleet, Commissioner, Poona. JD, vol. 282, compilation no. 545, pt I, 1894, 'Riots at Nasik between Hindus and Mahomedans', MSA.

roads and to be made up of people playing a variety of instruments. It would pass along the road where the Patel's mosque was situated, a route that had been used 'for the above purpose from ancient times.'[124] According to the petitioners, this year the practice had been violated: about 500 Muslims wielding sticks and knives told the Salis, who led the procession, that they would prevent them on pain of death from passing the Patel's mosque. An appeal had been made to the authorities, the petition continued, whose place it was to protect them, but who, through inexperience and incompetence, 'were unable to restrain the Mahomedans from invading the religious rights of the Hindoos'.[125] Muslim petitioners also employed the same language of protection from interference. In the words of the commissioner-in-charge in Poona, 'Yeola Musalmans . . . claim that their mosques are practically always open for prayer and preaching, and that consequently they must never, at any hour on any day, be disturbed by Hindu music,' something Winter saw as 'an innovation in consequence of the Bombay riots.'[126]

Having deemed it their duty to protect the customary rights of communities, officials struggled to determine exactly what these rights were. Whitworth noted that in Yeola an order had been passed regarding the music question that directed: 'when passing a mosque, the Hindu procession should play only cymbals and tabors and that all other music should be stopped when the procession was within 15 paces' distance from the mosque on either side.'[127] However, he went on, this represented 'the nature of a compromise rather than an adjudication to any existing custom', and stemmed more from a concern for 'the maintenance of order in the use of public streets'.[128] This practice contradicted the rulings of the sadr and high courts to allow music when it was objected to as disturbing the public worship of any community, but he maintained that neither the 'playing of music by

[124] Ibid.

[125] Ibid.

[126] Commissioner-in-Charge in Poona to the Secretary to Government, 17 November 1893, Demi-official correspondence, ibid.

[127] Whitworth's letter, 16 February 1894, JD, vol. 284, compilation no. 545, pt III, 1894, MSA.

[128] Ibid.

Hindus in front of a mosque or by Musalmans in front of a temple [were part of] a religious observance, in the exercise of which . . . either community has a right to be protected'.[129] As long as the people of Yeola were on good terms with each other, he wrote,

> questions as to the right of Hindu processions to play music when passing Muhammadan mosques did not trouble them much. Such questions were avoided because, from respect for the feelings of Muhammadans, Hindus of their own accord gave up the use of music, or at all events, the use of noisier kinds of music when passing mosques. And if they ever played cymbals or tabors while stopping louder music which might have been objected to, no offence seems to have been taken by the Muhammadan community because it was obvious that no offence was ever intended.[130]

However, now that relations in the town had become fraught, Winter saw fit to survey the residents of Yeola to determine what the customary practice of the playing of processional music should be. Those interviewed had at one point or another occupied a range of positions of authority—as police inspectors, sub-judges, head constables, older residents, and so on—in the town.

Balkissan Amirsing, who had been a police inspector for eleven years, stated that the general custom was for large instruments to stop playing but tals would continue.[131] Haphijuddin Jhulphikar Ali, head karkun (police constable) at Yeola, stated that until that year there had been no disturbances around processions. He had not seen if tals were played or not, but thought that they had not been 'because no dispute arose.'[132] Ramji Khanoji, a Hindu Maratha, had been the head constable at Yeola for two and a half years and had a different view. He said he had witnessed no dispute between Hindus and Muslims, although at 'the tabut time [i.e. Muharram] some Mussulmans objected to other Mussulmans playing before the Multanpuri mosque and the music was accordingly stopped.' He added that he had seen the Balaji's procession pass by two mosques and the music was stopped because

---

[129] Ibid.
[130] Ibid.
[131] Testimonies, ibid.
[132] Ibid.

'tals . . . were not played—nor were *mridangs*, in fact no music was played before the mosques but the Hindus passed calling on the name of their god. The Mussulmans would have objected to music.'[133]

Officials sought to remain faithful to the particular history of Yeola by looking for answers in the locality. However, the competing claims made it apparent to Assistant Collector Hayward that custom was 'not so clear as might have been desired'.[134] They addressed this problem in a number of ways. In the attempt to find a local solution, it was suggested that 'if there is no custom on which the authorities can rely, then get the opposing parties to agree to an arrangement which in the course of time will become a custom'.[135] But since agreement was not forthcoming, Hayward turned to the practice in neighbouring districts in an attempt to set a benchmark for policy in Yeola. In November 1893 he recommended that all music be prohibited before mosques at all times, prayer or non-prayer. Permission to play music, he argued, had only been granted to the Hindus 'after a successful agitation' and concluded that in fact there was no established right to this since 'it is never allowed anywhere else that I can hear of, the references have been made to Bombay, Poona, Ahmednagar, Satara and Belgaum.'[136] District officials reported that in these areas the playing of musical instruments, including tals in front of mosques, was not accepted practice or part of an ongoing right, and Hayward was inclined to agree. The commissioner in Poona strongly urged that Yeola adopt the same policy as that of Khandesh, where music was stopped in front of public buildings as well as mosques, as this would make it a policy that was born out of 'courtesy and not any religious grounds'.[137] And, it was proposed, any further disputes where there was no identifiable custom should be guided by rulings made in 1880 and 1882 by the high court of Madras.[138]

[133] Ibid.

[134] Government Resolution, March 1894, JD, vol. 282, compilation no. 545, pt I, 1894, MSA.

[135] Demi-official correspondence, ibid.

[136] Hayward to Winter, 3 November 1893, ibid.

[137] Commissioner's letter, Satara, 14 March 1894, JD, vol. 284, compilation no. 545, pt III, 1894, MSA.

[138] These were in the cases of Sundaram Chetti etat *v.* Reg. and Ponnusami

Hayward's attempt to look beyond Yeola as a way to understand the conflicts in the town was significant for it disengaged them from the particularities of their social context and categorized them as part of a larger phenomenon. But the events between September 1893 and February 1894 in Yeola were specific to the town, and they took place between people who moved in overlapping social and economic worlds. In November 1893 Ramchandra Ganesh Barve, the sardeshmukh, began a boycott of Muslim traders and artisans. By January 1894 the boycott appeared to have been discontinued, but on 2 February, at a meeting held by Barve and his colleague Krishnarao Vakil, it was resolved to fine Hindus who had traded with Muslims. Discussions also took place about the 'banding together of 150 well to do Hindu traders to prevent Mahomedans from being able to purchase silver and gold thread which they needed to embroider their pagris.'[139] Four days later, on 6 February, the defilement of the mosque triggered the outbreak of rioting. The events of 6 February, then, clearly had a relationship with those of the preceding five months. As the revenue superintendent, Barve was a prominent figure and was using his influence to isolate a community whose livelihood based on weaving and embroidery was integral to the economic life of the town. The recent history of cattle disease and crop failure, together with increasing competition from recently arrived migrant weavers and the lapsing of the autonomous revenue structure, meant that the way in which social rifts and alliances were expressed were quite particular to the town.

Yet the issue of processional music had emerged at the centre of local politics in Yeola precisely because of extra-local events. Numerous petitions related the conflicts to the effects of the cow protection riots in Bombay and to the Ganpati festivals that had taken place across Maharashtra. Pandurang Yogiraj Sant, owner of the Shri Vithoba temple in Yeola, wrote one such petition to the governor of Bombay. He argued that the temple had been in Yeola for 200 years, and during that

---

Chetti etat v. Reg. (I.L.R. VI Mad 203). Quoted in demi-official correspondence, JD, vol. 282, compilation no. 545, pt I, 1894, MSA.

[139] Gibbs, District Superintendent of Police for Nasik, to Fleet, the Commissioner in Poona, 12 February 1894, JD, vol. 284, compilation no.545, pt III, 1894, MSA.

time: 'The procession of Shri Vithoba has all along passed by the Patel's Masjid with all *tom toms* uninterrupted till the 24 July 1893. . . . The recent riots of Bombay has [*sic*] caused a bad feeling in the minds of the Mahomedans here and encouraged them to follow the example of their Bombay co-religionists. They have now made up their minds to prevent the procession of Hindoo Idols from passing by any Masjid with musical instruments.'[140] Haphijuddin Jhulphikar Ali also saw the influence of events elsewhere. When asked what the established custom on the playing of music had been, he said that he was not sure, but he felt that 'The riots in Bombay were due to the music playing in a Hindu temple near the Jumma Masjid and I think the Hindus wanted to start a new thing at Yeola viz. playing music before mosques, and I look upon the riots at Yeola as an off shoot of those in Bombay.'[141]

The key figure in all of this appears to have been Barve, who had been identified by colonial officials as a leading agitator in the politics of cow protection at least since the previous August. One of the most telling ways in which the particularities of the conflicts in Yeola became subsumed under the rubric of a more broad-reaching 'Hindu' politics was the association with cow protection. The conflicts around processional music must be understood as locally situated. However, their particular character was complicated not only through the alignment with wider conflicts around processional music, but also in the way they slipped so easily into being part of cow protection. In the middle of March 1894 the commissioner in Poona reported that 'the Hindus are seeking now to drag in a fresh point, connected directly with the cow-killing agitation'.[142] Even though officials struggled to keep the two issues separate—'the Commissioner considers it highly impolitic that anything connected with the cow-killing agitation should be officially recognised as part and parcel of the processional music question'—they understood them as related.[143] District Magistrate

[140] Petition to the Governor of Bombay from Pandurang Jogiraj Sant, owner and worshipper of the temple of Shri Vithoba at Yeola Taluka Yeola Zilla, Nasik, JD, vol. 282, compilation no. 545, pt I, 1894, MSA.

[141] Testimonies, ibid.

[142] Commissioner, 14 March 1894, JD, vol. 284, compilation no. 545, pt III, 1894, MSA.

[143] Ibid.

Winter saw the request from certain Muslims that music before mosques be prevented at all times of the day as 'altogether unreasonable and . . . an innovation in consequence of the Bombay riots.'[144]

A key community in all of this was the Salis, about half of whom were relatively recent migrants who had come to Nasik some two generations earlier. District officials had received a number of petitions to which Ganesh Barve was the main signatory. The Salis, who had led the procession in front of the Patel's mosque during the Ganpati festivals in September 1893, had authored one of these. In it they alleged that the proclamation of 1858 had been violated. They pointed to the aggression of Muslims who had prevented the proper practice of their religion and related this to the cow protection riots in Bombay. They signed themselves as Salis, but throughout the petition referred to themselves as Hindus. The question, however, is why would this community align itself with the politics of someone like Ganesh Barve, as well as adopt the politics of cow protection and the language of upper-caste Hinduism? They were not caste fellows, nor were many from a region where such reform movements had emerged. But the Salis had seen a number of other weaving communities in Nasik, along with many of their own, having to abandon their occupation because of pressure from the manufacture of piece goods. Economic pressure had forced many on to the land, where they were now small farmers or even day labourers.[145] They faced competition for weaving licences from a number of other communities, including the Momins—Muslim weavers who had migrated to the presidency after 1857 and who were presumably on the receiving end of Barve's boycott. For the Salis, to align with the politics of influential local figures appears to have been a way to stake a claim in this environment.

Nandini Gooptu argues in her study of the urban poor of North India in the early twentieth century that Shudras adopted a politics of militant Hinduism not because of any powerful commitment to a religious identity, but in 'their quest to carve out a more prominent

[144] JD, vol. 282, compilation no. 545, pt I, 1894, MSA.

[145] *Gazetteer, Nasik*, p. 53; R.E. Enthoven, *Tribes and Castes of Bombay, Vols 1–3* (Bombay, 1920), p. 310; and Syed Siraj al-Hassan, *Castes and Tribes in HEH the Nizam's Dominions* (Haryana, 1990 [1920]), p. 543.

position for themselves in urban society'.[146] As a Hindu religious idiom became increasingly important to the ways in which commercial classes asserted their power, so lower-caste appropriation of this idiom was a way to 'match or confront the power of the merchants symbolically'.[147] I would argue that this was true even in smaller towns such as Yeola and significantly earlier than Gooptu's focus on the 1920s would seem to indicate. However, it is important not to understand the participation of the Salis as simply instrumental. There were several other, often relatively prosperous, non-Brahman castes in Nasik—Shimpis (tailors), Sutars (carpenters), Kasars (coppersmiths), and Sonars (goldsmiths), for instance—who had begun to adopt the practices of an upper-caste Hinduism: abstention from meat and alcohol, the prohibition on widow remarriage (except the Kasars who allowed it), and wearing the attire of Maratha Brahmans.[148] The Salis seemed not to pursue such practices: they ate meat (other than beef) and allowed widow marriage. But they had begun to adopt Brahmanical surnames and gotras.[149] It was at the nexus of changing social perceptions and material insecurity that some also chose to lead a Ganpati procession and present themselves as defenders of Hinduism. This is not to suggest the emergence of a cross-caste Hindu identity; rather, that it provides some indication of why a community such as the Salis appropriated a formulation of high-caste Hinduism in their locality, and how, framed by the language of the state, this formulation could carry beyond it.

Conclusion

It was in a context of profound social, political, and intellectual change that the cow protection societies and reformed Ganpati festivals found fertile ground in western India in the late nineteenth century. They

[146] Nandini Gooptu, *The Politics of the Urban Poor in Early Twentieth-Century India* (Cambridge, 2001), p. 196.

[147] Ibid.

[148] *Gazetteer, Nasik*, pp. 46–60.

[149] Enthoven, *Tribes and Castes*, vol. I, p. 305. A gotra is the lineage assigned to a Hindu at birth and applies only to Brahman families. The system is patrilineal and indicates which one of the original seven or eight rishis of the Vedas the individual is related to.

were strikingly similar in terms of their emotive symbols and vocabulary. Their idioms emphasized the tenets of high-caste Hinduism. They defined India as the land of the Aryans and Hindus as reviving a down-trodden religion in the face of illegitimate foreign rule, both Muslim and British. What was significant about this collection of ideas was its claim to speak for all Hindus. It sought to be geographically broad-reaching and in terms that were explicitly anti-Muslim. It was the repli-cation of these idioms by a range of castes across the region that served to bring them into a shared political space. This articulation was particularly Maharashtrian in its formulation, but this did not mean that it was a Maratha identity alone. What emerged was the articulation of a regional, potentially cross-caste Hindu community, albeit drawing heavily on—and attempting to recast—collective memories of the past exploits of Maratha people and their heroes. However, the influ-ence of this formulation of Hindu community was heavily circums-cribed: the participation across castes ranged widely and the presence of Shudras in cow protection and Ganpati festivals was short lived. Moreover, rifts between Hindus and Muslims were often healed after outbreaks of violence and so did not appear to mark a permanent shift in local relationships.

A consideration of the music before mosques question in late-nineteenth-century western India shows that meanings created by conflicts and cultural innovations were not homogeneous or hegemonic. By themselves they illuminate little in terms of how the experience of local conflict altered people's self-perception in relation to the universal categories of Hindu and Muslim. Nevertheless, that a variety of castes chose to appropriate the idiom of upper-caste Hinduism is significant. Such protest movements and public displays provided avenues through which local grievances could be articulated. The proclamation of 1858 provided a framework for this. The promise of non-interference in religious custom framed the language with which Indians sought ac-countability from their rulers. In arguing their case to colonial offi-cials, local activists in Yeola were forced to engage in the language given to them: that of religious tradition and its violation. In adjudicating future practice, officials began with the premise that they would ad-here to local custom. In their attempts to determine what this was, they met what seemed an irreconcilable set of contradictory opinions, and so looked to neighbouring districts from which to extrapolate their decisions. It was in this way that people refashioned the categories of Hindu and Muslim in particular localities. These in turn framed and gave meaning to particular historical experiences. It was the way this dovetailed with shifting perceptions among a range of Shudras about what it meant to be Hindu that the conflicts became simultaneously local and translocal events.

2

Regionalism to Nationalism

Swadeshi and the New Patriotism
in Maharashtra 1905–1910

I n 1896 Bal Gangadhar Tilak and his associates inaugurated a
festival centred on Shivaji (1627–80), the legendary warrior-king
and founder of the Maratha state. The participation of non-
Brahmans was negligible and the festival was largely confined to a
small circle of upper-caste men. This commemoration of Shivaji joined the cow protection movement and the new Ganpati festival to form
a particular historical moment in late-nineteenth-century western
India. In their engagement with Christian missionaries, upper-caste
Hindu reformers earlier in the century had turned a critical gaze on
their own society. By the 1890s Brahman and non-Brahman intellectuals
alike had begun to mobilize history in the service of a reimagined
Maratha community.[1] For the upper castes, newly reworked ideas of
history and identity went hand in hand with an emerging critique of
colonialism. This was reflected in a proliferation of historical works
eulogizing Shivaji's role in forging the expansionist Maratha state. In
this representation, Shivaji was the torchbearer of a Golden Age of
Hinduism. He had overthrown Muslim invaders, freed Maharashtra
from the foreign yoke, and established swaraj. He had been the saviour
of Brahmans, of the cow, and of Hindu religion, all of which were again

[1] See O'Hanlon, *Caste, Conflict and Ideology*, chapters 9 and 10; and Deshpande,
Creative Pasts.

under threat.[2] Cow protection and the Ganpati and Shivaji festivals articulated a community that was simultaneously Maharashtrian and Hindu. Although the Hindu element gave it the potential to reach beyond the borders of Maratha country, it was a regional identity— distinctively Maharashtrian in the historical and cultural signifiers of its patriotism. It was with the Swadeshi movement that this would change. Begun in Bengal in 1905 but then pushed forward in Maharashtra and Punjab, the Swadeshi movement made it possible for patriotisms that had until then been articulated in a regional idiom to speak in a language that was now explicitly national.

The Swadeshi platform emphasized 'boycott', 'passive resistance', and the founding of 'national schools'. Indians were urged to buy and use only Indian-made goods in order to check the drain of wealth from India to Britain brought about by foreign imports such as Manchester cloth.[3] They were also told to resign from official posts, leave their schools, and end all co-operation with colonial rule. Calls for the boycott of foreign goods, particularly cloth, were made in Bengal as early as 1873. The abolition of cotton import duties in 1882 and of the excise tax in 1896 led to widespread calls for boycott, particularly in the Bombay and Poona papers, by the Poona Sarvajanik Sabha and members of the Indian National Congress.[4] However, as the idea was popularized, it became part of a broader, more militant programme for political as well as economic change. In Bengal the campaign comprised myriad interconnected strands, from the politics of petitions and public meetings, through the proliferation of patriotic literature, poetry and

[2] Of these histories of the Maratha period, M.G. Ranade's *The Rise of Maratha Power* (Delhi, 1971, first edn Poona, 1891) is the most well known in English. Works in Marathi include Antaji Ramachandra Haradikar, *The Triumph of Shivaji* (Bombay, 1891); Sitaram Narahar Dhavale, *A Play about the Child Shivaji* (Ratnagiri, 1884); Dattadas, *Ballads on the Life and Exploits of Shivaji* (Nagpur, 1908). See O'Hanlon, *Caste, Conflict and Ideology*, chapter 10.

[3] On the issue of cloth and its relationship to nationalism, see C.A. Bayly, 'The Origins of Swadeshi (Home Industry): Cloth and Indian Society, 1700–1930', in Bayly, *Origins of Nationality*; and Bernard Cohn, 'Cloth, Clothes and Colonialism', in B. Cohn, *Colonialism and its Forms of Knowledge: The British in India* (Princeton, 1996).

[4] Sumit Sarkar, *The Swadeshi Movement in Bengal: 1903–1908* (Delhi, 1973), pp. 96–7.

songs, to the tactics of revolutionary terrorism.[5] The Swadeshi movement in Bengal captured the imagination of a generation of young, upper-caste, urban men. Muslims, lower-caste communities, and the rural population remained largely indifferent. Nevertheless, the leaders of Swadeshi, boycott, and passive resistance in Bengal gave patriotism a meaning that would echo in the years to come.

In 1905 Tilak launched a parallel movement in Maharashtra. Although it is acknowledged that mobilization around the issue of Swadeshi was widespread in Maharashtra, scholarship has centred on Bengal and consequently there has been no close study of its various articulations in western India. Accounts of the movement in Maharashtra are noted only in more general histories.[6] As in Bengal, it was marked by intense political activity: demonstrations and rallies, the publication of pamphlets and articles, theatrical performances, industrial strikes, and organized conspiracies, all culminating in the assassination of a government official in 1909. The language of Swadeshi in Bengal was steeped in the cultural signifiers of the region. Likewise, Swadeshi patriotism in Maharashtra relied heavily on references to the martial traditions of the Marathas and the exploits of Shivaji. There were campaigns elsewhere in India—Madras, for example—but they were most keenly experienced in Bengal, Maharashtra, and Punjab. Bipin Chandra Pal of Bengal, Bal Gangadhar Tilak of Maharashtra, and Lala Lajpat Rai of Punjab, the 'Lal-Bal-Pal' triumvirate, were central to the movements in their respective regions. They were close compatriots and so-called 'extremists' because they were all similarly critical of the 'moderate' politics of constitutional gradualism that had hitherto been the approach of the Indian National Congress. The divide between the moderates and extremists was a historic one, resulting in a split in the Congress itself in 1907. Extremists emphasized indigenous values

[5] For studies on the Swadeshi movement in Bengal, see Amales Tripathi, *The Extremist Challenge: India Between 1890 and 1910* (Delhi, 1967); Sarkar, *Swadeshi Movement*; Leonard Gordon, *Bengal: The Nationalist Movement 1876–1940* (New York, 1974); and Rajat Kanta Ray, *Social Conflict and Political Unrest in Bengal 1875–1927* (Delhi, 1984).

[6] See A.I. Levkovsky, 'Beginning of Mass Liberation Struggle (The Swadeshi Movement)', in I.M. Reisner and N.M. Goldberg (eds), *Tilak and the Struggle for Indian Freedom* (Delhi, 1966); Cashman, *Myth of the Lokamanya*; and B.R. Sunthankar, *Maharashtra, 1858–1920* (Bombay, 1988).

and knowledge over those of the West, arguing that submitting paltry petitions to the ruling power was degrading and that Indians had to take their destiny in their own hands. They also held an understanding of India's history as one of many tolerant peoples sharing a common civilization that was abruptly interrupted by a series of foreign invasions, first Muslim and then British.[7]

The Swadeshi movement in Maharashtra failed in its economic goal to dent the profits on Manchester cloth. It failed also in its ideological aim to have Swadeshism embraced across creed and caste. Nevertheless, while there is no denying that its ideals were espoused overwhelmingly by high-caste men, there is some evidence that towards the end of the movement around 1910 the dominant ideas of patriotism and anti-imperialism had begun to be taken on board by urban working and artisanal classes. In the movement for cow protection and during the Ganpati and Shivaji festivals, ideas of Hindu community were formulated within a language of Maharashtrian regionalism. In its sisterhood with Bengal and in its formulation as an anti-imperialist movement, the Swadeshi movement in Maharashtra, while retaining many of the markers of Maratha identity, began to articulate a patriotism that was 'Indian' in its formulation. It was during this period that Shivaji festivals began to travel—to Bengal for instance—and in this sense also became national events.[8]

As definitions of what India was and who counted as an Indian became increasingly important, it was the particular ways in which the ideals of patriotism were formulated that were ultimately to prove far-reaching. It is here that the question of just whose nationalism this was becomes important. Shivaji emerged as a central element of a particular cultural idiom at the end of the nineteenth century, which was then incorporated into the Swadeshi movement in Maharashtra. This representation broadly reflected a discourse that excluded Muslims and lower castes. It was vehemently challenged by non-Brahman campaigns.

[7] For Swadeshi's ideological trends, see Bipin Chandra Pal, *Swadeshi and Swaraj: The Rise of the New Patriotism* (Calcutta, 1954); Aurobindo Ghosh, *Doctrine of Passive Resistance* (Pondicherry, 1948); Lala Lajpat Rai, *Writings and Speeches*, edited by V.C. Joshi (Delhi, 1966); Bal Gangadhar Tilak, *The Arctic Home in the Vedas: Being Also a New Key to the Interpretation of Many Vedic Texts and Legends* (Poona, 1903).

[8] On this, see C.A. Bayly, 'Patriotism and Nationalism', in *Origins of Nationality*.

Shivaji had long held an important place in the popular imagination of Maharashtrians. Indeed, Shivaji's prowess in battle, his lower-caste origins, and his ethic of social justice were central to Jotirao Phule's representation of his importance for non-Brahmans. The bahujan samaj, loosely translatable as the 'community of the majority', an organization with a genuine popular base taken from older devotional cults, arose from within the Satyashodhak Samaj around 1906 to challenge Tilak and other Brahman nationalists for their appropriation of the image of Shivaji.[9] Throughout the nineteenth century, peasant revolts against rent payment and the conditions of tenancy frequently drew on the languages of an older ethics to challenge both Brahman dominance and colonial rule.[10] However, by the early twentieth century popular challenges to the emerging definitions of nationalism and patriotism were branded 'anti-national'.[11] It is in this sense that the Swadeshi movement can be said to be self-consciously 'nationalist', adamantly rejecting anything that stood outside of its logic, whether posed by non-Brahmans or by Muslims.

Shivaji

The legend of Shivaji's exploits had long been an integral part of popular consciousness in rural Maharashtra, often recounted there in the ballad, or pavada, tradition. Scholars of the literary history of Maharashtra have shown that pavadas were part of a tradition accessible across castes.[12] In their evocation of Maratha history, pavadas functioned to integrate the different castes—the Brahmans, Prabhus, Marathas, Kunbis, and Mahars—into society as the followers of Shivaji.[13]

[9] Gail Omvedt, *Cultural Revolt in a Colonial Society: The Non Brahman Movement in Western India, 1873–1930* (Bombay, 1976), pp. 3–5, and chapter 6; Bayly, *Caste, Society and Politics in India*, pp. 240–2.

[10] See Ranajit Guha, *Elementary Aspects of Peasant Insurgency in Colonial India* (Delhi, 1983); David Hardiman, *The Coming of the Devi: Adivasi Assertion in Western India* (Delhi, 1987).

[11] Omvedt, *Cultural Revolt*, p. 124.

[12] Prachi Deshpande, 'Narratives of Pride: History and Regional Identity in Maharashtra *c.* 1870–1960', PhD dissertation, Tufts University, 2002, pp. 36–55.

[13] O'Hanlon, *Caste, Conflict and Ideology*, chapter 10.

Shivaji's broad appeal came not only from being acknowledged as a victorious warrior-king but also from the fact that all classes and castes could lay claim to him due to his own ambiguous identity as both Kshatriya and Shudra.[14] O'Hanlon has shown the way his role in Maratha history lent itself to myriad reinterpretations. In his exploits might be seen the past glories of the Kunbis and Marathas of western Maharashtra who formed the bulk of his armies, with the decline of Maratha power being attributable to the growth of Brahman influence as leadership passed to the peshwas. Alternatively, the strength of the Maratha polity could be attributed to Shivaji's Brahman mentor Ramdas. The wars against Muslim rule, therefore, could be read as having been fought with the intention to protect cows and Brahmans. His leadership of the Maratha and Kunbi armies all over India could be interpreted as a means of extending the power of these castes. Or Shivaji's attempt to balance the power between high and low castes allowed an interpretation of Maharashtra's historical and cultural traditions as emphasizing social harmony and a synthesis between local tradition and classical Hinduism.[15] Thus, the memory of Shivaji appealed not only to Kunbis but also to the Maratha princes and sardars of the Deccan, many of whom also owed their status and landed estates to him.[16]

The first Shivaji festival was held on 15 April 1896. Preparations had been made in all districts of Bombay Presidency, but the main celebration was to be at the historic hill-fort of Raigad, the place of Shivaji's coronation and his cremation. The date marked his birthday and, claimed the *Mahratta*, 'commemorate[d] the memory of the greatest Hindu hero of modern times, and the founder of the mightiest Hindu Empire.'[17] The celebrations were to last three days and comprise sermons, readings from Ramdas's chief work *Dasbodh* and Shivaji's chronicle *Shiv Vijaya*, theatrical performances, the singing of historical ballads, and the demonstration of gymnastic exercises reminiscent of

---

[14] On Shivaji's ambiguous varna status, see ibid., p. 168.

[15] Ibid., p. 167.

[16] The sardars were landed aristocrats of Maharashtra who performed military services for the state in pre-colonial times.

[17] *Mahratta*, 31 December 1895, from the *Report on Native Papers Published in the Bombay Presidency* (henceforth *Report on Native Papers*), week ending 4 January.

those practised by Shivaji's troops. Only swadeshi products were to be allowed at the festival and visitors were warned that those wearing non-swadeshi articles would not be allowed into the inner shrine containing the idols of Ramdas and Shivaji.[18] In his opening speech Tilak said that the object of the festival was to 'bring together all Marathas and foster a feeling of regard and confidence which would be conducive to the maintenance of their religion and institutions.' It was to be a festival for all Marathas, aimed, in Tilak's own words, to foster 'a spirit of nationalism'.[19] Several thousand attended the festival. The *Mahratta* claimed that Shivaji's birthday would from then on be one of the most sacred days in the Hindu calendar. It marked the dawn of freedom for Maharashtrians 'smarting from the vigour of Muhammadan tyranny'. Hindus were once again facing foreign oppression and it would only be by emulating the courage of Shivaji's life that they could cast off the weakness of centuries.[20]

Interest in the festival faded quickly, however, and subsequent celebrations were sporadic. Support had come from the princes and sardars at the outset of the fund-raising campaign, but contributions waned as early as December 1895. When it became clear that colonial officials disapproved of the implicit parallel that the festival drew between the supposed Muslim tyranny of the seventeenth century and their own, they dried up completely.[21] In addition, the form the festivals took—sermons, gymnastic exercises, and kirtans (hymns) on a hill—was removed from the concerns of ordinary Maharashtrians, urban or rural. The commemoration of Shivaji's birth was thus relatively short lived.

In 1897 Tilak was prosecuted for two allegedly seditious articles published in *Kesari*. In one, 'Shivaji's Utterances', Shivaji awakes in the 1890s after a long sleep to find the country in ruins. During his time, Shivaji had cultivated valour, fearlessness, and patriotism. He had believed that these would provide the foundation for a strong and moral society. But on his return he found not benevolent rule and

---

[18] *Kesari*, 3 March 1896, *Report on Native Papers*, week ending 7 March.
[19] SAPI, Kolaba, 27 April 1896.
[20] *Mahratta*, 19 April 1896, CSAS, Cambridge.
[21] Cashman, *Myth of the Lokamanya*, pp. 109–10.

unity among the people but famine and persecution. Foreigners were bleeding the wealth of the country and death through epidemic disease was commonplace. Women were ill-treated and rulers had become effeminate. Moreover, the Brahmans, his religious teachers, and those whom he had protected were being incarcerated, and the cow that he worshipped as his mother and protected with his life was being wantonly slaughtered.[22] Tilak was found guilty and sentenced to eighteen months imprisonment. His journalism had depicted Shivaji as the hero of an India under siege. It articulated what the fatherland was and who it belonged to. As the protector of the faith and the vanquisher of illegitimate rule, Shivaji became central to how an idiom of patriotism evolved in Maharashtra.

Non-Brahmans

After Phule's death in 1890, non-Brahman politics in Maharashtra continued primarily in its reforming vein under the leadership of the maharaja of Kolhapur, Shahu Chhatrapati, a dynast who claimed direct descent from Shivaji.[23] Shahu would become an important figure in the non-Brahman and untouchable movements, presiding over the All-India Depressed Classes Conference inaugurated at Nagpur in 1920 and later offering his support to B.R. Ambedkar's movement. Kolhapur's administration under the peshwas had been run largely by non-Brahmans. The state was annexed in 1827 and its army disbanded, curtailing the employment of large numbers of Marathas. Throughout the presidency Brahmans had been the disproportionate beneficiaries of colonial policies in education and employment, and Kolhapur, although a native state, was no different. By 1894, ten years after Shahu's coronation, Brahmans effectively ran the administration. After the formal transfer of power to crown rule in 1858, native states had been allowed to retain a measure of autonomy. Thus, Shahu perceived that

[22] From the evidence of the proceedings for the trial: Imperiatrix *vs* Bal Gangadhar Tilak and Keshav Mahadev Bal, L/P&J/6/462, file 2291 of 1897, reprinted from *Kesari*, 15 June 1897, OIOC.

[23] There is very little scholarship on non-Brahman politics between the period of Phule's death and the 1920s, but see Dhananjay Keer, *Shahu Chhatrapati, a Royal Revolutionary* (Bombay, 1966); and Omvedt, *Cultural Revolt*, pp. 124–36.

a threat to his own authority would more likely appear from local Brahmans than from the British.[24]

Soon after his ascendancy, Shahu introduced policies supporting the education and employment of Marathas. Omvedt argues that although the practice of rulers patronizing their caste fellows was commonplace in the neighbouring states of Baroda and Gwalior, Shahu's promotion of Marathas was resisted by Brahmans in Kolhapur as well as nearby Bombay and Poona. Among the opponents were Congress liberals who questioned whether Marathas were adequately qualified to be taking their jobs. But the maharaja formulated a full criticism of Brahmanism only after what became known as the Vedokta controversy in 1900.[25] The controversy arose when Shahu realized that he was receiving only the Puranokta rites because the palace priests insisted that, as Shudras, this was all that he and his family were due. He demanded to be given the Vedic rites. When his chief priest refused, Shahu responded by revoking his inam lands. When the priest's decision was upheld by another of the four high priests of Kolhapur, he too had his lands confiscated. Shahu saw the priestly viewpoint as an insult to the purity of his lineage and insisted on being recognized as a Kshatriya. In order to have their lands returned to them, the two priests reversed their decision. But the episode convinced Shahu that he needed to shore up non-Brahman influence. In 1902 he reserved 50 per cent of vacancies in the administration for 'backward castes'—as the beneficiaries of these provisions were now to be called.[26] The rise of the new Shivaji festival and the Swadeshi movement was contemporaneous with the opening years of Shahu's rulership of Kolhapur. Upper castes, particularly Brahmans, dominated both movements, neither of which had seriously addressed peasant and low-caste concerns. Shahu's policies of favouring Marathas angered Brahman nationalists. His support for the investigation of the assassination of a government official in 1909, moreover, only confirmed him in their eyes as a puppet of the British.

[24] Naito, 'Anti-Untouchability Ideologies', p. 183.

[25] Vedokta refers to the Vedic rites to which all twice-born castes are entitled. Puranokta are the rites that Shudras are allowed.

[26] Omvedt, *Cultural Revolt*, p. 127. By 1922 this measure had completely altered the caste balance of Kolhapur's administration.

The non-Brahmanism of the Maratha nobility in Kolhapur allied with the Satyashodhak Samaj as it became further radicalized in the early twentieth century. The education of non-Brahmans had been central to the samaj's programme. Leaders also campaigned for religious rites to be performed without the presence of Brahmans—something that found widespread popular support. By 1913, 266 marriages and more than 1,500 other ceremonies had been performed without the assistance of Brahmans.[27] These were conducted in defiance of Brahman authority, but their use of the sacred thread reflected the continued desirability of Kshatriya status and the acceptance of caste as a principle of social organization. Until around 1920 the movement among non-Brahmans emphasized social reform, not nationalism per se.[28] There were elements of this that were radical—self-performance of ceremonies was one example, the maharaja openly taking tea with untouchables another—but ultimately the movement remained caught within a logic of reform and 'uplift'. Nevertheless, it offered a profound critique of Brahmanism. Its opponents were often Brahmans who defended caste hierarchy or refused to allow that issues of social reform could have a place in nationalism. They depicted the politics of non-Brahmanism as separate from—and antithetical to—an emerging politics that had begun to call itself nationalist.

Swadeshi

Curzon's partition of Bengal in 1905 provoked an outraged response from the bhadralok, the educated high-caste Hindus of Calcutta. In its aftermath Bengal was swept with public demonstrations and acts of terrorism directed at the colonial state. Tilak, harnessing the momentum, founded the Swadesha Wastu Pracharini Sabha (Society to Promote the Use of Swadeshi Goods) in August 1905. At a meeting in Nasik he

[27] Ibid., p. 128.

[28] A number of scholars have made this argument for Maharashtra: Jayashree Gokhale, *From Concessions to Confrontation: The Politics of an Indian Untouchable Community* (Bombay, 1993); Gail Omvedt, *Dalits and the Democratic Revolution: Dr Ambedkar and the Dalit Movement in Colonial India* (Delhi, 1994). Others have made similar arguments for Non-Brahman movements elsewhere in India. See Saurabh Dube, *Untouchable Pasts: Religion, Identity and Power among a Central Indian Community, 1780–1950* (Albany, 1998).

expressed sympathy for the Bengalis 'in their national calamity arising out of the partition of Bengal'.[29] It was important that Indians made common cause with each other, he said, 'for the good of the country'. In Kolhapur, when it was suggested that the movement in Maharashtra should dissociate itself from that in Bengal, one speaker disagreed, arguing that all Indians must band together, and that, if they separated now, later agitations in Bombay would lead to reprisals by the British.[30]

However, the partition of a distant region held little meaning for the majority of Maharashtrians, so the movement in western India emphasized more the issue of home-manufactured products and boycott as part of the religious duty of patriots. Swadeshi rallies and demonstrations typically attracting several thousand people at a time were held in Bombay, Nasik, Belgaum, Kolhapur, Sholapur, and elsewhere in Bombay Presidency. True patriots were exhorted to buy only swadeshi articles and boycott the use of English-manufactured goods.[31] At a meeting in Poona in October 1905 a large crowd gathered to hear Tilak denounce the use of these; they should not be given away to the poor either, he said, because this went against 'patriotism and religion'.[32] The crowds then consigned foreign-made goods—from clothes and caps to umbrellas and lead pencils—to a bonfire and the meeting concluded with cheers of 'Shivaji Maharaj-ki-jai!' (Long live Shivaji Maharaj!)[33] During the 1906 Ganpati festival Tilak met Brahman community leaders in Nasik and exhorted them to take an oath before their goddess that they would use only 'country sugar and other indigenous goods'.[34]

Tilak knew that if the campaign was to make a dent in the profits on Manchester cloth, he had to recruit Bombay's merchants and manufacturers to the cause. He had approached Dinshaw Wacha to persuade millowners to supply dhotis to the Indian market at a

[29] SAPI, Nasik, 3 September 1905.

[30] SAPI, Kolhapur, 9 September 1905.

[31] SAPI, Bombay, 21 August; Nasik, 3 September; Belgaum, 9 September; Kolhapur, 9 September; Sholapur, 10 September 1905.

[32] SAPI, Poona, October 1905, para 984.

[33] Source Material of the History of the Freedom Movement in India, vol. II (Bombay, 1957), pp. 609–10.

[34] Kesari, 4 September 1906, Report on Native Papers, week ending 8 September.

reasonable rate, but was rebuffed on the grounds that the movement had a 'political colour'. This jeopardized the support of the government and the European mercantile community. However, with the launching of the Swadesha Wastu Pracharini Sabha, forty-four new factories and joint stock companies were set up in the region. The Bombay Swadeshi Cooperative Stores Company Ltd., founded in December 1905 with a capital outlay of Rs 250,000, drew together four prominent Bombay millowners among its directors: Ratanji Tata, Goverdhandas Khatan, Manmohandas Ramji, and Dwarkadas Dharamsi—although they did not go so far as to join the movement. Much was made of the importance of the merchant classes in the movement, for the onus was on them to substitute foreign for swadeshi goods in their shops. They would be the hardest hit, the *Mahratta* often acknowledged, but in a national movement some sacrifices would have to be made and the merchant, particularly the small trader, would be the hero of the piece.[35] Yet support from Gujaratis and Parsis, who together dominated Bombay's commercial life, was negligible. None of the secondary leadership was from these communities, with only a few small traders fully joining the cause.[36] As one district magistrate noted, 'I don't think the Gujarati Bania cares a brass farthing about the Bengal Swadeshi movement except as a means for putting money into his own pocket. Hence he is adding new weaving sheds to his mills and building new mills.'[37]

The success of the movement was seen to depend on the ability to appeal to different religious communities. To this end there were some efforts to reach out to non-Hindus. Organizers composed 'national' anthems that were sung on many occasions. One, written by Waman Sakaram Khare, a lawyer in Nasik, invoked various names for the Almighty, saying that India belonged to all religions: 'Bow to Hindustan, my pretty motherland, dear to me as my own life. . . . May the Almighty, Alla, Hormuz and the Lord, all protect my dear pretty Hindustan beloved by all. . . . Hindustan belongs to the Hindus, Mussalmans, Parsis, Christians and the Jews (all alike).'[38] 'Hindu–Muhammadan unity'

[35] *Mahratta*, 24 September 1905, CSAS, Cambridge.
[36] Cashman, *Myth of the Lokamanya*, pp. 174–6.
[37] SAPI, Ahmedabad, 9 September 1905.
[38] SAPI, Bombay, 7 April 1906. Similar sorts of pamphlets and songs circulated in Bengal: see Sarkar, *Swadeshi Movement*, chapter 6.

could be achieved, activists argued, if both communities boycotted foreign goods. The manufacture of foreign sugar was said to use 'the blood of cows and bulls and the bones of swine' and was 'therefore unfit and improper for the consumption of Hindu and Moslem alike'.[39] Leaders discussed the similarities of creed and custom between Hindus and Muslims, often presenting Ram and Rahim as the same deity.[40] Occasionally, Muslims also took to the podium: Maulana Ali Muhammad, a prominent supporter of swadeshi, presided over a meeting of 4,000 Muslims and Hindus in Nasik and urged the crowd to abstain from liquor and boycott British goods and foreign sugar.[41]

However, most Muslims across the presidency remained unconvinced. In Ratnagiri, one Abbas Khalipe was asked to take the chair. He refused and advised other Muslims not to attend—none did.[42] In Sholapur, Munshi Shaik Mahtab, once a supporter, had given up preaching swadeshi as none of the Muslims there would let him pray in the masjid or come to any community dinners until he did so.[43] The general reluctance on the part of Muslims to embrace swadeshi is not difficult to understand. As much as its leaders promoted the need for unity, there was a way in which Muslims were merely an appendage to the movement rather than integrated within it. Muslims were often spoken of at best as extraneous to the body politic, at worst as marauding invaders. Dr Shivram Paranjpe, the editor of *Kal*—an 'extremist' Marathi paper and one of Tilak's right-hand men—gave a lecture in Nasik where he argued that historically India had not been fortified, which was why foreigners had come and plundered her resources:

> We should have been at Attock, Cuttack and Cape Comorin. The Muhammadans invaded this country from the North and for five or six hundred years ruled with a rod of iron, breaking down our holy shrines and treating our religion with contempt, yet some accepted favours at their hands and served them. Some sank even so low as to inter-marry with them.

[39] SAPI, Nasik, 17 December 1905.
[40] Ibid.
[41] SAPI, Nasik, 31 January 1906.
[42] SAPI, Nasik, 23 October 1905.
[43] SAPI, Sholapur, 1907, para 310d.

Shivaji . . . freed the country of the Mussulman and protected kine [i.e. cows] and Brahmans, and . . . a great portion of India came under his sway.[44]

In another lecture Paranjpe argued that when Muhammad of Ghazni conquered the Punjab, Hindu religion and 'the nation' became weak. The language changed 'from Sanskrit to Urdu' and people were converted from Hinduism to Islam. 'Our religion', he declared, 'is the oldest in the world but it is deteriorating.'[45]

Despite calls for unity, there appeared to be little allowance for the social practices and economic position of Muslims.[46] A letter received by the superintendent of police in Bombay from a friend in Wai taluka, Satara district, communicated the fears of local butchers:

> Yakub, the beef butcher, was here yesterday, and he says that B.G. Tilak . . . is very busy again. He has got all the Brahmans in Wai to join together, form a fund, and have collected some Rs 20,000 to Rs 25,000 to buy up cows in every bazaar round about and prevent them being sold to the butchers. The butchers have appealed and petitioned the Collector, but no reply has yet been given. Not a single cow has been sold to the butchers in Wai for the last six weeks. They began operations in Wai, now they are beginning in Poona . . . They, the Poona Brahmans, are boasting that they have arms and weapons and will rise and kill the *sahib log* some night . . . I don't think it will be long in coming. Yakub is frightened out of his life every day he goes to Wai. All the Brahmans are armed with big bamboos, walking about the cattle market.[47]

[44] SAPI, Nasik, 1906, para 124. Paranjpe was a prolific writer who wrote over a thousand essays for his journal. He also wrote eight plays, mostly on historical subjects, as well as novels, poetry, historical works on battles fought by the Marathas, and literary essays, and he edited works in Sanskrit. His writings offered fierce critiques of British rule. See B.G. Gokhale, *The Fiery Quill: Nationalism and Literature in Maharashtra* (Bombay, 1988), chapter 3; and B.G. Gokhale, 'Shivram Mahadeo Paranjpe: Nationalism and the Uses of the Past', *Journal of Indian History*, 48, 143, 1970.

[45] SAPI, Sholapur, 1906, para 147.

[46] SAPI, Nasik, 23 October 1905.

[47] SAPI, Bombay, 2 January 1906. Sarkar argues that relations between Hindus and Muslims in Bengal during the movement became especially hostile. See Sarkar, *Swadeshi Movement*, chapter 7.

Elsewhere, at a meeting in Ratnagiri, Narayan Shivram Barve, a prominent Swadeshi activist and Congress extremist, argued that the meaning
of 'gaurakshan' needed to be broadened: more than simply cow protection, it should be promoted as 'self-protection'.[48]

Efforts were also made to attract lower castes to the movement.
Damodhar Ganesh Padhye, an organizer in Poona, described caste distinctions as an 'obstacle to patriotism'.[49] He appealed to them in the
language of Arya reformism, maintaining that caste distinctions had
not existed before the British. Caste had been a purely spiritual affair:
a Kshatriya could become a Brahman and a Brahman a Kshatriya by
his actions. But now, even though Indians were being 'crushed by
foreigners', they remained divided. If such distinctions were to be
observed, he said, they should be 'in spirituality and not in social reforms', so 'patriotism will not suffer.'[50] Caste should be to Hindus
what the different religious sects in Europe were to the state: 'In Europe
there are sects of religions, but they do not come in the way of social
reforms. This example we should follow. Pollution of water by the
lower classes or undertaking of a journey to a foreign land should not
be considered against religion. The interests of society should be looked after. Intermarriages should take place in sub-sections. A convert
should be admitted back into caste.'[51] Like Chiplunkar and Dayanand,
Padhye advocated that caste hierarchy be dissolved for the purposes of
national unity, but retained the idea of caste as a system of differentiated
social roles working together in an organic harmony. This was a profoundly Platonic vision whose emphatically upper-caste interpretation
of the varna system left most non-Brahmans cold. Very few responded
to such appeals to join the Swadeshi movement.

The Swadeshi movement therefore remained an overwhelmingly
upper-caste affair. It was for this reason that district officials did not
regard it as a serious threat to the political order. They frequently
reported its narrow support base and dismissed the efforts made to
change this: 'the Poona and Satara agitators are busy devising a system
for disseminating the doctrines inculcated in papers like the *Kesari*,

[48] SAPI, Ratnagiri, 19 January 1906.
[49] SAPI, Bombay, 28 May 1907.
[50] Ibid.
[51] Ibid.

Kal, Bhala etc. by sending them into the mofussil to read and explain to villagers the content of the leading papers.'[52] But access to such arguments, one official argued, 'by no means always implies sympathy with their views: they are to a large extent popular because they are good reading.'[53] 'Mussalmans and Borahs', it was believed, 'only read their own newspapers.'[54] In Poona it was reported that although the Swadeshi movement was attracting a lot of attention, 'those who advocate entire boycott of foreign goods are not supported by large numbers who sympathise with the movement to foster indigenous industries.'[55] And when the people of Yeola were asked why they were not using swadeshi cloth, leaders were told that they were poor and vilayati cloth was cheaper.[56]

Swadeshi in Maharashtra therefore faced significant constraints both as an economic and a political movement.[57] Whereas Bengal could boast a sizeable decline in Manchester imports for the year after 1905, Bombay actually witnessed an increase.[58] Nevertheless, while the vast proportion of Maharashtrians failed to respond to the call for boycott, what did arise from this period was an emerging formulation of patriotism, or swadeshabhiman. What remained would be to define the nature of that *patria* and who would belong to it.

Tilak on Patriotism

The 'narratives of pride' produced in the late nineteenth century lay at the heart of the patriotism that was fashioned at the beginning of the twentieth. Tilak's conception drew on ideas of belonging that had

[52] SAPI, Satara, 1906, para 547c.

[53] SAPI, District Magistrate, Belgaum, 16 June 1906.

[54] SAPI, Khandesh 1906, para 452.

[55] SAPI, District Magistrate, Poona, 28 October 1905.

[56] SAPI, Nasik, January 1906, para 59.

[57] Parallel arguments have also been made for Bengal. While merchants and zamindars seem to have been more enthusiastic in their support for Swadeshi in Bengal than in Maharashtra, their participation also dwindled quickly. And as in Maharashtra, the movement in Bengal failed to hold any appeal to the larger population of peasants. See Sarkar, *Swadeshi Movement,* chapter 10.

[58] Cashman, *Myth of the Lokamanya,* pp. 176–7. From *Kaiser-i-Hind,* 24 February 1907. Even the success in Bengal was temporary; by 1908 the imports to India of all main goods had risen far above the 1905 totals.

emerged in the previous generation. In a lecture delivered in 1906 he argued that patriotism presupposed an idea of nationality.[59] What, then, constituted a nation? A nation, 'so far as the affairs of this world are concerned', was 'an independent political unit'.[60] In places like Europe, people were defined as a nation based on certain shared characteristics: 'men coming from one ethnological race, moved by the same traditions, same ancient history, same ideals and professing the same faith, and socially living in the same style, make up a nation.'[61] In India, however, these shared circumstances did not exist, and so according to modern definitions India was not a nation but a mere '"congeries of nations" . . . a group of so many different nations.'[62] However, Tilak maintained that although language, religion, and social custom were not universally shared, it could still be argued that India was a nation. But what, if not these, were the elements that unified India?

A dominant factor was the presence of the British. In earlier times, several empires had existed in India simultaneously. But the British had transformed the meaning of empire, unifying India through its administration: 'empire now means one rule from Himalayas to Cape Comorin, and the subject races are governed by the same rules, same regulations and the same laws. . . . An empire like that never existed before.' Earlier rulers, Tilak argued, had extracted certain dues from their kingdoms, but, 'besides this . . . there was no other mark of subjection. There was complete autonomy in each of these provinces. . . . An empire . . . did not mean an assumption of the internal administration of a province by the Sovereign power.'[63] Colonial rule, aided by the introduction of 'western literature, western arts and western sciences', transformed a land that was once a geographical unit into 'a single administration under the control of the British Government.'[64] Thus,

[59] 'Lecture on Patriotism', 1906, pp. 1–17. Delivered to the Bellary Literary Society, reproduced in pamphlet form as *Speeches of Srj. B.G. Tilak Delivered at Bellary* (Bellary, n.d.), P/T 607, OIOC.

[60] Ibid., pp. 1–2.

[61] Ibid., p. 5.

[62] Ibid., p. 2.

[63] Ibid., p. 3.

[64] Ibid., p. 5.

the peoples of India were joined by the fact of their subjection. Hindus, 'whether they be in Bengal or Maharashtra or Madras . . . live in the same land though they do not speak the same language, and are under the same Government . . . and their grievances are the same.'[65] And, just as grievances against the imperial regime were shared by Hindus across India, so they also proved a common element 'between the Hindus and the Muhammadans and between Parsis and Christians': 'When you find your worldly interests bound up together . . . then there is certainly one reason why we should all work together and share in the benefits which are sure to be conferred by our joint action.'[66]

The tie of worldly interest provided the grounds for what Tilak called a 'composite patriotism'. This was an almost instrumental nationalism that called on Indians to put their minor differences behind them. 'The days are gone,' he wrote, 'when Mahrattas can work for the Mahratta nation, the Bengalis for Bengal, Rajputs for Rajputana or for the matter of that the Madrasis for Madras. We must be more Liberal, more broadminded and include in our programme work for the good of all the various races living in the difference provinces of the country and in that sense it is a "composite patriotism".'[67] The proposal that people should be Indians first and Marathas or Bengalis afterwards sounded not unlike European-style nationalism. However, this was not the intention. Tilak opposed historical change that followed the trajectory of Western societies. The crass opportunism of interest groups and a politics devoid of spirituality could not be the foundation of an Indian national identity. This had to draw on indigenous values—and for these he looked to ancient India. Patriotic sentiment should be inspired by ideals that were 'higher' than mere political interest. This higher form of patriotism was an 'altruistic' and 'non-egoistic' love of the nation.[68] It involved working for ideals that went beyond oneself or one's family unit, and was more spiritual than worldly in nature. Although in ancient and medieval India, '[b]eyond the ideal of a province there was no ideal of the whole country', there was the *spirit* of altruism. There was 'a kind of unity' which was

[65] Ibid., p. 7.
[66] Ibid., p. 8.
[67] Ibid., p. 12.
[68] Ibid., p. 3.

founded on non-egoistic ideals and love of humanity.[69] This ideal was exemplified in the Bhagvadgita, Mahabharata, and Ramayana, and in the great truths of the Vedas.

Vedic religion, according to Tilak, was 'the religion of the Aryans', and the purest rendition of the values of Hinduism. It exemplified the highest human values, and in the term sanatan dharma, 'spiritual wholeness', represented the unity of life and tolerance for all religions.[70] Hindu dharma was not a doctrine, but teachings for a way of life. Each aspect and element of the universe had its own individual dharma or inner truth, but each was related to the other 'as so many sons and daughters of one great religion.'[71] Despite differences of language, sect, and region, it was dharma and the teachings of the Vedas that was the thread that tied people across India together: 'Now take for instance the Hindus by themselves. So many of them are at least governed by the Shastras held sacred all over the country: there are no doubt minor differences. But there is agreement in this, viz., that all Hindus whether they be in Bengal or Maharashtra or Madras are actuated by ideals pointed in our *Puranas* and *Vedas*.'[72] The great religious texts provided a 'moral as well as social tie', and held the ethical and philosophical foundations for nationalism in India.

For Tilak, it was out of the relationship between dharma and history that Indian civilization evolved. It was this that all Indians shared, providing the foundation from which a modern patriotism could emerge. Vedic society represented satyug, the era of truth. In Vedic times, he argued, there had been social as well as spiritual unity. But philosophical attacks on Hinduism by Buddhism and Jainism had weakened religion and society from within. Subsequent accretions and corrupt practices in Hinduism itself led to a further weakening of its truths, while subjection under Muslim and British rule meant that 'unity has disappeared bringing on us great degradation. . . . We think ourselves separated and the feeling of that unity which was at the root of our advancement in the past is gone.'[73] Hindus had forgotten what

[69] Ibid., pp. 3–4.

[70] Speech to the Bharata Dharma Mahamandala, Benares, 3 January 1906, in *Bal Gangadhar Tilak, His Writings and Speeches* (Madras, 1919), p. 35.

[71] Ibid., p. 36.

[72] Lecture on Patriotism, p. 7.

[73] Speech to the Bharata Dharma Mahamandala, pp. 36–7.

and who they once were. If they were to be strong again, they had to 'restore the lost and forgotten union . . . [for] in the absence of unity India cannot claim its place among the nations of the world.'[74] The strength of Hindus lay also in their numbers. If the different sects could unite on a common platform 'and let the stream of Hindu religion flow through one channel', India would be triumphant: 'If we lay stress on [our common heritage] forgetting all the minor differences that exist between different sects, then by the grace of Providence we shall ere long be able to consolidate all the different sects into a mighty Hindu nation. This ought to be the ambition of every Hindu.'[75]

For Tilak, then, India was the land of the Aryans and Hinduism the religion of the Aryans. India, by right, belonged to the Hindus. But who were these Hindus? Tilak argued that racial mixing had taken place over millennia and rendered differences between 'Aryans' and 'Dravidians' meaningless. Through migration and intermarriage, the people of India, north and south, were now of the same stock.[76] Caste distinctions were similarly insignificant: 'The races have become mixed up in course of time, and to speak the truth there is no real *Sudra* as there is no real Brahman. . . . Both stand ethnologically on the same level and to rake up the divisions now and tell one class of people that they are of such and such race and inferior to certain other race is the height of absurdity.'[77] Thus, everyone raised on the soil of India, regardless of position, was a Hindu. This was an argument that merged race with culture. Hindus were a race that shared a civilization dating back five thousand years. It was an argument that could also be extended to the Muslim and Christian communities. Muslims and Christians had brought their religions to India and through centuries of proselytizing and coercion had converted sections of the population. However, the existence of large numbers of converts did not mean that Islam and Christianity had become indigenized and could be accepted as Indian religions alongside Hinduism. Rather, their conversions of the 'original' population of India from a religion as ancient as the Vedas meant that Muslims and Christians were from the same stock as Hindus and, at their core, Hindus themselves. The religion may be different, but the

[74] Ibid., p. 37.
[75] Ibid.
[76] Lecture on Patriotism, p. 9.
[77] Ibid.

civilization was the same: 'Whatever the differences in religion, whatever the differences in languages or whatever other provincial differences and social customs may be, they are not the essentials. They are something like the dress in use. Your turban or *dhowati* may be different from mine and we may put them on in different ways, it matters not in which ways we use them. The inner man is the same.'[78] Thus, converts would always be Hindus. Significantly, the proselytizing religions themselves would always be separate from the spiritual essence of India.

Crucially, Tilak resolved the questions of religious and caste difference by erasing the space between 'Indian' and 'Hindu'. Hindu dharma was the historical, spiritual, philosophical, and social basis for Indian nationality. And he saw civilization and dharma as inextricable. Dharma, loosely and inaccurately translated as religion, was not doctrinal in the way that Islam and Christianity were, but could be defined as outlining one's duties in this life in preparation for the next. Its all-encompassing nature meant that it was also inherently tolerant, for it acknowledged the truth-value of other religions. The qualities of Hindu dharma were such that it was broad enough to hold within it the beliefs of different peoples, to absorb them and make them its own as it had done for millennia. As people had come to India over thousands of years, from Central Asia and beyond, it was the adaptive and accommodative qualities of Indian civilization, born of its dharma, that had allowed this. Tilak's rendering of Indian history did away with any worldly basis to social identity. Caste and religious difference were superficial, underlain by a dharmic universalism which tied all Indians together. This alignment of Indian with Hindu through re-reading ancient history served as the foundation for the politics of this emergent patriotism.

Popular Patriotism

Patriotism or swadeshabhiman had become the watchword of the times as Tilak and his group sought to popularize its ideals. The elements which constituted ideas of patriotism were consistent and recurring: a historical narrative that depicted India's past as the degradation of its once great religion and people; an evocation of Hindu gods

[78] Ibid., p. 10.

and heroes and resistance in the face of illegitimate and immoral foreign rule; the call for unity amongst the classes and castes of Hindus (and, occasionally, Muslims); and the need to stand up and bear arms if necessary. When read together these created a series of ideas not only about who the enemy was (the British) and why (because they had drained the wealth and now controlled the resources of India), but also about what it meant to be Indian and to belong.

In addition to passive resistance and boycott, 'national education' was the third pillar of the Swadeshi movement. The purpose of education, Tilak argued, was not merely to teach the student to read and write, but to teach nationality.[79] Colonialism had created a psychological weakness and self-doubt that continued to undermine society. Government schools had only educated Indians to be servants in the colonial bureaucracy. National schools would impart knowledge about the greatness of India's past and the achievements of her people in science, religion, and war. They would teach Indian literature in the vernacular languages, develop scientific and industrial knowledge, and strengthen the student population through gymnastic exercise. Educational institutions that emphasized the importance of indigenous knowledge for the evolution of inner strength amongst Hindus dated to the late nineteenth century and were the intellectual precursors to the schools of the early 1900s. After the protest against the Age of Consent Bill in 1891, the New Preparatory Classes were founded in Poona in memory of Chiplunkar. By 1905 they became a school known as the Maharashtra Vidyalaya. The school was to impart religious training as envisioned by Chiplunkar and infuse a 'spirit of patriotism' among its scholars.[80] The institution outlined its founding principles thus:

> To impart to the youths of the country a course of instruction, comprehensive in its scope and complete in its parts and on the most approved methods, to mould their minds and build up their character under strict discipline and in harmony both with the best traditions of the past and as the higher national requirements of the present and the future, so as to fit them to take their proper place in the public life of the nation, and thereby to help to maintain and elevate the national standards of conduct ... The education to be so imparted should be both theoretical and

[79] Ibid.
[80] SAPI, Bombay, 1905, para 1012.

practical—literary and scientific and technical and should include religious and moral instruction as a necessary part of the course. Physical training has to be carefully attended to and right discipline which is a matter of fundamental importance in an educational institution requires careful attention. The general medium of instruction should be the learner's vernacular.[81]

Associations with similar objectives, such as the *Sadavartan* Pravartak Mandali and the San Mitra Samaj, were founded around 1896, with classes conducted by Congress extremists and those involved in the revived Ganpati festivals. One Mahatma Agamya in Bombay had advocated that the younger generation should establish a society in Poona for 'the Political Emancipation of India'. Vinayak Damodhar Savarkar, a 22-year-old Brahman from Nasik, graduate of Fergusson College and a member of the San Mitra Samaj, was to lead the society. At a meeting in Bombay he gave a passionate speech and, quoting a verse written by Shivaji, urged the audience to 'Collect many men, make their thoughts one, and fall together'.[82] Indeed, there was significant overlap between the Society for the Political Emancipation of India, the San Mitra Samaj, and the Maharashtra Vidyalaya. Tilak, Bhopatkar, and Dr Paranjpe spoke regularly to the students of these institutions about their religion and 'initiate[d] them into political movements such as the Swadeshi movement, the Dassera Holi, the burning of foreign clothes, Ganpati melas and the new Indo-European movement of Mahatma Agamya.'[83]

The Maharashtra Vidyalaya's sister institution, the Samartha Vidyalaya, had 110 boys—all were Brahmans except for two Marathas and one washerman.[84] Each student carried copies of lectures by Bipin

---

[81] From the statement of purpose of the Maharashtra Vidyaprasaraka Mandal, written by J.V. Oka, Secretary, compiled in a letter from Du Boulay, Secretary to the Government of Bombay, Judicial Dept, to Secretary to the Government of India, Home Dept, 5 June 1910, L/P&J/6/1011, file 2081, 1910, 'Samartha Vidyalaya' of Talegaon, Poona District, proclaimed as an unlawful association, OIOC.

[82] SAPI, Bombay, 3 March 1906.

[83] Ibid.

[84] 'Proposed Declaration of the Educational Institution known as the Samartha Vidyalaya situated at Talegaon in the Poona District to be an unlawful association

Chandra Pal and Tilak, and all owned copies of pamphlets containing selected writings from *Kal*, the Marathi-language paper edited by Paranjpe. The library contained all the important Marathi publications of 'extremist' opinion: *Kesari, Kal, Mumuksha, Bhala, Vande Mataram,* and *Rashtramat.*[85] A study of ancient Indian history was central to the curricula of national schools. Such knowledge of the past, it was argued, 'would tell people that they were once rulers themselves. . . . Education should be such that the men of the future should become so many warriors like their ancient heroes Shivaji and others.'[86] Physical exercise was a crucial part of moral education—Indians had to be physically as well as mentally strong. Daily visits to the gymnasium were compulsory, and around the gym were mounted pictures of 'national' heroes: Tilak, Bipin Chandra Pal, Lala Lajpat Rai, Ramdas, Chiplunkar, Shivaji.[87]

The government declared the Samartha Vidyalaya a seditious organization and banned it. The Bombay judicial department named a series of Maharashtrians who were involved in the school and who were also 'all shareholders in Bepin Chandra Pal's Hind National Agency' in Bengal. Balkrishna Keshav Kulkarni 'was chosen by the Bombay National Union as a delegate to the . . . Extremist Congress at Nagpur. . . . Another master, D.V. Patvardhan publicly advocated boycott in Bijapur in 1908.'[88] The annual reports also showed that the

---

under section 16 of the Indian Criminal Law Amendment Act, 1908'. Extract from notes taken at the time of the search, in the letter from E.H. Ingle, District Superintendent of Police, Poona, to District Magistrate, Poona, compiled in a letter from DuBoulay, Secretary to the Government of Bombay, Judicial Dept, to Secretary to the Government of India, Home Dept, 5 June 1910, Bombay Judicial Department Proceedings, Confidential Branch (henceforth Bo Judl Procd, Confdl), May 1910, serial no. 7, pp. 277–86, Z/P/3206, OIOC.

[85] Ibid.

[86] Ibid. From the second annual report which carried extracts of a speech by a teacher, B.V. Phadke, who had spoken of the main objectives of the education students received there.

[87] Ibid.

[88] 'Professor Bijapurkar was the founder of the [Samartha Vidyalaya] and the . . . translations of two documents, found when his house was searched, show that his object was, by a system of national education, to prepare the way

school was supported by Vidya Prasarak Mandali, an organization founded by Tilak, Bijapurkar, and other activists. The aims of 'national education'—to foster indigenous knowledge and patriotism—were thus integral to the Swadeshi movement and part of a wider programme of change. The prospect of such change served to radicalize a generation of young men, some of whom established networks of underground organizations.

Conspiracy and Assassination

The Swadeshi movement also spawned a network of underground political organizations. The most renowned case of conspiracy emerged in Nasik with the assassination of Mr Jackson, the local collector. On the evening of 21 December 1909 Jackson went to the Native Theatre where a farewell performance had been organized. As he entered, 'a young man who had been sitting not far from the door jumped up and rapidly fired a number of shots at him from a Browning automatic pistol. Death was practically instantaneous.'[89] The assassin was one Anand Laxuman Kanhere, a 17-year-old Chitpavan Brahman and arts student at Aurangabad. In his confession to the police Kanhere stated that his motive in coming to the performance that evening was to murder Mr Jackson because he 'oppressed the ryots'.[90] He said that 'it was through reading *Kesari* and other newspapers of similar tone that he formed the idea that Mr Jackson had suppressed the Dasara procession in Nasik and in other ways dealt harshly with the liberty of the people.' Although Kanhere insisted that he was not part of any society in Aurangabad, investigations revealed that not only was there such a secret society, but that it was one of many chapters of an organization, Abhinav Bharat, which spread across Maharashtra and as far as London. The murder of Jackson developed into a much larger case of conspiracy: thirty-eight men, all except one of whom were Maharashtrian Brahmans, were arrested and faced charges that they had 'advocated,

---

for the overcoming of England.' Letter from DuBoulay to the Secretary to the Government of India, Home Dept, 12 May 1910, L/P&J/6/1011, file 2081, 1910, OIOC.

[89] Assassination of Mr Jackson. Discovery of conspiracy at Nasik Discovery of Conspiracy at Nasik, L/P&J/6/978, file 4762, 1909, OIOC.

[90] Ibid.

prepared for, and conspired together to bring about an armed rebellion or revolution and . . . to overawe the Government by criminal force or show of criminal force.'[91] Support for a 'revolutionary conspiracy' was found to exist in Nasik, Bombay, Pen, Poona, Yeola, and elsewhere. The masterminds of this conspiracy were identified as the Savarkar brothers.

Abhinav Bharat had its origins in Mitra Mela, begun in 1903. An organization of young men, Mitra Mela was led by Ganesh and Vinayak Savarkar and reproduced many elements of similar associations in the Deccan. Members received gymnastic training—provided incidentally by a Muslim from Baroda. Songs prepared for the Ganpati and Shivaji festivals were sung in temples and during processions. Meetings were held where members read the biographies of Mazzini, Shivaji, Ramdas, and the works of 'patriotic revolutionists', and debated the means for attaining independence for India.[92] Mitra Mela was active until June 1906, when Vinayak Savarkar left for England on a scholarship from Shamji Krishna Varma, the founder of India House at Highgate. Before Savarkar's departure, Mitra Mela had become Abhinav Bharat, or Young India Society, a title borrowed from Mazzini's 'Young Italy'.

Abhinav Bharat was an underground organization that had remained out of the purview of government until the assassination of Jackson. Oaths of secrecy were administered to all members. In his confession, one Chutterbhuj Jhaverbhai Amin, a Gujarati tailor from Bombay, described the ritual of oath-taking. At the time of oath-taking he had been working in London at India House as a cook, at which time Vinayak Savarkar was the manager there. Meetings would take place regularly and were open to all. Then, after the meeting, 'they used to discuss how the English could be driven out of India. . . . The means suggested were the collection of arms, killing Englishmen by arms or bombs . . . and not to mind the loss of fifteen natives if only one Englishman was killed.'[93] At one point, Savarkar pressed Chutterbhuj into taking an oath:

[91] From the Judgement of the Savarkar Case, Trial and Conviction and Question of Extradition in case of failure at the Hague, L/P&J/6/1069, file 778, 1911, OIOC.

[92] Ibid.

[93] Statement of Chutterbhuj Amin, L/P&J/6/978, file 4762, 1909, OIOC.

He closed the room from inside. Then he placed a lamp with ghee in it on the mantelpiece and put a picture of Shivaji beside it. He made me sit near the fireplace beside him . . . Poured some water into the shallow of my palm . . . and recited Sanskrit sloks for ten minutes. He then translated them into Hindustani. He said that . . . there was in India a secret society the members of which were spread all over the world that he was the leader of it and that from that day I was a member. It was called the Abhinav Bharat Society . . . Every member was to be ready when called on to war against the Government and should come with such weapons as he may have, sacrificing life, family or possessions. By drinking the water which he had poured into my hand I became a member . . . I took the oath of Shivaji . . . He asked me to make a report of my progress and promised to pay all expenses. I was to report personally once a year what I had done for the country.[94]

The details of the ritual of oath-taking were corroborated elsewhere in the presidency as other local conspiracies came to light.[95]

By September 1908 Savarkar and his associates had produced a number of typed copies of a pamphlet with instructions on how to prepare bombs. These were posted to various destinations in India.[96] When Chutterbhuj Amin left London for India in 1908, Savarkar instructed him to pack a parcel containing twenty Browning automatic pistols, plus ammunition. Savarkar was also in contact with a number of Indian anarchists living in Paris, one of whom he tried to induce to take another consignment of pistols to India, eventually only succeeding in persuading him to take one (others were despatched from elsewhere). The pistols were intended to reach his brother Ganesh in Nasik via a contact in Bombay. They arrived safely, as did the manuals, one of which was found in Ganesh's house early in 1909.[97] It was later confirmed that one of these pistols had been used in the assassination of Jackson.

What emerged from the investigation was evidence of an intricate network of communication. One particular case came to light in Bombay: on 15 June 1909 Balkrishna Hari Athavale was found travelling

[94] Ibid.
[95] See for example the Aundh Conspiracy Case in Satara, L/P&J/6/1034, file 3421, 1910, OIOC.
[96] Ibid.
[97] Ibid.

on a train without a ticket. When removing him from the train the conductor, on feeling that his trunk was inordinately heavy, asked Athavale what it contained. Books, came the reply, which were the property of Krishnaji Datatraya Bhosekar, a student at the Victoria Jubilee Technical Institute. His suspicions aroused, the conductor forced the trunk open: it contained '8 bottles of phenol and one bottle of Hydrocyanic Acid, 4 tins of Plaster of Paris, one paper packet of Manganese Dioxide, two porcelain dishes for mixing chemicals, 23 copies of the Russian Secret Organisation Rules, one manuscript copy of the rules of the "Abhinav Bharat" and articles of wearing apparel.'[98] Bhosekar initially denied everything, but then confessed. He said that in May 1908 he had met Ganesh Savarkar on a train. The two began conversing and on hearing that Bhosekar was a student of chemistry at the institute, Savarkar became intensely interested. He 'immediately plunged into the subject of Swadeshi and Swaraj, and before parting exacted a promise from Bhosekar that he would always further the cause of the Motherland and promised to meet him again.'[99]

They met several times in Bombay. Savarkar subsequently administered the oath of secrecy and initiated him into Abhinav Bharat. At another meeting Savarkar gave him several copies of the Russian Secret Organisation pamphlet for distribution to 'carefully selected friends', a copy of the rules for Abhinav Bharat, and Rs 20 for the purchase of chemicals.[100] Savarkar was found guilty on two counts: 'abetment of waging war, the providing of arms and the distribution of instructions for the manufacture of explosives', and 'conspiring with others . . . to overawe by criminal force the Government of India and the Local Government.' He was sentenced to transportation for life and the forfeiture of all property. Of the others, eight were acquitted, the rest were sentenced to between six months and fifteen years imprisonment.[101] Not all of the thirty-eight men arrested for conspiracy were involved in the same projects: some were part of local chapters of Abhinav Bharat and

[98] Arrest of Balkrishna Hari Athavale in possession of explosives at Kalyan Railway Station (Thane), confidential letter, Poona 3 July 1909, from Du Boulay to Secretary to the Government of India, Home Dept, Simla, L/P&J/6/953, file 2735, 1909, OIOC.

[99] Ibid.

[100] Ibid.

[101] Judgement of the Savarkar Case, L/P&J/6/1069, file 778, 1911, OIOC.

some appear to have organized their own terrorist plots. Nevertheless, what was clear was that the different groups shared a political programme and common ideology which they employed for the purposes of recruitment and mobilization.

Extending Patriotism

To what extent did the acts of such young patriots resonate with other Maharashtrians? Did their ideals reach beyond a small circle of high-caste men? The official feeling was that they did not. Reflecting on recent events, the district magistrate of Satara, S.R. Arthur, wrote: 'Satara is probably typical of many Deccan districts. The vast majority of the population know nothing and care nothing about politics. Of the educated classes, any natives of culture are perfectly loyal to Government; a certain element chiefly consisting of Brahmin pleaders may be classed as passively disloyal.'[102] Despite his protestations to the contrary, however, Arthur was disturbed by what he saw as the potential for these opinions to be shared: 'There can . . . be no question that students generally in India are being imbued from their earliest years with bitter hatred of the sovereign power, some by their parents, some by school masters, some by listening to seditious speeches, all by the native press, and I know cases of sons of loyal parents being taught sedition very much against the will of their parents.'[103]

That the elements of early-twentieth-century patriotism in Maharashtra were defined by, and largely limited to, a small group of high-caste men is clear. Yet by 1908 there was some evidence of the acceptance of these ideas by a wider spectrum of individuals and communities. In October 1909 two Konkanasth Brahman girls from Kolhapur ran away from home. Godu, aged 16, and her friend Manu, aged 15, set out one night on a mission to assassinate Europeans. They were found by the police dressed as male sadhus and declared that their ambitions

[102] Report by S.R. Arthur, Collector and District Magistrate, Satara, regarding the trend of events and the measures necessary to the tranquillity of the country, sent to A.C. Logan, Commissioner, Central Department, 7 August 1907, Bo Judl Procd Confdl, September 1907, serial no. 7, pp. 255–60, Z/P/3203, OIOC.

[103] Ibid.

were to serve their country. In her statement Godu said that she and Manu 'used to read together books and newspapers and discuss different topics'.[104] They were familiar with the stories of the Rani of Jhansi, Baikache Bund, Panipatche Mukabala, Vikram Shashika, and Gulbankavali—all of which featured dynamic women protagonists. The girls sought to model themselves on such women:

> Great changes have occurred in the kingdom on account of attempts made by women for their country; women can do anything without being suspected; ideas of this nature occurred to me and I spoke to Manubai. We . . . were a good deal troubled at home and so we both thought that we should leave the house quietly, disguise ourselves like Sadus, go to Rajas like the Nizam, induce them to join a big conspiracy, collect Europeans in one place and blow them up. If we succeed in acquiring a great kingdom in this way, we felt confident that we would be received with great pleasure and joy by our husbands and relations.[105]

The two clearly came from politicized and literate households. They said they had read newspapers such as *Kesari, Bhala, Mumuksha, Kal,* and *Hindoo Punch,* which Godu's father-in-law, Yedneshwar Paranjpe, brought home from the library. Paranjpe was a 'follower of Swadeshi custom'—'he wears swadeshi cloth and does not eat foreign sugar'— and would converse with his friends about Swadeshi.[106] It was 'on account of my reading [these] . . . books and newspapers, and on account of hearing conversations about the Swadeshi movement in the house, [that] I began to think of doing something for my country', Godu confessed.[107] Unfortunately, neither was able to realize these aspirations: they were handed over to Godu's father after their 24-detention expired, after which they presumably returned home.[108]

A strike of millhands in Bombay in July 1908 that brought the city to a standstill provided further evidence of the broadening reach of the

[104] Adventure of two young Brahman young women who set out on a mission to assassinate Europeans for political motives, L/P&J/6/977, file 4669, 1909, OIOC.

[105] Statement of Godu, ibid.

[106] Ibid.

[107] Ibid.

[108] L/P&J/6/977, file 4669, 1909, OIOC.

new patriotism.[109] On the mornings of 15 and 16 July 1908 anonymous placards were found pasted at the entrance and in the latrines of the Jacob Sassoon Mill. One read as follows:

> Satya Narayan and Shivaji ki Jai . . . This is to inform all the head jobbers that owing to your holding a meeting Tilak came to Bombay, for that reason Government desires to imprison him, for that purpose 17th instant has been appointed. Therefore all mill-hands are warned not to come to the mill for work. He who goes to the mills for work is the son of the Governor, or bhangi. He who tears this notice will drink cow's blood. If a Mahomedan tears this, he will eat pig's flesh. Do not tear; do not tear. Remember this. This will bring you good luck. God will do you good.[110]

Tilak had been arrested on 24 June 1908 for sedition. It was alleged that several of his articles condoned revolutionary acts against the state. His trial opened on 13 July, and on 17 July millhands struck in 28 of Bombay's 85 mills. During the next few days there was sporadic violence across the city. Millhands from the Lakhmidas mills went about in gangs stoning windows and breaking the furniture of mills where workers had defied the strike. An estimated 35,000 out of a total of 100,000 millhands in the city were on strike. Europeans were assaulted and their businesses sabotaged.[111] Notices in Marathi were found posted in latrines in Tardeo urging millhands to fight back against colonial power: 'Why are you Asleep!', they read: 'Awake, be ready, and assist your Parel comrades. Defile the mothers of the European police.'[112]

[109] Trial of Mr Tilak, Editor of *Kesari* Newspaper. Conviction and sentence for sedition. Appeal to Crown, L/P&J/6/877, file 2436, 1908, OIOC. On the 1908 strike, see L.A. Gordon, 'Social and Economic Conditions of Bombay Workers on the Eve of the 1908 Strike', in Reisner and Goldberg, *Tilak and the Struggle*; and Cashman, *Myth of the Lokamanya*, chapter 8.

[110] Bombay Government, Special Dept, weekly letter 22 July 1908: anonymous placards in Bombay informing the millhands that Mr Tilak was being prosecuted on their account, L/P&J/6/888, file 3122, 1908, OIOC. Bhangis, a caste of scavengers and sweepers, were considered the lowest of all untouchables.

[111] Europeans at Currey Road Station had been attacked and had taken shelter in a liquor shop that was later wrecked. Elsewhere, coolies employed in godowns at the Grain Bazaar prevented the passage of carts carrying goods belonging to Europeans. L/P&J/6/877, file 2436, 1908, OIOC.

[112] Ibid.

On 23 July Tilak was found guilty and sentenced to six years' transportation. On hearing the verdict, cloth-shop employees in the Mulji Jetha market, primarily Gujaratis and Parsis, passed a resolution to stop work for six days. Gujarati and Parsi businessmen did likewise in the cloth and grain markets and in the freight and share markets; the Cotton Exchange too closed its businesses. Small shopowners also closed and over the next two days workers in seventy-six of the city's mills were on strike. Black bunting hung throughout the streets and Tilak's photograph was prominently displayed in shop windows. Gangs of millhands in their thousands wandered through the streets chanting 'Tilak Maharaj-ki-jai, Chhatrapati Tilak Maharaj-ki-jai!' It was reported that some believed Tilak to be an incarnation of Vishnu.[113] Several attempts were made to disrupt transportation in the city. One group attacked Curry Road railway station, delaying the Poona Mail carrying reinforcements to the Bombay garrison. Workers from the nearby railway workshops joined the millhands. But by 29 July the latter, facing 'military reinforcements, heavy rains and economic deprivation', returned to work.[114]

Communities across the city had demonstrated against Tilak's sentencing, especially millworkers and traders who had been conspicuously absent from the Swadeshi movement. But support for the strike was far from universal. On 25 July a prominent Parsi businessman, Sir Vithaldas Damodar Thackersey of the Bombay Native Piece Goods Association, called a meeting where it was decided to reopen businesses the next day. The next morning, Ranchondas Madhanji, a Gujarati, opened his shop but a protest against him forced him to close again. Elsewhere, as business people attempted to reopen their shops, they were prevented by their own workers. Amongst millhands, Hindus, primarily Marathas and Gujaratis, participated in their thousands, but Muslim workers were overwhelmingly absent. Tilak had been actively organizing in the Bombay mills since the 1890s, establishing the Bombay Millhands Defence Association, which had played a part in

---

[113] Sir George Sydenham Clarke (1843–1933), Secretary to the Colonial Defence Committee 1885–92, member of the War Office Reconstruction Committee (1904), to Lord Morley, Secretary of State, quoted in Cashman, *Myth of the Lokamanya*, p. 180.

[114] Ibid.

planning the strike. He spoke regularly on the issues of Swadeshi and boycott, vehemently attacking the colonial administration, blaming them for workers' poor conditions and speaking to their resentment of government officials for their interference in tax and social policies.

It is difficult to gauge the motives of the various communities of Bombay for such large-scale action. It appears that motivations differed between workers from different mills, and among individuals from the same mill. Workers could have been spurred on by the grand idea of an independent India, by resentment towards the colonial government, or by anger at cruel working conditions. Rather than an ideological unity amongst the participants, what the strike served to highlight was the ways in which an idea of patriotism was harnessed in the naming of the events of July 1908 as 'nationalist', and how the issues of labour, religious duty and belief, national heroes, and a regional anti-imperialist politics interlocked. Workers were encouraged to be proud warriors like their 'national' hero, Shivaji. They were told it was a religious duty to support 'Chhatrapati Tilak Maharaj'. They were reminded of their economic oppression by the colonial state. Their militancy was associated with Shivaji's warrior tradition, political action, and religious duty. It was named by Tilak—and accepted by colonial officials—as evidence of mass disaffection with the colonial state and an embracing of emergent patriotic ideals.

Conclusion

The cow protection movements, Ganpati festivals, and conflicts over the question of music before mosques in the 1890s had articulated broad-based, regional ideas of Hindu community. In taking up these ideas and in employing cultural signifiers specific to Maharashtra, the myriad articulations of patriotism in the first decade of the twentieth century identified what it meant to be an Indian and to belong to a patriotic community. The Swadeshi movement in Maharashtra drew on upper-caste histories of ancient India that had recast Shivaji as a Hindu patriot and his Muslim enemies as foreign interlopers. Its leaders asserted that lower-caste Marathas should see themselves as Hindus, identified India as the land of the Aryans, and argued that the incorporative qualities of Hinduism meant that even Muslim and Christian converts were essentially Hindu. Thus, Tilak's idea of composite patriotism gave way to dharmic universalism. Any space that could have existed between the emerging identities of 'Hindu' and 'Indian' was effectively erased.

The Swadeshi movement enjoyed limited economic success, its appeal limited primarily to young Brahman men. The ideas of patriotism with which it was linked resonated only briefly with broader communities of labourers and merchants. More generally, moreover, Swadeshi found little long-term resonance with non-Brahman communities. Neither did it attract the support of Muslims. The way in which Muslims were represented as alien meant that they remained resolutely outside the movement. Furthermore, activists did not take seriously the very real issues that divided high and low castes, be they exploitation of labour, control of land, or the hierarchies of ritual and custom. The Non-Brahman movement therefore took little interest in, or was actively hostile to, Brahman political organizing at the turn of the century. For them, Shivaji was the protector not of Brahmans but of the true sons-of-the-soil, the Maratha Kunbis.

Campaigns by the Maratha nobility to be recognized as Kshatriyas, as well as those by Satyashodhak peasants who took to performing their own ritual ceremonies, marked them out as beyond the sphere of nationalist politics. Shudras, whether from the nobility like Shahu, from the small missionary-educated class like Phule, or from peasant communities, attached their own meanings to the past. They formulated ideas about land, religion, and community on their own terms. What this tended to mean, at least for the first decade of the twentieth century, was that high-caste men owned the language of patriotism. Their discourses were about the nature of the colonial state: the drain of wealth, the immorality of rulers concerned solely with worldly matters, and the legitimacy of India as a nation. Non-Brahmans were not directly engaged in this arena of knowledge production. Their critiques about land and caste were dismissed by nationalists as anti-national and understood by the colonial state as social reform issues. In this sense, the exigencies of appropriating and transforming liberal models of nationalism, and of portraying India's diverse population as a nation, dictated an agenda for Indian nationalism that was already showing considerable rigidity.

But the national and the communal were defined together, and it is to the question of how the category 'communal' came to be so closely associated with the Muslim minority that we now turn.

PART II
Communalism

3

From 'Religious Community' to 'Communal Minority'

Muslims and the Debates around Constitutional Reform 1906–1909

T he British colonial government had long held that Indian society was constituted by its communities. Muslims also had a clear sense of themselves, in their myriad sects, as being distinctly 'Muslim'.[1] However, in 1906 this distinctiveness was just that: perceived differences between religious communities, or conflicts arising therein, were not termed 'communal'. Nor was the term attributed as a quality inherent to Muslims. It was in the course of the debates that preceded the constitutional reforms of 1909 that this transition took place.

The debates begun in 1906 on constitutional reform in India arose out of three sets of events. First, the terrorism and political unrest witnessed during the Swadeshi movement had unsettled colonial officials, forcing them to look for potential allies in Indian society. Second, while Congress extremists had rejected the politics of constitutional gradualism, moderates continued to push for electoral reform. The new viceroy, Lord Minto (1905–10), in contrast to his predecessor Curzon, saw the need to be responsive to such political demands.[2]

---

[1] See M. Mujeeb, *The Indian Muslims* (Delhi, 1985); Farzana Shaikh, *Community and Consensus in Islam: Muslim Representation in Colonial India, 1860–1947* (Cambridge, 1989); Jalal, *Self and Sovereignty*.

[2] The colonial government had created the beginnings of a representative structure in 1892. In 1905, Congress sent its president Gopal Krishna Gokhale

Third was the emergence of distinctively Muslim political concerns. Uneasy about the prospect of electoral reform, which had worked against them in the act of 1892, a deputation of prominent Indian Muslims met Minto in October 1906 to state their case. They argued that, in any further electoral reform Muslims should, on account of their status as a minority in India and their historical significance to Indian society, be considered an electoral category in their own right. Minto, in very vague terms, agreed.[3] It was on the basis of this agreement that the members of the deputation founded the All India Muslim League in December 1906.

For its part the colonial government of India had a dual—and fundamentally contradictory—agenda. On the one hand a sense of realpolitik meant that in order to offset the potentially destabilizing effects of political unrest, it needed to ensure the loyalty of the more conservative groups in society. On the other the profession that the purpose of colonial rule was to educate and enlighten Indian society to reflect the values of Britain and to gradually school the population for self-government meant pursuing reform in line with the principles of liberal representative democracy.[4] These two conflicting agendas initiated a discussion on the nature and purpose of constitutional

---

to communicate its case for further council reform. Gokhale argued that Congress demands were in line with the stated objectives of British rule, namely to prepare Indians for self-government. In response, in his budget speech of 1906, Secretary of State Morley emphasized the importance of expanding 'the representative element' within Indian legislative councils. Shaikh, *Community and Consensus*, pp. 121–2.

[3] On concerns about electoral representation on the part of Muslim reformers dating back to the 1890s, see Shaikh, *Community and Consensus*, p. 119; Rafiq Zakaria, *Rise of Muslims in Indian Politics: An Analysis of Developments from 1885–1906* (Bombay, 1970); Francis Robinson, *Separatism Among Indian Muslims: The Politics of the United Provinces' Muslims, 1860–1923* (Cambridge, 1974), pp. 135–47.

[4] By 'liberal representation' I mean a political structure that in theory represents individuals, as opposed to class or community interests. James Mill and his son John Stuart Mill were proponents of this view and wrote extensively on India: see James Mill, *The History of British India* (London, 1858); and John Stuart Mill, *Considerations on Representative Government* (New York, 1862). For an analysis of their views on India, see Uday Singh Mehta, *Liberalism and Empire: India in British Liberal Thought* (Cambridge, 1999).

reform in India, culminating in the council reforms of 1909 and the creation of a separate electorate for Muslims.

The historical controversy surrounding the 1909 reforms has been centred on the institution of a separate electorate for Muslims—a provision much maligned for its apparent role in the 'communalization' of Indian politics. Scholarship on the reforms has argued variously that they were evidence of Britain's 'divide and rule' policy, pitting Hindus against Muslims;[5] that they marked a turning point after which Hindu–Muslim relations would become increasingly hostile;[6] that the granting of separate electorates to Muslims signified an incredible 'success' on the part of a small and very young organization, the All India Muslim League;[7] that they were evidence of a basic 'communal' or 'anti-national' character on the part of Indian Muslims;[8] and that they marked a 'high point' of Muslim 'separatism'.[9] It was during this period that a corporate Muslim identity was formalized in Indian politics—this much is widely recognized. Consequently, 1909 holds a prominent place in scholarship not only on Muslim identity formation but also in the story of Partition.[10] However, in focusing solely on the history of Muslim representation or 'separatism', scholarship on this period has not identified the process by which 'communalism' came to be associated with the behaviour of the 'Muslim minority'. While some scholars have located the emergence of communalism in the 1920s and 1930s,[11] others have referred to all inter-community riots as 'communal'.[12] In contrast, I argue that it was in the period 1906–9 that the category was given its

[5] Ram Gopal, *Indian Muslims: A Political History (1858–1947)* (Bombay, 1959); M.N. Das, *India Under Morley and Minto: Politics Behind Revolution, Repression and Reforms* (London, 1964).

[6] Pardaman Singh, *Lord Minto and Indian Nationalism (1905–1910)* (Allahabad, 1976).

[7] Syed Reza Wasti, *Lord Minto and the Indian National Movement, 1905–1910* (Oxford, 1964).

[8] Das, *India Under Morley and Minto*.

[9] Robinson, *Separatism*.

[10] David Page, *Prelude to Partition: The Indian Muslims and the Imperial System of Control, 1920–1932* (Delhi, 1982); Moin Shakir, *Khilafat to Partition: A Survey of Major Political Trends Among Indian Muslims during 1919–1947* (Delhi, 1983).

[11] Pandey, *Construction of Communalism*; Freitag, *Collective Action*.

[12] Bayly, 'A Pre-History of Communalism?'

current meaning. In contemporary debates, the term is taken to mean the political organization of a religious community to the furtherance of its own ends, often in the most hostile and violent ways. By 1909 its meaning was already heavily imbued with negative connotations: to be communal implied an irrational attachment to pre-modern, religious identities rather than to a modern national identity. Prior to this period the term was value-neutral and extended to non-religious corporate 'interests' such as those in commerce and land.[13] In 1906, at the outset of the debates on council reform, discussion centred on the idea of creating separate electorates for a series of 'communities of interest' or 'communal' interests, of which Muslims represented only one. These interests were those that British officials saw as being 'stable', that is, conservative and therefore loyal, as well as those requiring assistance in representing themselves in the new electoral structures.

This chapter charts the trajectory of the debate that culminated in the 1909 reforms. It argues that this process was central to the definition of Indian Muslims as 'communal', and that it was during the course of these debates that a decisive shift in the meaning of the term took place. The reforms of 1909 were neither the reflection of an inevitably widening gap between Hindus and Muslims in India, nor a milestone on the road to Partition. However, what this period represented was the historical moment when Muslims began to be identified as a 'communal minority' rather than a 'religious community'. It was in the process of the discussions that took place between 1906 and 1909 between Viceroy Minto, Secretary of State for India Lord Morley, local representatives of the colonial state, and the self-styled representatives of Hindu and Muslim communities that the term communal became associated solely with the perceived sub-national and separatist aspirations of Muslims.

Morley and Minto on Constitutional Reform

In a letter to Morley in March 1907, Minto detailed his thoughts on the purpose of 'political representation for natives'.[14] This was a time

[13] Shaikh, *Community and Consensus*, chapter 4; Robinson, *Separatism*, chapter 4.

[14] Correspondence with Morley on the question of Council Reform, Calcutta,

of great political change, he argued: 'A new spirit is abroad everywhere in the Eastern world and novel influences are making themselves widely felt.' This new spirit was one of self-determination: the Indian National Congress, whose aim was the gradual establishment of self-government, had 'done much to promote the growth of a sentiment of common nationality'. Western education had also precipitated great changes, creating a new class of 'moderate, thoughtful and loyal men'. Indians were not ready for self-government, Minto argued, but the recent unrest meant that 'the permanence of [our] administration depends upon a sound appreciation of the changing conditions which surround it.' Thus, if the longevity of the British presence in India was to be assured, modes of governance that had become routine would have to be reconfigured.

Minto's strategy lay in creating allies in 'stable' sections of society in order to offset the effects of the recent militancy. Alongside growing ideas of 'nationality', he believed that there existed a 'great body of conservative opinion' amongst men still loyal to the government. It was by sustaining the allegiance of this conservative element—represented by the 'great agricultural classes', namely the landlords—that Minto felt the current pace of political change could be stemmed. It was the representation of their interests that should be made central to any political reform. Minto's overriding concern, then, was preservation rather than change. The purpose of reform was to ensure stability. The framework of reform had to reflect rather than seek to alter long-established social formations, and would have to be, in Minto's words, in line with the 'conditions of the country'. Theodore Morison, an adviser on council reform, had argued similarly: 'institutions which are not in accordance with the actual distribution of power in society do not change society'; rather, 'it is the institutions which come to grief'.[15] Morison maintained that while conferring political power to the landed aristocracy would mean privileging a narrow oligarchic elite,

---

21 March 1907, Home Dept., Public Branch. Mss Eur 573 John Morley Papers, vol. 32 (October 1906–August 1907), OIOC. Henceforth Morley Papers.

[15] T. Morison's confidential note appended to the 'Scheme for Representation of the Principal Communities of Indian Society', proposed by Sir William Lee-Warner, 18 April 1907, Morley Papers, vol. 32.

contemporary Indian society *was* 'oligarchical and aristocratic', as Britain had been in an earlier age, and in this sense such reform would be appropriate to India's stage of development.

That reform should be 'appropriate' was of central concern. In 1892 the government had introduced elections to the provincial legislative councils. As we have seen in chapter 1, these made some provision for the representation of significant group interests that had hitherto gone unrepresented. Nevertheless, it was the urban, Western-educated professional classes, especially lawyers, who came out best. Rural interests, such as those of the big landlords, as well as those of Muslims, had gone almost completely without representation. Out of 54 members elected to the provincial councils, only 10 were landholders, while 36 were barristers.[16] Minto continued that while it was true that any system founded on democratic principles held a tiny minority responsible for the interests of the majority, the results of the 1892 reforms represented a glaring failure of the system: elections had unfairly favoured the interests of one group, and consequently misrepresented the character of Indian society.

Minto's proposals were therefore cast in the language of pragmatism and fair play. On the one hand there was a concern for self-preservation: if a framework of representation could be devised accurately to reflect the interests and classes of Indian society as they were understood by the British, then, once such institutions were firmly in place, they would be regarded as 'a precious possession round which conservative sentiment will crystallise and will offer substantial opposition to any further change . . . and any attempt to democratise Indian institutions.' On the other he saw it as the responsibility of government to structure a system that would fairly represent—and draw into formal politics— a wider array of social groups whose interests had been wholly alienated from it. But what would be the foundational unit of reform? Minto attributed the limitations of the 1892 reforms to their being a 'Western importation uncongenial to Eastern tastes'.[17] One of his advisers, Sir William Lee-Warner, deemed Indian society unsuited to such forms of representation for it 'thinks, lives and acts according to

[16] Minto to Morley, 21 March 1907, Morley Papers, vol. 32.
[17] Ibid.

castes, races and religions'.[18] These were the 'natural compartments' of society and could provide the foundation for a system where the principle of territorial voting had been tried and had failed. Indian society was such that it could not be thought of as one nationality, but was, rather, an 'imperial federation of various groups', each of which was fiercely protective of its own 'domestic concerns', or customs.[19]

Furthermore, it was believed that since India from time immemorial had been in the hands of absolute rulers, both Hindu and Muslim, reform would need to respond to recent political demands but simultaneously remain autocratic. Minto put this rather more euphemistically. The responsibilities of the British administration in India, he wrote, were twofold. Firstly, as 'trustees of British principles and traditions' it was duty bound to consult and represent 'the wishes of the people . . . so far as they are articulate'. But equally, its duty was to remain within the bounds of 'Indian history and tradition'. Could these two principles—British constitutionalism and Indian autocracy—be fused into what Minto called 'a constitutional autocracy'?[20] Such an autocracy would be a far cry from the 'Asiatic despotism' of earlier times. A constitutional autocracy would bind itself 'to govern by rule which admits and invites to its counsels representatives of all the interests which are capable of being represented and which merely reserves to itself in the form of a narrow majority the predominant and absolute power which it can only abdicate at the risk of bringing back the chaos to which our rule put an end.'[21] This would provide 'some-thing that may be called a constitution' for India that would be framed along 'sufficiently liberal' lines as to satisfy the demands of 'all but the most advanced' while at the same time retaining the support of the more conservative elements of society.

Minto thus sought a framework that would reflect the institutions of Indian society and at the same time reassert British control. These institutions were the broadly community-based, or 'communal

[18] Sir William Lee-Warner, Governor of Bombay, in his 'Scheme for Representation of the Principal Communities of Indian Society', 18 April 1907, Morley Papers, vol. 32.

[19] Ibid.

[20] Minto to Morley, 21 March 1907, Morley Papers, vol. 32.

[21] Ibid.

interests'—be they landholding, commercial, educational, or religious—that were seen to comprise Indian society. The failure of earlier
attempts at reform had reinforced for Minto the idea that not just anybody could represent the interests of any group. Indians were not yet
able to set aside their group affiliation to represent the interests of others, and so 'the multifarious groups . . . which make up the people of
India can be represented in the fullest sense of the word only by persons
who actually belong to them.'[22] Differences within groups would die
away as members came to identify the solidarity of their interests.
Significantly, representatives would behave simply as intermediaries
between the interests of their communities, however defined, and the
colonial government. Thus, they had little real power to direct policy,
for they were to function as advisers and were not elected by a general
public. Minto recognized that the attempt to balance the interests of
various communities flew in the face of the principle of non-interference
professed in 1858. However, this 'complete departure from our attitude
of neutrality as between races and sects' was justified precisely because
Indians were not seen to share any 'general sentiment of common nationality'.[23] Certain Muslims, Minto argued, had recently become sus-
picious of 'Hindu' political activities, as evident in the formation of the
Indian National Congress, the cow protection movements, and the
Swadeshi movement. Thus, if a Hindu was nominated to the council,
Muslims would soon claim their right to a seat 'in order to preserve the
balance'. But Minto also justified a departure from the principle of
non-interference as government fulfilling its responsibility: it was its
duty to right the wrongs created by the hierarchies of traditional institutions.

The idea of balancing interests implied a certain parity among the
communities. So, while Hindus were a numerical majority, India,
being constituted by its communities, was bound to represent their
interests in roughly equal ways.[24] The most significant interests to have
been consistently passed over since the creation of municipal councils
were those of the Muslims and the landlords. It was they who were seen

[22] Ibid.
[23] Ibid.
[24] Shaikh, *Community and Consensus*, pp. 156–8.

to represent the conservative elements in Indian society, and it would be the creation of 'an additional electorate recruited from the landed and monied classes and from the Mahomedans' that would provide the 'requisite counterpoise' to the disproportionate influence that professional men currently exerted on the various councils.[25] It was this principle that emerged at the centre of the negotiations.

The Legislative Councils and the Question of Representative Authenticity

Once it was determined that the 'communal interests' of Indian society would form the basis of the new constitution, it had to be decided which of these would receive representation on the various councils, and in what proportion. Lee-Warner proposed that any caste or religious community that accounted for at least 20 per cent of the local population 'should have the right of choosing its own members from its own groups'.[26] In cases where their numbers were less, the government would decide whether or not that group was 'so influential . . . as to deserve a special right to a seat'. The purpose was not to ensure 'mathematical precision', but a presence for the principal groups in society. The qualifications for voting had already been determined, and a new electoral register would be drawn up according to communal group. Nomination by government, it was believed, would diminish over time as elections proved increasingly successful in drawing new people into public life. Significantly, the term 'community' referred to all 'interests' in society, rather than being necessarily a confessional category. Lee-Warner argued that such interests must be considered, for as long as one or two 'advanced' classes or castes enjoyed a monopoly of political power at the expense of groups—such as the Muslims or, in western India, the Maratha peasantry who also existed entirely outside this new arena of politics—ideas of 'due representation' were meaningless.[27]

It was decided that provincial governments would determine the interests to be represented in their regions, the population of which in

[25] Minto to Morley, 21 March 1907, Morley Papers, vol. 32.
[26] Lee-Warner, 'Scheme for Representation', 18 April 1907, vol. 32.
[27] Ibid.

turn would be able to elect one of their own to represent them. It was important that the methods of selection ensured that someone properly representative of the group would come forward. Minto felt that although Muslims had been elected to provincial and imperial legislative councils in earlier years, they were 'not really representative of their class', and nominations to supplement their number had also frequently failed to secure the appointment of the 'most appropriate' representative.[28] He suggested that the only means of securing accurate representation of the group was 'by assigning to each important class a member specially acquainted with its views'.[29] Changes in Indian society had accelerated and 'added to the complexity of the problem by bringing to the front classes which were then backward and by making them more keenly conscious of their individual interests and more disposed to claim separate representation by means of special electorates.' Therefore, he argued, it seemed to be less and less possible to have a representative who did not entirely reflect the views of his group or was drawn from outside it.

On receipt of Minto's dispatch, Morley appointed a committee in London to consider the proposals. It was made up of Sir David Barr as chairman, Lord MacDonnell, Sir James La Touche, Sir James Thomson, Sir Lawrence Jenkins, K.G. Gupta, Sir Walter Lawrence, and S.H. Bilgrami. MacDonnell and La Touche had wide experience of provincial administration, Jenkins was a lawyer, Lawrence served the government at Simla and Thomson in the Madras Presidency. Bilgrami and Gupta were to be the 'Muslim' and 'Hindu' representatives: Nawab Imad-ul-Mulk S.H. Bilgrami, in collaboration with Mohsin-ul-Mulk, had drawn up the final version of the memorial that the Muslim deputation presented to Lord Minto on 1 October 1906, and K.G. Gupta had been a senior civil servant in the revenue department.[30]

The new imperial and provincial legislative councils were therefore to be devised around communities of interest. The Imperial Council was to have 62 members that would include 31 official members. Of the non-official members, 28 were to be elected. The elected members

[28] Minto to Morley, 21 March 1907, Morley Papers, vol. 32.

[29] Minto to Morley, 1 October 1908, Morley Papers, vol. 33 (October 1908–May 1909).

[30] Wasti, *Lord Minto*, pp. 150, 69 and 147.

were to function in an advisory capacity and would be drawn from
various communal interests in the following proportions: professional
middle class 12; landholders 7; Muslims 5; European commerce 2;
and Indian commerce 2. Three seats would also be reserved for what
were called 'minorities, special interests or experts'. At the provincial
level, the councils to be reformed were those of the Bengal, Bombay,
and Madras presidencies and the United Provinces, and would reflect
the same principles as the Imperial Council. In Bombay the communal
groups to be represented were municipalities and district boards, the
presidency corporation, the university, landholders, Muslims, the
Bombay and Karachi chambers of commerce separately, millowners
associations for Bombay and Karachi alternately, and the Indian commercial community.[31]

Representatives were to be selected in one of three ways: election,
nomination, or association. Election was deemed the most favourable
method, being the most accurate reflection of the group's will.
    ever, where electorates could not be formed, members would
be selected through associations. This raised the problem of which
    ciation was to conduct the election, and what to do if a rival
association claimed a greater right. A further problem was corruption.
There was the possibility that the association 'may be captured by a
small ring of politicians . . . its original character may be transformed
by changing the conditions of membership or by manipulating . . .
admissions, or . . . the whole organisation may exist ..."more on paper
than in practice".'[32] Where there were no representative associations,
and electorates could not be formed, the option of nomination was put
forward, 'until the community . . . developed sufficiently to be fit for a
more independent system'. However, this was felt to be unsatisfactory
since there was nothing to ensure that the nominee would be properly
representative.[33] In the case of landowners there was little uniformity
in the different provinces, with some opting for election proper and
others for election by associations. Most were in favour of election by
a constituency which comprised landowners who either paid a certain

amount of revenue or derived a certain income from their land, although doubts were expressed by 'some Governments and several landholders as to the possibility of working such an electorate over an area so large as an entire province.'[34] Selection for the Muslim constituency would follow similar principles. The Imperial Legislative Council would have five Muslim elected seats, one for each of the provinces with the largest population of Muslims, namely Bengal, Eastern Bengal and Assam, Punjab, and the United Provinces, and one nominated seat given alternately to Madras and Bombay where the Muslim population was smaller, more scattered, and unorganized. In course of time it was hoped that electorates could be formed, but until then proportional representation would be achieved only through nomination.

The idea that a community shared a set of core interests—material, political, and ethical—inevitably raised the question of authenticity: who could be deemed to reflect properly the interests and values of a group? The arguments for separate electorates for Muslims were that they were 'much more than a religious body', forming 'an absolutely separate community, distinct by marriage, food and custom, and claiming in many cases to belong to a different race from the Hindus'.[35] Thus, it was not enough simply to be born a Muslim, for one's views may be more 'Hindu' than 'Muslim'. One had to live in the 'absolutely separate' way to be considered truly representative. But this position had its own problems. If Indian society was to be locked into representing itself through a system of separate electorates for a variety of communities, what were the implications of, say, a Muslim landowner being elected? If he was elected for the landowning constituency, would the interests of Hindu and Muslim landowners be understood as identical? If not, then how could Hindu landowners ensure that the elected individual represented their interests equally? Likewise, if a Muslim landowner were elected to the Muslim seat, what would ensure that he worked in the interests of poor Muslims and not simply his fellow zamindars? If a Muslim were elected to a landholding seat, would that mean seats allotted to a Muslim electorate should be cut by

[34] Minto to Morley, 1 October 1908, para 12 on Provincial Advisory Councils, Morley Papers, vol. 33.
[35] Ibid.

one, and that it be assumed he would work for both interests simultaneously? And, most importantly, would the provision of a separate electorate preclude Muslims and other communal interests from voting in the territorial electorates that would be made up by the rural and municipal boards, or would they be entitled to a 'double vote'? Minto, concerned that the separate electorate would permanently foreclose the possibility of communities participating in the broader electorate, defeating the very purpose of the reforms, insisted that they were indeed entitled to a double vote.[36]

Responses to the Proposed Scheme

All provincial administrations approved of the proposals for the special representation of Muslims.[37] The overwhelmingly positive reception on the part of the beneficiaries of the new reforms seemed to vindicate the perception of India as a society comprising communal interests. Muslim representatives approved of the provisions—although they felt they did not go far enough; and landowners, both Hindu and Muslim, welcomed the separate representation of their interests. In contrast, commercial and industrial classes, both European and Indian, felt that they had been under-represented. That the landowners registered their response as a body rather than as confessional subsections is testimony to the idea that 'community' was not necessarily a religious category. However, the urban professional class, overwhelmingly upper-caste Hindus, reacted bitterly to the proposals, calling them 'medieval', 'denationalising', and evidence of an imperial conspiracy of *divide et impera*. They demanded instead 'the formation of territorial constituencies on a scale which would render their own influence predominant.'[38] The Bombay Presidency Association accused the government of prejudice, suggesting that 'the aim of the reforms should not be cleavage or

[36] Morley to Minto, 27 November 1908, Morley Papers, vol. 33.

[37] There was a difference of opinion, however, regarding the method of selecting representatives. Wasti, *Lord Minto*, pp. 168–9. This difference, Wasti argues, was mainly due to local conditions. While some of the provinces wanted to form Muslim electoral colleges (Bengal, UP, and Punjab), others preferred to use the recognized Muslim associations (East Bengal and Assam); Madras and Bombay preferred simple nominations.

[38] Minto to Morley, 1 October 1908, Morley Papers, vol. 33.

counterpoise but the re-adjustment and expansion of the proportionate representation of the different communities so as . . . to enable the Government to secure the benefit of the knowledge, experience, advice and co-operation of the most capable and the best trusted representation of all classes and interests.'[39]

These opinions were widely expressed in the Indian press and re-produced across India.[40] Editorials within a wide spectrum of political opinion claimed that reserved seats for communities would hinder the quality of representation and would prevent the best candidates from being chosen: 'A ward may be inhabited by a majority of Hindus, but it will be a serious disability if they are prevented from electing a Muhammadan gentleman who may be better qualified for the place than any of them. Or it may be the other way.'[41] If Muslims had not taken advantage of the opportunities afforded to them by colonial rule, they had 'only themselves to blame for the consequences of their neg-lect'.[42] Improvement, progress, merit, and enlightenment, according to this view, were all values embedded in a model of society whose foundational unit was the individual and not the community. The indigenous press accused the state of abandoning its policy of non-interference.[43] This explicitly partisan behaviour, many argued, violated all that the government claimed to stand for in India. It was supposed to be a progressive, unifying, and even-handed force. Its role was to inculcate a modern approach to politics. Yet it had fostered retrograde and divisive tendencies and encouraged the public expression of reli-gion at the expense of politics: 'The State should not penalise political opinions and favour religious beliefs. British rule in India will be de-prived of one of its most potent justifications if it ceased to exercise a unifying influence on the heterogeneous people of the country. The

---

[39] Bombay Presidency Association to the Government of Bombay, 24 February 1908, para 12. Public Letters from India, 1908, vol. XXXVII, quoted in Wasti, *Lord Minto*, p. 162.

[40] Wasti, *Lord Minto*, chapter 4.

[41] *Oriental Review,* para 22, week ending 14 January 1905, *Report on Native Papers*.

[42] Ibid.

[43] *Oriental Review*, 2 October 1907, *Report on Native Papers*, week ending 5 October.

ideals it is bound to keep before it are modern, not medieval.'[44] That there were to be separate electorates for numerous other interests and classes was eclipsed by the perception that the government was pitting the two 'great communities', Hindu and Muslim, against each other.

Over and above a violation of the promise of non-interference, the proposals were seen as a fundamental contradiction to nationalism. 'A priori there is absolutely no conflict between Muhammadan progress and Hindu progress in the field of politics', argued an article in *Mahratta*. 'But we must in all earnestness point out to the organisers of the Muhammadan deputation that the time chosen by them for the movement is somewhat prejudicial to the cause of the whole Indian nation. . . . Muhammadans are Indians first and Muhammadans afterwards.'[45] Any expression of group interest was 'denationalising'. A piece in *Indu Prakash* pointed to the example of the Aga Khan, the spiritual head of the Ismaili community of Shia Muslims. He was, it acknowledged, an erudite, forward-thinking man who had been at the forefront of political change. But his involvement in the negotiations for separate electorates was evidence of his having descended into the ranks of sectarian politics: 'As the religious head of the section of the Muhammadans and as a recognised statesman of European reputation, we would have preferred His Highness the Aga Khan occupying the position of an all-India man rather than that of a luminary of a clannish clique. To lose the position of an all-India man and to come to be regarded as a leader of a denationalising movement is to descend from the high pedestal of popular esteem.'[46] In a model of society where individuals are citizens before they are anything else, the assertion of group interest was seen to contradict the pursuit of a greater social good and was dismissed.

However, while those who challenged the idea of the level playing field were deemed divisive, the defence of separate electorates demonstrated that there was nothing neutral or even-handed in a liberal system

[44] *Indian Social Reformer,* 4 November 1906, *Report on Native Papers,* week ending 10 November.

[45] *Mahratta,* 23 September 1906, *Report on Native Papers,* week ending 29 September.

[46] *Indu Prakash,* 18 August 1908, *Report on Native Papers,* week ending 22 August.

of representation. In 1908 Mohamed Ali, a young nationalist Muslim who had studied at the Aligarh Muhammadan Anglo-Oriental College and at Oxford, wrote a passionate letter to Congress leader Gopal Krishna Gokhale explaining how hollow he felt the arguments opposing separate electorates were.[47] Gokhale had initially supported separate electorates for Muslims. By 1908, however, he felt that Muslim demands were unreasonable and reversed his position. In his letter Mohamed Ali chastised Congress nationalists for their opposition to the scheme favouring separate representation for Muslims.[48] Referring to a meeting that had been attended by Muslims, Hindus, and Parsis alike, he wrote that it was at times like this that he saw the 'possibility of a working unity—not the sentimental rubbish that is too often talked on the subject—between the various "interests" (not properly called races or religions or sects) of India.' People from different worldly communities were not always representatives of their spiritual communities. 'Unity', then, should be pragmatic: as interests coincided, so different groups would collaborate. To talk of an undifferentiated electorate as a reflection of unity was 'absurd': 'Each community if it feels that it is an "interest" by itself and cannot trust another to choose its representative must be allowed to choose its own and if that community is based on a racial, religious or caste difference its desire should be considered quite as legitimate as if the difference was occupational. Unity will not come if the Mosalmans are refused the permission to select their own advocate in *litigation*—as unfortunately much of our politics is at present.'[49] The political structure should reflect 'what *is*', Mohamed Ali argued, and not 'what *ought to be*'—that is, it should reflect denominational rather than territorial interests. He looked to the 'practical unity of Canada' as a possible model for India. What was the use of India's leaders professing fine emotions towards each other, he asked, when these were empty gestures? At best they were mere niceties, at worst they hid rampant prejudice. The Indian National Congress met three days every year, and during that time 'there is nothing but fraternity and love and all that'. But what went

[47] For more on Mohamed Ali, see chapter 4.
[48] Maulana Mohamed Ali to Gokhale, 8 February 1908, file 341, no. 3, Gokhale Papers, NAI.
[49] Ibid.

unexposed was that 'many of the patriots are as narrow, as selfish and as caste-ridden during the remaining 362 days as any Mosalman whom they denounce as a fanatic.' Rather than staging such demonstrations of 'false fictitious unity', he urged Gokhale to put together 'a powerful and really representative organisation consisting of some hundred or two hundred men all united on the principal questions.' It was within such a body, whose creed would be 'justice to all', and not merely 'India for the Indians', that an *entente cordiale* between Muslims and Hindus would be found.[50]

Gokhale's opposition demonstrated the nature of the problem as one of the rigidity of liberalism. In a letter to William Wedderburn in December 1909, Gokhale wrote of his grave concern that the weightage being accorded Muslims in the councils was so excessive as to be 'monstrously unjust'.[51] Representation in Bombay, he argued, was structured so that three out of four members sent to the viceroy's council would be Muslims, when their proportion in the population of the presidency was only one-fifth. This was more than likely an inaccurate charge based on counting the number of seats in different constituencies that may have yielded a Muslim candidate—the Muslim, Karachi Chamber of Commerce, and special interest constituencies, for example. Such a calculation betrayed Gokhale's acceptance of the position that Indians, in this case Muslims, were bound by their ascriptive identities and would be compelled to act by them. By implication, Gokhale believed that even if a Muslim were elected to, say, a seat for the chamber of commerce, that should be considered a Muslim seat. The difference in the franchise for Hindus and Muslims was also something that pained him: while in the city of Bombay every Muslim with an annual income of £135 could elect a member to the council, 'no Hindu or Parsee, however wealthy, or whatever his position in other respects, has a vote,

[50] Ibid.
[51] Gokhale to Wedderburn, 3 December 1909, file 203, part II, no. 159, Gokhale Papers, NAI. Sir William Wedderburn (1838–1918) served in the Indian Civil Service from 1859 and acted as a judge of the Bombay high court. He founded the Indian National Congress along with A.O. Hume and served as its president in 1889 and 1910. He was chairman of the Indian Parliamentary Committee, founded in 1893, where Indians could air their views on the problems they faced.

unless he is a member of the three or four bodies which have been called upon to return a member. And it is the same throughout the country.'[52] Gokhale's objection was not that Muslims were recognized, but that measures such as a lowered franchise or the absence of parallel electorates for Hindus or Parsis, were unequal and unjust. But in arguing for equality in a strict sense, Gokhale was arguing for the 'denominational interest' of his own community.

Electoral Colleges: The Debate Continued

As the proposals stood, Muslims would vote in a separate as well as a general electorate. It was this double vote that was seen to be unfair. To address these concerns Morley suggested an alternative scheme of electoral colleges. This would retain a single electorate rather than the several that were being proposed, while accommodating the concerns for communal representation. He outlined the scheme as follows: if one were to imagine a hypothetical province whose population was twenty million, of which fifteen million were Hindus and five million Muslims, with twelve representatives to be elected, then, the population being in a ratio of 3:1, nine Hindus and three Muslims would have to be elected.[53] To obtain these members, the province should be divided into three electoral areas, each of which would send forward three Hindus and one Muslim. There would be an electoral college within each of the three areas which would work to preserve the proportion between the two groupings. Thus, each electoral college would comprise, say, 100 members, 75 of whom would be Hindus and 25 Muslims. The electoral college would be made up of the different electorates such as substantial landowners paying not less than a fixed amount of land revenue, the members of rural or subdivisional boards, the members of district boards, and the members of municipal corporations, all of which would return to it the candidates of their choice. After the election, those 75 Hindus and 25 Muslims obtaining the majority of the votes would become part of the college. In the event that the Muslims elected failed to provide the full 25, the number would be supplemented

[52] Ibid.
[53] Morley to Minto, 27 November 1908, Morley Papers, vol. 33.

by nomination. The electoral college of 100 members would then be called upon to select, by a method of one member one vote, three Hindus and one Muslim from its body who would go forward as representatives at the provincial level. The idea was that 'minorities would be protected against exclusion by majorities, and all larger and important sections of the population would have the opportunity of returning members in proportion to their ratio to the total population.'[54] Morley argued that the proposal was not such a departure from what already existed and would provide important advantages: allaying the concerns of Hindus while simultaneously being able to accommodate 'further claims for representation by special classes or association'. Thus, it was also a scheme for the fair representation of minorities.

Those speaking on behalf of Hindu opinion greeted the revised proposals enthusiastically. But many colonial officials had misgivings. In early 1909 Minto wrote that the 'scheme of electoral colleges . . . has been fully examined by ourselves and by all Local Governments. . . . All Governments are unanimous in their condemnation of the system and lay stress on the fact that it has given rise to the gravest dissatisfaction among the classes affected by it, specially the Muhammadans and the landholders.'[55] Muslim organizations from around the country, including the All India Muslim League, protested vehemently against the scheme, asserting that there was nothing in it that would prevent them being 'swamped' by the weight of Hindu opinion. What, for example, was there to prevent a 'pro-Hindu Muhammadan' from being nominated whose election could easily be secured by the Hindus on the electoral college, over that of a candidate selected by the vast majority of Muslims? An editorial in the London *Times* supported Muslim fears that under this scheme their representation would be illusory: 'The type of Muslim who secures Hindu support secures it by virtue of his utility to Hindu rather than Muslim interests; yet this is the type most likely to be elected under the provision of Lord Morley's scheme.'[56] However, to achieve proportional representation, the electorate that made up the municipal and district boards had to consist of

[54] Ibid.
[55] Minto to Morley, 8 February 1909, Morley Papers, vol. 33.
[56] *The Times*, 29 December 1908, quoted in Wasti, *Lord Minto*, p. 173.

'at least as large a proportion of Muhammadans as the electoral college itself'—still something of a distant reality.[57] Moreover, in order for Muslims to be voted onto municipal and district boards, it required that they be concentrated within the same districts and not scattered in distant towns and villages, as was more often the case. Bombay Presidency exemplified this problem. Outside Sind, Muslims made up only between one-tenth and one-twentieth of the population, and were widely dispersed over the region. This would mean that if the Muslim vote was scattered, their numbers, and in turn their influence, would be overwhelmed by other interests.[58]

Many observed that the scheme would create a great sense of disillusionment with the government. The Muslim League, at its Amritsar session in 1908, maintained that the implementation of electoral colleges would 'mark the first breakdown of that implicit faith which Muslims have for so long placed in the care and solicitude of the Government.'[59] Anger was directed against officials for their seeming willingness to renege on the pledge of separate electorates made by the viceroy in 1906. Minto had first agreed to the general principle that the 'Indian Muhammadans ought to be represented as a community on the basis not merely of their numerical strength, but also of their historical and political importance' when he was visited in Simla by the deputation of Muslims in October 1906.[60] He had said:

> The pith of your address . . . is a claim that in any system of representation whether it affects a Municipality, a District Board or a Legislative Council in which it is proposed to introduce or increase an electoral organisation the Muhammadan community should be represented as a community. You point out that in many cases electoral bodies as now constituted cannot be expected to return a Muhammadan candidate and that if by chance they did so it could only be at the sacrifice of such a candidate's views to those of a majority opposed to his own community whom he would in no way represent and you justly claim that your position should

[57] Minto to Morley, 8 February 1909, Morley Papers, vol. 33.

[58] Ibid.

[59] Resolution 3, the All-India Muslim League Session, Amritsar, 1908, quoted in Wasti, *Lord Minto*, p. 172.

[60] Minto to Morley, 22 July 1909, Morley Papers, vol. 34 (July–December 1909), OIOC.

be estimated not merely on your numerical strength but in respect to the political importance of your community and the service it has rendered to the Empire, I am entirely in accord with you.[61]

However, the form this representation would take had been unclear:

Please do not misunderstand me; I make no attempt to indicate by what means the representation of communities can be obtained, but I am as firmly convinced as I believe you to be that any electoral representation in India would be doomed to mischievous failure which aimed at granting a person enfranchisement regardless of the beliefs and traditions of the communities composing the population of this continent.[62]

Three years later, in January 1909, a deputation of the London Branch of the All India Muslim League paid Morley a visit, once again to present its views on representation in councils. This time Morley gave a much more definite pledge to meet their demands 'in full'. 'The Muhammadans demand three things. . . . They demand the election of their own representatives to these councils in all stages. . . . Secondly, they want a number of seats in excess of their numerical strength. Those two demands we are quite ready and intend to meet in full.'[63]

And in a letter to Morley, Minto upheld the principle that Muslims should be assured a separate electorate: 'we believe that separate representation is less likely to accentuate [class differences] than a system of joint representation under which the minority would be constantly struggling to wrest from the majority a fair recognition of its claims. If the Muhammadans elect their own representatives they are likely to be on better terms with the Hindus than if every election gives rise to a conflict between the two communities. . . . [A]nd we would urge on you the necessity of applying the same principle to the case of the landholders.'[64]

The proposal for electoral colleges had unnerved Muslim representatives in India and was harshly criticized by the London Committee of the All India Muslim League. Thus, in 1909, despite Morley and

[61] From T. Morison, 'Note upon the Pledges given to the Muhammadans', Morley Papers, vol. 34.
[62] Ibid.
[63] Ibid.
[64] Minto to Morley 8 February 1909, Morley Papers, vol. 33.

Minto's assurances, Muslims put forward a dramatic proposal. In a petition presented to Morley in January that year, the London League Committee declared that as long as Muslims were assured of separate electorates they did not need to be represented in a general electorate, in which case the concern over double-voting would be redundant: 'Save as regards University representation in which both communities have the privilege of double voting, the Muhammadan subjects of His Majesty, so long as they can obtain adequate and substantial communal representation on the Council, the Rural and District Boards and Corporations *with the right of electing their own representatives* do not ask for double votes.'[65] But Minto was keen that Muslims continue to vote in mixed electorates. And it should not be seen as granting undue favour, he argued, since the majority population was Hindu. The double vote could be understood as 'satisfying Muhammadan claims to be represented in proportion, not merely to their numbers, but also to their political and historical importance.'[66] Furthermore, the Muslim community should not be singled out since the double vote also applied to the other communities—landowners, commercial bodies, and electors for the university.

Morley proposed that if the electoral colleges were not to go ahead, then the number of Muslims on the council should be increased and the double vote disallowed.[67] Whereas Minto had opposed it being dispensed with altogether, Morley assured him that he had not intended 'to disallow the double vote so far as Presidency Corporations, Landholders and University [were] concerned', merely for the Muslims. For while 'special privileges' seemed 'justifiable' in the cases of 'property and education', it was 'undesirable to give the privilege of double vote to the adherents of any particular religion merely as such.'[68] It was the issue of so-called special privileges for religious groups on which the debate turned. On the one hand Morley argued that the Muslims should not be eligible for a double vote on the grounds that they were

---

[65] T. Morison, 'Note upon the Pledges given to the Muhammadans' (italics in original). From a petition presented by the London Committee of the All India Muslim League to Morley on 27 January 1909, Morley Papers, vol. 34.

[66] Minto to Morley 8 February 1909, Morley Papers, vol. 33.

[67] Telegram, Minto to Morley, 11 February 1909, Morley Papers, vol. 33.

[68] Ibid.

a religious group. On the other Minto was loath to remove from Muslims the possibility of voting in mixed electorates as well as their own. Hindu representatives had, since the outset, been largely opposed to separate electorates for Muslims. The decisive shift in the discussion came here, as Morley accepted the position that Muslims represented a 'religious' group rather than their prior designation as one 'interest' group among many.

In April 1909 a telegram from the Government of India was read in the House of Commons about the methods of obtaining representatives: 'the method proposed is simply that in general electorates such as municipalities, district boards and members of provincial Councils, all sects and classes, including Mahommedan, will vote together. By this means some, but not sufficient, representation will be obtained for Mahommedans. In addition a certain number of seats will be reserved for Mahommedans, and none but Mahommedans will have a voice in filling these.'[69]

What this implied, as Minto himself put it, was that 'Mahommedans must depend upon the general electorates in the first place, and that their own electorates would only give them a sort of second chance.'[70] However, the Government of India's recommendations had been 'separate Mahommedan electorates in the first place, which were to secure for them their proper proportion of representation, and beyond that again was their chance of winning seats in the general electorates, and also nomination.'[71] But the information that had been communicated to Muslim delegates was that the former rather than the latter was the case. Consequently, Bilgrami, fearing that separate electorates were now to provide the supplementary and not the main body of Muslim representation, stated that Muslims no longer had any interest in voting in mixed electorates, and communicated this to Morley. In a telegram to the viceroy, a startled secretary of state wrote that the 'question of Mahomedans has caused serious difficulty. . . . Proposals thus outlined are regarded by Mahomedans here and in India also,

[69] From 'Note Upon the Pledges given to the Muhammadans', by T. Morison, Morley Papers, vol. 34.

[70] Telegram, 20 May 1909, Minto to Morley, Minto Collection, quoted in Wasti, *Lord Minto*, p. 181.

[71] Ibid.

according to Bilgrami, who has just returned, as violation of pledges given by you and reaffirmed by me. It now appears that Mahomedans have all along regarded Government of India's original proposals as even worse than electoral colleges, and that our pledges were understood to mean entire elimination of Mahomedans from general electorates right down to rural boards.'[72] And Morison counselled that 'now that the Muslims had been aroused nothing would satisfy them except complete fulfilment of the promises given to them.'[73]

Between October 1906 and January 1909 the attempts made to structure a system of representation for Muslims by reservation of seats, whether they would be filled through election or nomination, in the imperial and provincial legislative councils, had always assumed that Muslims would continue to participate in the general electorate. While maintaining complete 'separateness' at all stages in their own constituencies, Muslims would still be allowed to vote for, and compete as, representatives in other electorates such as landowners, commercial bodies, and the university, as well as in a general poll. Separate electorates had been intended as a temporary measure to ensure the representation of hitherto unrepresented interests and to draw members of those groups into representative politics. These electorates would work to create a level playing field. However, once these communities were able equally to compete, members would no longer be bound to represent only the interests of 'their' group. Morison argued: 'As other classes of society came to the front and were able to enforce their right to a share in the control of public affairs, the constitution of the Council of Notables might be widened and in this way the privileges of the few might in time by a natural process be expanded into the liberties of the many.'[74] Participation in this arena of politics would create a sense of collectivity that would supersede provincial identities. For the Muslim electorate to participate in a representative system simply amongst themselves, then, was anathema to Minto, who felt it would consolidate their isolation and exclusion from political life.

[72] Telegram, Morley to Minto, 27 April, 1909, Morley Papers, vol. 33.

[73] T. Morison, 'Note Upon the Pledges Given to the Mahommedans', Morley Papers, vol. 34.

[74] T. Morison's note appended to Lee-Warner's 'Scheme for Representation of the Principal Communities of Indian Society', 18 April 1907, Morley Papers, vol. 32. This would, of course, still apply only to men of property.

The problem was twofold and lay in the lack of clarity as to what the various pledges meant. First, the pledge to represent Muslims in excess of their numbers was inconsistent with that of the 'community' electing 'its own' since there was a dearth of viable Muslim representatives, and 'far from being in excess of their ratio to population [their proportion] is actually below it in all but two Councils.'[75] Second, Muslims rejected the proposal to supplement any shortfall through elections in mixed electorates or by nomination on the grounds that 'Muhammadans so elected would not be their representatives at all; the only genuine Muhammadan representatives are those whom they elect themselves, and these it has been shown are less, not more, than they were promised.'[76] Thus, the idea of supplementing Muslim representation through any method—mixed electorates or nomination—however much in excess of their numbers, was considered illegitimate. Instead, the London Branch of the Muslim League pushed to increase separate seats in all councils—a position the viceroy accepted since 'the trend of recent discussions . . . have unfortunately emphasised the differences between communities, and will probably impair the chances of the Muhammadans in the general electorates.'[77]

The provision to secure seats for Muslims beyond their proportion in the population provoked a strong negative reaction on the part of the professional class of Hindus. This was articulated by K.G. Gupta, who sat on Morley's advisory committee in London. Arguing against Morison, Gupta contended that, far from falling short of the pledges made to Muslims, the Councils Bill actually exceeded them. If Muslims had been accorded 'special protection' on the grounds that they were a minority, then it followed that in regions and provinces where they were a numerical majority—Punjab, Bengal, and the North West Frontier—reservations and separate electorates could not be justified. On the contrary, by this logic, in those same provinces the 'admittedly

[75] T. Morison, 'Note Upon the Pledges Given to the Mahommedans', Morley Papers, vol. 34.

[76] Ibid.

[77] Letter, Minto to Morley, 22 July 1909, Morley Papers, vol. 34. On the imperial council, the number would increase from five to six, thereby ensuring one representative each for Madras and Bombay; and in the provincial councils, the number would increase from three to four in Bombay, and from two to four in Bengal and Eastern Bengal and Assam.

influential Hindu minority should receive special consideration'.[78]
Furthermore, continued participation in mixed electorates, allowing
Muslims the opportunity to be represented in a proportion over and
above that dictated by their numbers, should not extend to other
electorates such as universitites, chambers of commerce, planters (in
East Bengal and Assam), landowners, and so on. These, Gupta argued,
were neither 'Hindu' nor 'Muhammadan' and it would be 'against all
reason and equity to include them in the aggregate number of elected
seats upon which the Muhammadan proportion is to be based'.[79]

Gupta proposed an alternative structure for the Imperial Legislative
Council where it would be divided into two classes. Class I would
comprise twelve members elected by the provincial legislative councils
and six members elected by the 'Muhammadan' electorate, making a
total of eighteen members. Class II would comprise seven members
elected by the landholding electorate, two elected by chambers of commerce, and one by Indian commerce, giving it a total of ten members
and the whole council a total of 28. Gupta argued that the 'Muhammadan proportion should be calculated not on 28, the aggregate of
elected seats of all kinds, but on eighteen, the total of I.'[80] Thus
Muslims would be entitled to 23 per cent (their percentage of the total
population of India) of eighteen seats yielding 4.4 seats, not the six
seats currently assigned. And elections to provincial councils would be
made similarly. By removing one-third to one-half of council members
from the calculation, Gupta could make a case for the reduction in the
number of reserved seats for Muslims while still comfortably arguing
that the pledges were adequately redeemed by the proposal. Numbers
would be supplemented only by the general electorates, and not by
inclusion in the other 'special interest' electorates.

The scheme preferred by those claiming to speak for Hindu interests—be they liberal newspapers, political associations such as the
Indian National Congress, or individuals such as Gupta—had been
that of electoral colleges. After it had been rejected and it was clear that

[78] Note on Muhammadan Representation by Mr Gupta, Morley Papers,
vol. 34.
[79] Ibid.
[80] Ibid.

distinct interest groups would be central to any reform, Gupta began to represent Hindus as an interest group in its own right. His frustration on the question of Muslim representation was obvious. By holding out the 'spectre of Muhammadan discontent', he argued, Muslims were trying 'to extort the full pound of flesh'.[81] But, he demanded, were they the only community to be considered? The reforms had been intended to extend electorates. However, Gupta contended, their effect would be to narrow, not broaden, the 'popular' electorate. By setting aside special interest electorates, that 'by no stress of imagination [could] . . . be regarded as popular or general electorates', the number of seats that were strictly mixed were whittled down from an ostensible twenty-five to twelve, of which one was for Burma, 'where there are no Hindus to speak of'.[82] Gupta's concern had to do with the bias he felt was being levelled against Hindus:

> The whole controversy—the whole demand for separate Muhammadan representation— centres round the assumption that in the elections the interests of the Muhammadan minority should be safeguarded as against the Hindu majority; and when it comes to determining the proper proportion of Muhammadan representation it ought in all fairness to be calculated on the seats given to general or popular electorates and not on the aggregate of elected seats of all kinds including constituencies that represent purely limited interests . . . in which the Hindus have no voice whatsoever; . . . true statesmanship requires that no *undue* favour is shown to one community at the *expense* of another.[83]

By using 'general electorate' interchangeably with 'Hindu community', Gupta could argue that seats for special interests meant that the councils would be agents of 'class' and not 'popular' interest. It was widely acknowledged that Hindus would overwhelmingly populate seats for interests other than those specifically for Muslims. However, by arguing that since they were for special interests they could not be considered part of a general electorate, Gupta was effectively arguing for an interest group for Hindus.

[81] 'Note of Dissent', by K.G. Gupta, 16 August 1909, Morley Papers, vol. 34.
[82] Ibid.
[83] Further note on Muhammadan Representation by K.G. Gupta, 10 August 1909, Morley Papers, vol. 34, emphasis mine.

Significantly, the argument was founded on the issue of numbers. For Gupta, 'minority' meant numerical minority. That Indian Muslims were a political minority everywhere in India, even in places where they were a numerical majority, was of little interest to him. The fact that they would be allowed to vote in all sections of all electorates meant that while they had been given the opportunity 'to elect their full representation in proportion with their numerical strength, the Hindus will have no such privilege.'[84] Rather, Hindus would have to compete with all other communities for the remaining eleven seats. This meant that even if they managed to secure most of the seats for landowners, the proportion open to them would still be 'far in defect of their numerical strength not to speak of their importance from the point of view of their influence and education.'[85] Gupta deployed the very same language of the Muslim League deputation of 1906 to legitimate his argument.

While Minto had been firmly against any suggestion that Muslims should not participate in mixed electorates, others seemed to be softening their position. In an unsigned letter, an individual wrote to him that while Muslim representative interests should be secured by all the various means provided, if 'that interest is fully provided for by exclusively Muhammadan electorates it seems clear that it must be excluded from voting in the general electorates.'[86] The letter suggested that a reordering of seats on provincial councils could ensure that a greater number would be reserved for a Muslim electorate, securing full Muslim representation. However, this would entail their exclusion from all mixed electorates. The author justified his position by arguing that if Muslims themselves were 'strongly set upon the principle of strictly Muhammadan electorates, there is some advantage in deferring to it.'[87]

The shift seemed to have come about for a variety of reasons. It should be recalled that the viceroy and secretary of state had had two goals for constitutional reform. First, to draw into politics the more conservative and loyal sections of society in order to counteract the

[84] Gupta, 'Note of Dissent', Morley Papers, vol. 34.
[85] Ibid.
[86] Letter to Lord Minto, from the India Office, London, dated only 1909, unsigned, Morley Papers, vol. 34.
[87] Ibid.

emerging anti-colonialism of an urban, professional, largely upper-caste Hindu elite. Second, to break down the barriers between the so-called 'water-tight' communities of caste and religion. By so doing, the reforms would introduce Indians to the idea of a public life. To bring into being a system which continued to represent an interest group as an impermeable category would defeat the whole purpose of the scheme. However, when it became apparent that Muslims, especially in provinces such as Madras and Bombay, would have to rely in signi-ficant part on representatives chosen through election or nomination from mixed electorates to fill the seats reserved for them, Bilgrami and the London Committee of the All India Muslim League recorded their vehement opposition. If the choice was between supplementary repre-sentation through mixed electorates and full representation through separate electorates with no double voting, then it was the latter that those of the London Committee preferred. Officials argued that this approach would not win them any seats in the mixed electorates, and so, to ensure their numbers would be complete, they determined that extra seats would be added to Muslim electorates in the imperial and provincial legislative councils.

These moves infuriated Gupta, who saw seats for 'general' electorates being whittled away in favour of 'class interests' and contended that what was left to Hindus was far less than was warranted by their nume-rical strength. Not wanting to alienate what they themselves had named the majority, government seemed to soften its stance on the point about double voting: if Muslims were given a greater number of seats in 'their' electorate, exclusion from mixed electorates could, at a pinch, be justified. Muslim representatives in London who had agreed to the community's exclusion from a general electorate provided they could separately elect all their representatives, also made this easier. Such a move could appease Hindu dissent, while at the same time ap-pearing to fulfil all their pledges to Muslims.

Conclusion

Minto had consistently opposed reforms that set Muslims outside the general electorate, arguing that it was impossible to give them 'an en-tirely separate communal representation'. In the event, the scheme that finally emerged was in line with the one originally put forward in

1907. It retained the principle that Muslims across the country would have separate electorates 'nearly representing that to which their numerical proportion in the population would entitle them', which would be supplemented through mixed electorates.[88] Seats would be filled by a combination of election and nomination, despite opposition to the second method. Government tried to appease these concerns by arguing that nominations were intended only as a temporary measure to be used in cases such as Madras where it seemed impossible to constitute electorates immediately. Seats gained through separate electorates would comprise the majority of Muslim seats, anything gained in mixed electorates being supplementary.

However, while the reforms of 1909 were not so different than what had been proposed in 1907, something significant had happened during the course of the debates. 'Minority', 'special', or 'communal' interests in 1907 had not been defined solely in terms of numbers—of majorities and minorities. Rather, the discussion had emphasized the integral importance of these interests in the definitions of an Indian constitution. It went beyond the determination of the relative numerical proportions of different interests, asserting not only their legitimacy in a representative structure but also that they were an essential part of one. In this sense, a certain parity among interests was recognized. By 1909, this had changed. It had become possible to entertain the idea that communal interests, specifically those of the Muslims, could be taken care of outside one main representative structure, and so were thus no longer seen as constitutive of it. In October 1909 it was stated that the 'special representation of Muhammadans was only claimed and only conceded on the ground that so important a minority required protection.' Thus, it could be argued that '[where] they are in a majority no special measure of protection is required.'[89]

It was in the intricacies of the debate between 1906 and 1909 that the question of representation shifted from being a qualitative one about what it meant to be a special interest or community in the Indian context, to being a quantitative one where minority came to be defined in numerical terms. Thus, it became possible to talk about Hindus

---

[88] Confidential note on the New Legislative Councils, Appendix II on Muhammadan Representation, Morley Papers, vol. 34.
[89] Ibid.

needing 'protection' from Muslims in regions where the latter's population was numerically greater. Issues of relative political power and access to it, all of which had contributed to the earlier discussions, were lost. In addition, the process by which the 'communal' Muslim interest became defined in numerical terms also created a new meaning for that term. There was an emerging perception on the part of a professional class of Hindus that representation for Muslims on councils in greater proportion than their percentage in the population was 'excessive', and 'at the expense of' the Hindus. This in turn served to associate the communal electorate—and the term communal itself—with divisive, 'denationalising', parochial ideas. As we saw in Chapters 1 and 2, by the early twentieth century a category of patriotism had begun to emerge, not only in Maharashtra but also elsewhere in India, which aligned an idea of India and Indianness with high-caste Hindu identity. The main arenas for the emergence of this idea were the popular mobilizations around the issue of Ganpati festivals, cow protection, and the Swadeshi movement. At the very highest echelon of political action, debates over imperial constitutional reform had begun to align the term communal with the Muslim community. Constitutional reforms were introduced by the British with the intention of maintaining control over a changing society. They were also presented as an act of imperial benevolence, aiming to create parity among India's communities. Ironically, they served to engender much clearer ideas of what it meant to be a majority population, as well as the characteristics and values of a minority.

Ten years later, Mohamed Ali and his brother Shaukat, with Mohandas Gandhi, spearheaded an anti-imperialist movement which rejected the very idea that majority and minority should characterize the relationship between Hindu and Muslim communities. The Khilafat movement was a popular protest movement across northern and western India that sought to define Hindus and Muslims as partners in an independent Indian nation, and in so doing to create a foundation for nationalism that was not determined by Western models of democracy. It is to the Khilafat movement and the post-Khilafat period that we now turn.

4

The Question of Muslim Autonomy

The Khilafat Movement and the Separation of Sind 1919–1932

As the First World War ended, rumours began to circulate in India that a harsh peace treaty was to be imposed on the defeated Ottoman empire. If true, such a treaty would endanger the position of the sultan as the khalifa of Islam and the safety of Mecca and the other Holy Places, the Jazirat al-Arab. In 1919 Muslims mobilized in a broad-based popular campaign the likes of which had not been seen before in colonial India. The Khilafat movement aimed to pressurize the victorious Allies to retain intact the boundaries of the Ottoman empire as they had existed in 1914 and to preserve the position of the khalifa as the temporal head of the Islamic world. Mohandas Gandhi was quickly drawn to the movement. His experiences in South Africa had convinced him that a challenge to colonial rule could only succeed if it was based on Hindu–Muslim unity. By supporting the Muslims of India in their concerns for the Khilafat, Gandhi sought to demonstrate his loyalty—and by extension that of the rest of 'Hindu' India—to this ideal. In the aftermath of the war, Gandhi also altered the Congress's structure and membership rules. He turned it from a debating society for the middle classes into an organization with committees in almost every district and the potential for building a mass following. Gandhi saw this as an opportune moment to undertake a parallel anti-colonial campaign. Thus, he gave his commitment to the movement to save the khalifa and launched another—non-violent Non-cooperation—alongside it.

The period 1919–22 is widely understood as the heyday of Hindu–Muslim unity in the anti-colonial movement.[1] The leaderships of Congress and the Khilafat movement often overlapped. Strikes, demonstrations, and satyagrahas took place around the country, while 'Hindu–Musalman ki jai' (Long live Hindu–Muslim unity) became a familiar cry. Unity, however, was ephemeral. After 1922 a series of differences between the Khilafat and Non-cooperation leaderships intersected with growing popular conflict between Hindu and Muslim communities. Unity was shattered, giving way to a period of 'communalism'. Scholarship on this period has tended to depict the demise of Hindu–Muslim unity as marking a turning point in the anti-colonial struggle. The bond of fraternity turned out to be an ad hoc coalition of interests with often markedly different aspirations.[2] The conflicts had 'revived old Hindu–Muslim antagonisms',[3] and 'irrevocably violated' the 'Hindu–Muslim understanding'.[4] For many, the unravelling of the Non-cooperation and Khilafat coalition reads as a milestone on the path to Partition.[5]

This chapter focuses on the Khilafat movement in Sind, the only Muslim-majority region in Bombay Presidency. It argues that to understand the end of the Khilafat and Non-cooperation movement as

---

[1] There is an extensive literature on these movements and the possibilities they were seen to represent. See for example P.C. Bamford, *Histories of the Non-Cooperation and Khilafat Movements* (Delhi, 1974 [1925]); Judith Brown, *Gandhi's Rise to Power: Indian Politics, 1915–1922* (Cambridge, 1972); Mushirul Hasan, *Nationalism and Communal Politics in India, 1916–1928* (Columbia, 1979); Gail Minault, *The Khilafat Movement: Religious Symbolism and Political Mobilization in India* (New York, 1982); B.R. Nanda, *Gandhi, Pan-Islamism, Imperialism and Nationalism in India* (Bombay, 1989); M. Naeem Qureshi, *Pan-Islamism in British Indian Politics: A Study of the Khilafat Movement, 1918–1924* (Leiden, 1999).

[2] Qureshi, *Pan-Islamism in British Indian Politics*, p. 345.

[3] Hardy, *Muslims of British India*, p. 195.

[4] Minault, *The Khilafat Movement*, p. 149.

[5] Nanda, *Gandhi*; Moin Shakir, *Khilafat to Partition: A Survey of Major Political Trends Among Indian Muslims During 1919–1947* (Delhi, 1983).

beginning the downward spiral of Hindu–Muslim relations is misleading. At its grassroots the Khilafat movement was made up of myriad alliances which were constantly shifting right from its inception. For some Muslims the movement was a pan-Islamic one whose goal was to retain the position of the Khilafat and the Sultan's control over the Jazirat al-Arab. For others it was about protesting against colonialism. Likewise, for some Hindus, Khilafat and Non-cooperation were two sides of the same coin. Others saw little worth in a union with Muslims. Scholarship that charts a trajectory from unity to fragmentation is misleading in its implication that when Muslims and Hindus pulled away from each other after the movement ended, they did so by virtue of their belonging to one community or the other.

I argue that there were varieties of divergent aspirations that made up the Khilafat and Non-cooperation movements, many of which had little to do with either Indian nationalism or Hindu–Muslim unity.[6] Nevertheless, this period proved critical for the ways in which nationalism would be formulated in the future. During these years, to be a nationalist did not require one to subsume smaller affiliations to the greater ideal of the nation. Rather, the movements sought to forge a nationalism that was built by its communities, where each, whatever its relative size, was a necessary part. By the end of the 1920s the possibility of such a federated nationalism was increasingly distant. For those within the Hindu Mahasabha, an organization with close links to Congress but founded on an explicitly Hindu nationalist agenda, the end of the movements demonstrated the incompatibility of 'extra-territorial' and Indian nationalisms. Loyalties to political bodies outside India, or Muslim aspirations to be recognized as such within India, were now seen as communalism.

This chapter begins with a background to pan-Islamism in India. It then turns to a study of the Khilafat and Non-cooperation movements in Sind. Finally, it considers the aftermath of the movements and the response in Sind and among nationalists in Delhi to the question of its separation.

---

[6] An important source is the recent publication of selected documents from different regions during the Khilafat period: Mushirul Hasan and Margrit Pernau (eds), *Regionalizing Pan-Islamism: Documents on the Khilafat Movement* (Delhi, 2005).

Pan-Islamism in India

Muslims had been part of the Indian National Congress since the first decade of its inception. However, Sir Sayyid Ahmed Khan took the position that while Muslims should work together with Hindus, they should remain outside Congress.[7] He felt that demands for representation on councils had been dominated by Hindu Bengalis and believed that the reformed councils would have no place for Muslims. Sir Sayyid and his Aligarh college were enormously influential in the intellectual world of Indian Muslims at the end of the nineteenth century. Consequently, many took his lead, maintaining a distance from Congress and professing loyalty to the Raj. At the same time, the Government of India made several decisions that would shake this loyalty. After the revolt of 1857, officials introduced policies aimed at undermining Muslim prominence in government bureaucracies. For instance, in the United Provinces in 1894, a ratio of three Muslims to every five Hindus in public service positions was introduced.[8] The Devanagari script was also put on an equal footing with Urdu and knowledge of both scripts became compulsory for upper-level administrative appointments.

Although Mohsin-ul-Mulk organized the October Deputation to Simla in 1906, demanding separate electorates for Muslims and professing their loyalty to British rule, many younger Muslims had begun to protest against British imperialism at home and abroad. Mushirul Hasan and Sara Ansari have argued that a series of policies—the annulment of the partition of Bengal in 1911, the opposition to a Muslim university in 1912, as well as the Italian invasion of Libya, an Ottoman province, in 1911—contributed to the growth of anti-government sentiment amongst Muslims.[9] In 1913 the Anjuman-i Khuddam-i Kaaba was founded in Lucknow. One of a set of organizations concerned with the future of Turkey and the Holy Places, it was led by Maulana Abdul Bari, a respected scholar at Lucknow's Firangi Mahal theological seminary. His associates were Shaukat Ali, a graduate of

[7] Lelyveld, *Aligarh's First Generation*.

[8] Mushirul Hasan, *Nationalism and Communal Politics in India, 1885–1930* (Delhi, 1991), p. 53.

[9] Ibid., p. 60; Sara Ansari, *Sufi Saints and State Power: The Pirs of Sind* (Cambridge, 1992), p. 78.

Aligarh who had resigned his government post in the opium department, his younger brother Mohamed Ali, and Mushir Husain Kidwai, a taluqdar who had published a book arguing that the principles of Islam and socialism were closely tied. All three would become central figures in the Khilafat movement.

At the centre of pan-Islamic and anti-imperialist activities during these years was Maulana Mohamed Ali.[10] Shaukat and Mohamed Ali occupied the centre of the intellectual world at Aligarh. M.A. Ansari, the Edinburgh-trained surgeon who led a medical mission to Constantinople in 1912, and Maulana Abul Kalam Azad, the religious scholar who had turned to a career in journalism, also influenced the radical thought of this younger generation.[11] Pan-Islamist and anti-imperialist sentiment found voice in a slew of new publications that included Mohamed Ali's English-language *Comrade*, Maulana Azad's Urdu-language *al-Hilal*, as well as the *Oudh Punch* and the *New Era*. Several stints in prison during the First World War allowed both to deepen their knowledge of Islam and Muslim history. Both believed deeply in their faith but also had strong rationalist and modernist approaches that allowed them to reconcile their religious beliefs with their commitment to Indian nationalism. For Sunnis—the overwhelming majority of India's Muslims—the khalifa was the temporal successor to the Prophet, responsible for the perpetuation of Sharia and for the Holy Places of Islam. If these were ever to be endangered, Mohamed Ali argued, it was the duty of every Muslim to ensure their safety and sanctity.[12] When in 1919 it became clear that the Ottoman empire would be dismantled, Maulana Mohamed Ali, Shaukat Ali, and many others decided to take a stand.

[10] For biographies of Mohamed Ali, see Afzal Iqbal (ed.), *My Life, A Fragment: An Autobiographical Sketch of Maulana Mohamed Ali* (Lahore, 1966); Afzal Iqbal, *The Life and Times of Mohamed Ali* (Lahore, 1979); Mushirul Hasan, *Mohamed Ali, Ideology and Politics* (Delhi, 1981).

[11] For scholarship on Azad, see Rajat K. Ray, 'Revolutionaries, Pan-Islamists and Bolsheviks: Maulana Abul Kalam Azad and the Political Underworld in Calcutta, 1905–1925', in Mushirul Hasan (ed.), *Communal and Pan-Islamic Trends in Colonial India* (Delhi, 1981); Ian Henderson Douglas, *Abul Kalam Azad: An Intellectual Biography* (Delhi, 1988).

[12] Hasan, *Nationalism and Communal Politics*, p. 113.

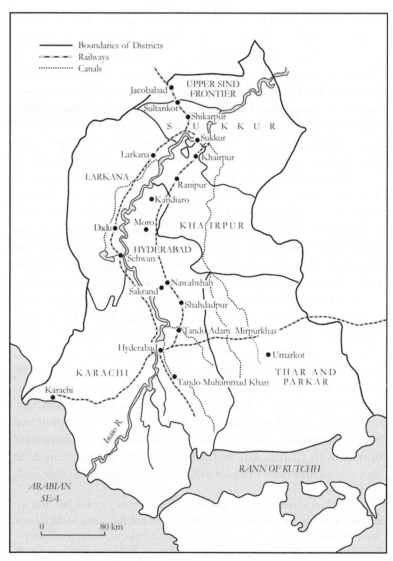

Map 2. Sind in the Colonial Period

Sind in the Nineteenth and Early
Twentieth Centuries

Sind, now part of Pakistan, was incorporated into the British empire in India in 1843.[13] Taken by Charles Napier from the Baluch Talpur dynasty, it lay on India's strategically important western frontier. Although part of Bombay Presidency, the province was separated from the rest of British India by a series of native states along its eastern border, its geographical isolation meaning that its commissioner enjoyed far greater autonomy than did those in the other divisions of the presidency. Sind, moreover, was overwhelmingly a Muslim province, with Muslims accounting for 75 per cent of the total population of 3.5 million in 1911.[14] Of Sindhi Hindus, David Cheesman paints a heterodox picture. The majority were descended from the Lohana tribe, recent immigrants from the Punjab, many of whom worshipped at Muslim shrines and followed a blend of Hinduism and the teachings of the Sikh Guru Nanak. There were few Brahmans, they had little knowledge of the shastras, most ate meat (except beef) and had few taboos about mixing with other castes or non-Hindu communities.

Hindus tended to be concentrated in urban centres and to belong to the professional (Amil) and merchant (Bania) classes. The Lohana Amils had held the highest administrative offices under Muslim rulers since the mid-eighteenth century. They spoke Persian, grew beards, dressed like Muslims, and were usually educated under Muslim teachers. After the British conquest Amils took to English-language education and continued to populate government positions. Banias, in contrast, were less integrated with Muslims. They wore the Hindu dhoti and were not generally familiar with Persian. Sind had long been important in trade with Central Asia and Banias had been dominant in these commercial networks. The port of Karachi, the capital of British Sind,

[13] There are surprisingly few histories of Sind written in English, but see Hamida Khuhro, *The Making of Modern Sind: British Policy and Social Change in the Nineteenth Century* (Karachi, 1978); R.D. Choksey, *The Story of Sind: An Economic Survey, 1843–1933* (Pune, 1983); Ansari, *Sufi Saints and State Power*; David Cheesman, *Landlord Power and Rural Indebtedness in Colonial Sind, 1865–1901* (Richmond, Surrey, 1997); Claude Markovits, *The Global World of Indian Merchants, 1750–1947: Traders of Sind from Bukhara to Panama* (Cambridge, 2000).

[14] Taken from the 1911 Census Report, Cheesman, *Landlord Power*, p. 35.

grew rapidly in the second half of the nineteenth century, in large part because of powerful Hindu trading firms which dominated trade and moneylending throughout the province.[15]

Muslims who lived in Sind's towns were usually artisans and labourers. The vast majority, however, were peasant farmers. Cheesman argues that by the late eighteenth century the importance of tribal institutions had diminished and rural Sind was no longer organized around the sardars but around waderos, landholders who owned some of the largest estates in British India and who rarely had any tribal connections with their cultivators. The latter were landless labourers (haris), 'tenants-at-will' who could be removed from the land at any point. The administration and revenue structure relied heavily on the waderos, jagirdars, and zamindars. Consequently, no legislation had been introduced to protect agriculturalists as it had been in the rest of the presidency under the Deccan Agriculturalists Relief Act.[16] Colonial policy aimed to cultivate the loyalty of landowners. Most had been allowed to retain their land, but the distribution of titles was equally important. Izzat—the maintenance of honour and status—was central to Muslim social life. It was especially important that those who were economically powerful should also be seen to be honourable. Ansari has shown how colonial officials appropriated the idea of izzat by creating a system of honours and gifts that were distributed to waderos and smaller landowners as rewards for co-operation.[17] By the end of the nineteenth century, however, as a consequence of legislation introduced after 1843 that conferred full property rights on landowners, waderos had become caught up in a cycle of debt to the Bania trading classes and had lost much of their land to them.

In addition to the waderos, the Sufi religious elite were central to the exercise of power in Sind.[18] These were the Sayyids and the pirs of the sajjada nashin families, both of Arab descent.[19] Following the advent of Islam in Sind, Muslim conversions had mostly been performed by Sufis. As a result, religious authority tended to be held by their

[15] Cheesman, *Landlord Power,* pp. 46–9.

[16] Ibid., pp. 36 and 60–71.

[17] Ansari, *Sufi Saints and State Power,* pp. 46–9.

[18] See Ansari, *Sufi Saints and State Power,* pp. 38–45.

[19] *Sajjada nashin* literally means 'one who sits on the carpet', but indicates the head of a pir family. Ibid., p. 7.

descendants, the pirs, rather than by the ulema. Their popular Islam had a strongly syncretic character, with Muslims and Hindus sharing many practices that were particular to the region. Sayyids, who claimed descent from the Prophet Muhammad, generally resided in towns and tended to be teachers and scholars. Many were also waderos, and the combination afforded them tremendous influence. In contrast, rural areas were the social base of pirs. These pirs were also landed, but those belonging to important shrines—generally the tombs of revered Sufis—wielded great moral and spiritual influence over local populations, both rich and poor. They were absolutely central to the social and economic life of Sind, often acting as adjudicators in local conflicts. A wadero would often consult his pir before taking any decision in complex cases, while a cultivator who wanted to approach his wadero would do so through his pir.[20] Pirs became mediators between the rulers and the population, rewarded by official patronage with grants of land.

It was during the pan-Islamic activities of the early twentieth century that the pirs of Sind began to be drawn into wider Muslim politics. Several had developed close ties to the ulema of the Dar al-Ulum at Deoband, the influential theological seminary in the United Provinces.[21] By the 1900s there was a network of Deobandi influence in Sind from Barchundi at the Punjab–Sind border to Sukkur and Hyderabad. Pirs such as Ghulam Mujaddid Sirhindi of Matiari, Turab Ali Shah Rashdi, and Ali Anwar Shah Rashdi of Larkana were followers of the prominent pan-Islamic leader Maulana Abdul Bari of Firangi Mahal. They supported the Sind branch of the Anjuman-i Khuddam-i Kaaba founded by Abdul Bari and worked to raise money in support of the safety of the Jazirat al-Arab. By 1919 Sindhi pirs were part of a wider framework of Muslim intellectual and political life in India. Most, however, were from the Qadiri and Naqshbandi Sufi orders that had emerged in the eighteenth and nineteenth centuries. Pirs from longer established shrines had shown less interest in pan-Islamic ideas. Nevertheless, because of their important position in rural society they were central to the widespread support for the Khilafat and Non-cooperation

[20] Cheesman, *Landlord Power*, p. 38
[21] Ansari, *Sufi Saints and State Power*, pp. 78–89.

movements in Sind. Involvement in these movements came from a variety of sources: conservative ulema, Western-educated professionals, zamindars, and urban businessmen. But the Khilafat movement in Sind would have been insignificant had it not been for mass support from the countryside, and it was for this that the pirs were responsible. They called on their murids, spiritual disciples, to participate in demonstrations and boycotts, toured rural areas, were prominent at Congress and Khilafat Committee conventions, all the while speaking of the dangers that faced Islam and the Holy Places and the need for Hindu–Muslim unity to combat it.

The Khilafat and Non-cooperation Movements in Sind 1919–1924

Protest against the fate of the Khilafat emerged from mobilization against the Rowlatt Act of 1919. The act was an attempt to make permanent the wartime restrictions on civil rights including detention without trial for minor offences such as the possession of seditious tracts. Gandhi declared that 6 April 1919 should be observed as a 'day of humiliation' and that satyagrahas should be held around the country.[22] On 6 April processions took place across Sind.[23] In the mofussil towns of Larkana and Shikarpur, a large proportion of shops remained closed. In Karachi a scheme was worked out to cut off the food supply to large sections of the population. Public meetings and demonstrations were attended by people in their thousands. Hindu and Muslim spokesmen came together to denounce the colonial state, the commissioner in Sind noting that 'the week has been distinguished by the

[22] On the 1919 Rowlatt satyagraha, see Ravinder Kumar (ed.), *Essays in Gandhian Politics: The Rowlatt Satyagraha of 1919* (Oxford, 1971). Satyagraha, literally 'truth in action', was the foundation of Gandhi's philosophy of non-violent non-cooperation. It was a form of civil disobedience based on the moral action of the individual born of truth (satya), non-violence (ahimsa) and self-sacrifice (tapasya). Satyagrahas had been tried in rural Bihar and urban industrial centres in Gujarat and Bombay with varying success since 1916, involving hartals (work stoppages), shop closures, and public demonstrations.

[23] Memorandum from H.S. Lawrence, Commissioner in Sind, Karachi, 13 April 1919, Home/Special, 521, part XII, 1919, MSA.

remarkable phenomenon of united assemblies of Hindus and Muhammadans in a Muhammadan mosque and a Hindu temple.'[24]

Gandhi drew on the success of the Rowlatt satyagrahas in order to integrate the goals of the Non-cooperation and Khilafat movements. Proponents of the latter had been preaching non-cooperation since its inception. They said that Islam was in danger and that there were three ways to save the faith:

1. Non-cooperation ie. to sever all connection with the enemy of 'Din' (religion ie. Islam).
2. Hijrat ie. to leave the country of the enemy of religion.
3. Jehad ie. to fight with the enemies of Din by drawing sword (Jazaq-Allah-Afrin).

Non-cooperation means that you should not have any kind of love with the enemies of Din . . . We have been obliged to sever connections with the Government, as the Government has become the enemy of our religion . . . If our religion is interfered [with] then we will not remain loyal under any circumstances . . . We know that this Government is nothing in comparison of that Government (God). If we are not afraid of God and are afraid of Government then we are Kaffirs and Mardud (cowards) . . . Non-co-operation is the first step and if we are firm on this then we will be able to do Hijrat as well as Jehad. We will have to undergo troubles owing to non-cooperation but we should be ready for the same.[25]

Gandhi took up the Khilafat position on non-cooperation in the mass satyagrahas of the early 1920s, insisting that Hindus would support Indian Muslims in their quest to retain the Khilafat. At a meeting held during satyagraha week, he proposed 'to cease cooperation with the Government if it took any part in dismembering the empire of the khalifa against the dictates of the Islamic law.' When on 19 April 1919, at Jallianwalla Bagh in Amritsar, General Dyer's troops killed 327 people, Hindu, Sikh and Muslim, who had been peacefully demonstrating against the Rowlatt Act, Gandhi continued: 'the Muslims and Hindus of India were not only united over the question of the Khilafat, but also on all political questions relating to their motherland—India.

[24] Ibid.
[25] Mr Jan Muhammad Junejo, barrister, speaking at a conference at Jacobabad, 'Khilafat Agitation in Sind', Home/Special 355-B, 1919, MSA.

This was the National Week in memory of the tragedies in the Punjab. The blood of Hindus and Muslims mingled in Jallianwalla Bagh and other places last year had cemented the Hindu–Moslem unity.'[26]

Gandhi reiterated at meetings around the province that the Khilafat was a Hindu question *because* it was a Muslim question. At a conference in Hyderabad he said that certain Hindus had taken the position that they would support the Khilafat cause only if Muslims stopped cow slaughter and mobilized around Jallianwalla Bagh. But, he maintained, their support should be unconditional—Khilafat was an Indian concern.[27] At the same meeting Muslim spokesmen announced that their co-religionists would adopt the Swadeshi movement as their own and boycott foreign goods. Many also declared that they had stopped eating beef. In several districts, at the encouragement of local ulema and the Khilafat leadership, some individual families also gave up beef in their diet.[28] Next to Gandhi were the Ali brothers, who spoke of the link between Indian freedom and Turkish freedom and emphasized the importance of Hindu–Muslim unity as a prerequisite for national unity.

The bond between Gandhi and the Ali brothers was reflected in other personal relationships at a local level. In Sind, three Hyderabadi men stand out in particular: Sheikh Abdul Majid, Dr Choitram Gidwani, and Javharmal Totiram Mansukhani, otherwise known as Swami Govindanand. Sheikh Abdul Majid, a recent Amil convert, was released from prison in March 1919, after being interned for 'pan-Islamic activities', resuming his editorship of a Sindhi-language paper sympathetic to the Khilafat and Non-cooperation movements, *al-Amin*.[29] He was one of the key organizers of the hartal in Hyderabad on 6 April and had tried to persuade the Baluchi sardars to join the Non-cooperation movement.[30] He spoke often at Khilafat conferences, urging Muslims to end all ties with government and unite with Hindus:

[26] SAPI, para 646, 1920.

[27] SAPI, Hyderabad, para. 168, 1920.

[28] However, Muslims in several municipalities resented the efforts by Hindu activists to make cow slaughter illegal. See *al-Wahid*, a Muslim-owned newspaper in Sind, 9 January 1921, *Report on Native Papers*, week ending 29 January.

[29] District Superintendent of Police, Hyderabad, Home/Special, 521, part XII, 1919, MSA.

[30] Ibid.

This is cunning British who first gave us promises that religious places will not be touched and we being simple men believed their word and helped them in every way. Our big zamindars as well as our poor men helped the Government in donations as well as in recruiting and thus we sacrificed the lives of our poor brethren for the interest of *khabis* British and now see they have changed their promises and have greatly injured both our Islam and the Sultan of Turkey . . . Now if you are weak and are not ready for your religion then you are cursed. Leave at once the posts of Honarary [*sic*] Magistrates of this cunning British. Hate his titles and hate him even and pray to God to ruin this enemy who has no religion at once . . . You and Hindus are in crores and what five lakhs of Englishmen can do to you . . . Now our Mussalmans and Hindus have realised and have united.[31]

Sheikh Abdul Majid worked alongside Choitram Gidwani, an ex-assistant surgeon removed from his position for refusing military service.[32] In 1907 Gidwani joined a secret society and, emulating Bengali revolutionaries, took a vow of celibacy. He played a prominent part in the Swadeshi movement, opening a swadeshi store in Hyderabad and founding a Brahmacharya Ashram modelled after the national schools in Bengal. The schools continued into the 1920s and their members were an integral part of the Non-cooperation movement in Sind:

> At every political meeting in Hyderabad, at every conference or Congress meeting in Sind, the boys of Choithram's Ashram are to be found working as volunteers and opening the proceedings with political songs. Also, on March 30th 1919 when the *hartal* was forced on the town by Choithram and his associates, boys of the Ashram and of the National School and College were employed to pelt with mud and stones those shopkeepers who refused to yield to softer persuasion.[33]

Javharmal Totiram Mansukhani was a friend of Choitram's and also worked closely with Sheikh Abdul Majid. He had been forced to leave his position as a professor at Fergusson College, Poona, and later to resign from Bankipore College on the grounds that his lectures were

[31] Khabis: Arabic for 'wicked' and 'malicious'. March 1920, meeting in Hyderabad, Home/Special 355-B(1), 1920, MSA.

[32] DSP, Hyderabad. 25 May 1919, Home/Special, 521, part XII, 1919, MSA.

[33] Ibid.

seditious. Interned during the war, in January 1919 he began campaigning for the Non-cooperation movement and was regularly seen at Khilafat meetings. After his release Mansukhani adopted the dress of a sadhu and became known as Swami Govindanand, travelling across Sind speaking at public gatherings. Like Sheikh Abdul Majid, he also spoke of the broken promises of the British and the need to stand unified in opposition to them: 'England desires that all other nations should be destroyed. India now demands swaraj. During the war, India was promised much. Without India's help England would have been defeated but now India is fettered; the British Government is proved to be false. Swaraj will be ours before the end of the war, if we are firm about satyagraha.'[34] The swami argued that armed resistance had been used in other contexts, but 'India can be freed by the writing of an order.' And if Indians held firm to the principles of non-violence and unity between the communities, 'power will return'.[35]

By 1920 the Khilafat and Non-cooperation campaigns were beginning to converge. In Delhi, Non-cooperation leaders were demanding that people resign their titles and civil appointments and withhold taxes, as well as encouraging the police and the military to refuse duty. Activists in Sind were doing the same. Large numbers were reportedly resigning from 'Government employments, honorary posts, titles, other distinctions and privileges as Chair, gun licences, membership of municipal and local boards.'[36] By mid-October a dozen Muslim students from Karachi had left their schools and it was rumoured that about 300 others, both Muslim and Hindu, would soon follow.[37] A campaign for the boycott of council elections was also in full swing.[38] Religious leaders provided the essential link between urban Khilafat activists and the rural Muslim population.[39] District officials reported

[34] Ibid. Extract from the reports of the Superintendent of Police, from a meeting in Sukkur, 28 April 1919.

[35] Ibid.

[36] SAPI, Secretary of Sind, Karachi, para 1163, August 1920.

[37] SAPI, Karachi, 18 October 1920.

[38] SAPI, District Magistrate, Karachi, 5 October 1920.

[39] On the role of ulema in the Khilafat movement, see Mushirul Hasan, 'Religion and Politics in India: The *Ulama* and the Khilafat Movement', in Hasan, *Communal and Pan-Islamic Trends*.

that 'The disloyalty amongst pirs, sayyids and mullahs is spreading. As meetings are generally held in mosques or idgahs in small towns it cannot be controlled. The extremists like Dr Shaikh Nur Muhammad and Shaikh Abdul Majid are giving up propaganda in Hyderabad for small towns and are working through pirs, sayyids and mullahs.'[40] In Karachi, Abdul Jabbar, Nur Muhammad, Aminuddin N. Munshi, Sheikh Abdul Majid, and Muhammad Hashim asked maulvis 'to pass a fatwa on the authority of the Koran, directing the boycott of Councils.'[41] Soon after, Pir Ghulam Mujadid Sarhandi, also a member of the Sind Provincial Khilafat Committee, declared that the authority of the Quran superseded that of the British: 'If we find anything being done against our religion we can no longer remain faithful to Government . . . "He who killed Mussulmans went to hell", so says the Koran . . . Mussulmans are not afraid of being hanged or going to jail for the sake of Khilafat . . . I would urge you to adopt non-cooperation and boycott the Councils.'[42]

Colonial officials were surprised at the intensity that the movement had achieved by 1920. 'The Caliphate agitation has assumed a gravity of which it is difficult to trace a parallel in the history of political unrest in this country', ran one report. 'Whatever the origins of the movement and the causes of its growth . . . it would be underestimating the situation to declare that it is confined to a few discontented Muhammadans. It is true in some parts the agitation is more violent than in others. Sind, for example, is the most affected part of this Presidency.'[43] However, despite the enthusiasm with which Sindhis appeared to take up the question of Khilafat and Non-cooperation, there were real ambiguities from the outset.

It was clear, for example, that participation was sometimes secured by coercion. When activists were organizing a Sind-wide hartal to take place in March 1920 in honour of Khilafat Day, Pir Mahbub Shah, a prominent figure in Hyderabad, announced that jihad

---

[40] SAPI, Hyderabad, 30 March 1920.

[41] SAPI, Karachi, 13 October 1920.

[42] SAPI, Karachi, 20 October 1920.

[43] SAPI, extract from weekly report of the special officer for Bolshevism, Poona, 7 May 1920.

would be declared on all Hindus and Muslims who did not observe the strike.[44] In Karachi a Memon friend of the assistant superintendent of police told him that 'the Caliphate leaders are trying to arrange that all Muhammadans who do not take part in the hartal should be excommunicated, no one should attend marriages or funerals in their families and they should be excluded from the burial grounds'.[45] Pir Ghulam Mujadid was reported to have decided with other pirs and maulvis 'that a party of Moulvis should visit the Thar and Parkar district and endeavour to force those harris who are working upon the lands of loyal zamindars to boycott them and work only for those zamindars who are pro-Caliphate.'[46]

Although evidence of support for the movements was everywhere, ignorance, apathy, political opportunism, and outright resistance were also evident. Even as people in mofussil districts gathered to listen to Non-cooperation leaders, audiences seemed unmoved by the ideals themselves. The district magistrate of Sukkur noted in November 1920 that while Non-cooperators' efforts would likely result in a diminution of votes polled in council elections, '[t]he chief drawback to their progress in a place like Shikarpur is that people who have for years been accustomed to promise their votes to both candidates find it quite easy to go a step further to refrain from voting as well.'[47] In Larkana the district magistrate was more definite about the indifference of many local people: 'so far these non-cooperation preachers have not cut much ice in this district outside towns of Larkana and Dadu and even there it is only certain noisy and quarrelsome groups of disaffected persons who support them with any consistency and vigour.'[48] Non-cooperation leaders, both Hindu and Muslim, communicated with their audiences in Sindhi. They were men of high standing in their communities. Nevertheless, they were ultimately urban men, often far removed from the lives of their rural audiences, most of whom seemed to know little or care even less for the fate of the Khilafat. Indeed, a

---

[44] SAPI, Hyderabad, 24 March 1920.
[45] SAPI, Karachi, 11 March 1920.
[46] SAPI, Karachi, 5 August 1920.
[47] SAPI, Sukkur, 8 November 1920.
[48] SAPI, District Magistrate, Larkana, 2 November 1920.

letter from one organizer stated that the Muslims of rural Sind were 'totally ignorant of the Khilafat'.[49]

Moreover, political alliances were complex. Zamindars, for instance, tended to remain aloof. In early 1920, when officials had begun to express fears about the possibility of open revolt, it was the zamindars they felt they could count on: 'It is the object of those manipulating the agitation to impress upon Government officers . . . the idea that there is widespread popular feeling and indignation . . . So far as the mass of Sindhi zamindars is concerned, the Commissioner [of Sind] believes that this is not yet the case; the zamindars as a whole, are to some extent indifferent, and to a great extent entirely loyal.'[50] There were also pirs and ulema who actively campaigned against the movement. In the Thar and Parkar district, for instance, Pir Pagaro of Kingri and Makhdum Muhammad Hasan of Multan, the mujawar of the shrine of Bahawal Haq, had forbidden their followers to contribute anything to Khilafat funds or attend meetings. And, in a telegram to the Sind provincial government, the managing committee of the Shia Anjuman indicated their opposition to the Non-cooperation movement: 'All Shia Mussalmans in Sind view with hatred the movement of Non-cooperation and are against it.'[51] There are two possible explanations for this expression of loyalty. First, the objections were in part theological. While all Sunnis accepted the existence of the Khilafat, Shias rejected its legitimacy, following only the teachings of the twelve imams directly descended from Ali. Second, at a time so soon after the 1918 constitutional reforms which had confirmed Muslims as a separate electoral category, Shias feared the loss of their recognition as a community in its own right. Tellingly, an influential Shia zamindar was reported to have said that the government had been mistaken in not giving Shias the option of separate representation. Shias, he said, wanted this as much as the Sikhs, and even more so since the birth of the Khilafat movement.[52]

Non-cooperation had been launched by Gandhi on the back of the Khilafat movement and the two campaigns came quickly to be part of

[49] SAPI, Nawabshah, 20 April 1920.
[50] SAPI, Karachi, 3 February 1920.
[51] SAPI, Karachi, 15 October 1920.
[52] Ibid.

the same anti-colonial project. Yet both movements were short lived, barely lasting two years. Scholars have argued that their decline in 1922 marked the beginning of a long-term parting of the ways between Hindus and Muslims. The evidence from Sind suggests that there was nothing so decisive: the coalition between Non-cooperators and Khilafatists seemed to founder almost as soon as it came together. In April 1921, when the campaigns were at their height, it was already apparent that many Muslims in Sind supported Khilafat but associated Non-cooperation with Hindus:

> The Muhammadans of Sind as a whole, especially the cultivating classes, are almost entirely unaffected by the non-cooperation movement . . . The Pir of Kingri who is perhaps the most important Pir in Sind, has not only openly declared himself against it, but he advises those who consult him to remain faithful to the British Government . . . There is an exception in Pir Mahbubshah of Hyderabad District who is responsible for considerable agitation . . . there is an interest in Khilafat but not non-violent non-cooperation. The reasons for men like Rashidullah Shah, the Jhande Pir, holding aloof from non-cooperation is that it is initiated and controlled by Hindus.[53]

The faultlines within the movement were visible all over Sind. In Karachi, Muslims were not adopting Non-cooperation but support for the Khilafat campaign continued.[54] On the Upper Sind Frontier, Hindus took an interest but no Muslims appeared at Non-cooperation meetings.[55] Zamindars, both Hindu and Muslim, as well as pirs, represented their opposition through aman sabhas, 'peace councils', set up by the government to combat Non-cooperation.[56] The declining support for the Non-cooperation campaign was matched by a reported 'increased activity in so-called pan-Islamic circles'.[57] The spirit in Karachi was said to have been ebullient, with large cheering crowds attending public meetings: 'the Non-cooperation movement loses momentum as the Khilafat movement becomes more intense and

[53] SAPI, Sind, 15 April 1921.
[54] SAPI, Karachi, 1 March 1921.
[55] SAPI, Upper Sind Frontier, 3 April 1921.
[56] SAPI, Hyderabad, 2 July 1921.
[57] SAPI, Sind, 14 May 1921.

more general. The general feeling of sympathy with the religious view of the Khilafat is widespread.'[58]

By late 1921 the coalition was in decline. Enlistment of volunteers had fallen off and meetings once attended by both communities were now attended almost exclusively by one or the other.[59] Rural areas such as Sakrand and Sinkhoro talukas were least affected by the movement, the most concerted support for it being found in talukas with towns or large villages such as Tando Adam, Shahadapur, Nawabshah, and Naushahro.[60] That the support for Non-cooperation was mostly from towns is something that can likely be explained by the fact that the large proportion of Hindus lived in urban areas. In this sense, participation in the movements was not necessarily ideological but was mobilized through chains of authority represented by pirs, mullahs, activists, and publicists. Thus as the support of pirs fell away, so did the participation of their murids. At the end of 1921, the year that swaraj was supposed to have been won, a report noted: 'It may safely be said that outside the big towns the great majority of the people of Sind . . . know little or nothing of the political and racial questions connected with the movement; the number of meetings and agitations is now comparatively small.'[61] By January 1922 Non-cooperation in Sind had come to a complete standstill.

The Ties Unravel

However brief and ambivalent, there was something unique about the period of the Khilafat and Non-cooperation movements. There was a sense of optimism about the possibility of forging a nationalism that could be shared by Hindus and Muslims alike. The commissioner in Sind had commented on it during the 1919 hartals: 'the movement in Hyderabad has this peculiar distinction that it aims at combining both Hindus and Muhammadans in one common cause.'[62] Mohamed Ali

[58] SAPI, Sind, 17 November 1921; Karachi, 20 and 23 December 1921.
[59] SAPI, Sukkur, 15 July and 26 August 1921.
[60] SAPI, Nawabshah, 4 November 1921.
[61] SAPI, Sind, 11 January 1922.
[62] H.S. Lawrence, Commissioner in Sind, to Secretary to Government, Political Dept, Bombay, Karachi, 27 April 1919, Home/Special, 521, part XII, 1919, MSA.

spoke about swaraj being the rule of not one community in particular but of all:

> If the reign of Sikhs is established in India it would not be called *swaraj* but it would be called the rule of the Sikhs. If the Rajputs win, it would not be *swaraj* but it would be the rule of the Rajputs. If the Mahomedans win it would be the rule of the Mahomedans, but it would not be called *swaraj*, and if the Hindus win, it would be called the rule of the Hindus, but it would not be called *swaraj*. *Swaraj* means the rule of all—the rule in which all are united, in which all are treated like brothers and equals. Such is the *swaraj* that we now want to establish.[63]

Anthems composed during this period reflected this. As late as August 1922 the Shikarpuri paper *Watan* published a poem called 'National Song' which expressed all the possibilities of that moment. It called on people to 'discard the fine silks and showy fabrics of foreign manufacture', to strive for 'education and freedom', to adopt non-violent non-cooperation, and for Hindus to unite with Muslims with God as their guide.[64]

As the joint leaderships pulled away from each other, however, unity unravelled. The reasons for this were twofold. First, dissension within the Congress ranks in Sind meant that its organization was breaking down in all districts except Hyderabad.[65] Second, events at an all-India level were having an unsteadying impact on the leadership in Sind. A Khilafat Committee meeting in Ahmedabad in December 1921 passed a resolution put forward by Hasrat Mohani that Muslims should abandon non-violence if it forced the government's hand and ensured a positive outcome for the independence of the Khilafat. Mohamed Ali, moreover, declared that Muslims would support an Afghan invasion of British India. This put the question of violence at the top of the Khilafat agenda, much to the discomfort of the Congress leadership.

---

[63] Prosecution of the keeper of the 'Hindu' press in respect of certain articles published in the *Hindu* newspaper. From 'Translation of an article from the Hindu dated 15th July 1921: Some points of the Speech of Mr Mohamed Ali', p. 231, BPCP, July 1921, P/Conf/62, 1921, serial no. 5, OIOC.

[64] Prosecution by 108 Criminal Procedure Code against Balandram Vasandmal, editor of *Watan* newspaper, published at Shikarpur, for an article on 9 August 1922, BPCP, August 1922, P/Conf/ 65 of 1922, OIOC.

[65] SAPI, Karachi, 23 February 1922.

The *Sind Vasi*, a moderate Sindhi daily in Hyderabad, reported that 'Hindus were surprised and grieved by the attitude of the Sind Mussulman members, in the Congress Subjects Committee. . . . Hasrat Mohani's resolution in the Khilafat Committee . . . passed by 48 votes to 23.'[66] The possibility of a more violent political programme put a strain on the relationship between Choitram Gidwani and Abdul Jabbar. The latter had upheld Hasrat Mohani's resolution and thus threatened to go directly against Gandhi's condition of non-violence.[67] Furthermore, negotiations between Britain and Turkey seemed to indicate that a successful resolution to the Khilafat question was imminent, adding to these suspicions: 'Moulvis and Mullas are showing some signs of lack of interest in the agitation since the success of Turkey and it is possible that if the terms of the Near East settlement are satisfactory the unrest among Muslims may die down to a great extent. It is obvious however, that the leaders do not regard with equanimity the possibility of their ceasing to be of importance and efforts are being made to transfer the interest in Khilafat affairs to National affairs. Their cry now is that the Khilafat will not be safe unless swaraj is attained.'[68] Mohani's resolution, Mohamed Ali's statement, and the potential outcome to the negotiations in Turkey resulted in many Muslims in Sind pulling out of Non-cooperation, sending nervous ripples through Hindu Non-cooperating ranks.[69]

Three further events were crucial. First, in the summer of 1920 Maulana Azad and Maulana Abdul Bari issued a fatwa calling for hijrat—that is, the withdrawal of Muslims from dar-ul-Harb (the land of unbelief) to dar-ul-Islam (the abode of Islam). In response, an estimated 60,000 Muslims from the rural areas of Sind, the United Provinces and the Frontier Provinces left India for Afghanistan. They had been told by their pirs and mullahs that Islam was in danger, that hijrat could be an alternative to Non-cooperation, and that Afghanistan and not India was within dar-ul-Islam. The migration proved a debacle. The refugees were mostly poor Muslims who sold their few possessions

[66] SAPI, Sind, 11 January 1922.

[67] Ibid.

[68] SAPI, Larkana, 28 October 1922.

[69] SAPI, Karachi, 25 January; Hyderabad, 1 February 1922. This point is emphasized in Jalal, *Self and Sovereignty*, p. 225.

in order to make the journey. As their caravans travelled through the Khyber Pass, many were attacked and looted by tribesmen. The Amir of Afghanistan soon issued a proclamation indicating that no more Indians should come. Several thousand muhajirin returned to India penniless, many others dying on the return journey.[70]

Second, the Moplah rebellion in Malabar strained the union between Hindus and Muslims, creating a backlash against Muslim communities around the country. Antagonism between the predominantly Muslim Moplah peasants of Malabar and their Hindu landlords was longstanding. After the First World War, Moplahs, many of whom were demobilized soldiers, had begun to declare their support for the Khilafat. Advocating non-cooperation, they also condoned violence in pursuit of redress against their landlords. In August 1921 the alleged desecration of a mosque led to violent conflict with Hindus. Khilafat flags were flown and reports highlighted religious rather than economic reasons for the rebellion.[71]

Third, the famous Chauri Chaura incident: in February 1922 peasants in Chauri Chaura in the United Provinces trapped twenty-two policemen in their station and burned them alive. Gandhi immediately called off the satyagraha that was to take place in Bardoli and suspended civil disobedience indefinitely, declaring that Indians were not yet adequately evolved spiritually for the discipline that non-violent non-cooperation required. The decision incensed Congress politicians such as Motilal Nehru and C.R. Das, who saw it as an arbitrary retreat just when the anti-colonial movement seemed to be gaining momentum. It also exasperated Khilafat leaders, who began to question Gandhi's position as leader of the movement.

In Sind itself, 1923 was marked by increasing antagonism between the Hindu and Muslim communities. The Arya Samaj had began aggressive shuddhi and sangathan (purification and unity) campaigns. Shuddhi was directed at reconverting those that Hinduism had 'lost' to other religions, specifically Islam. This was supported by the Hindu Mahasabha, an explicitly Hindu nationalist organization founded in

[70] See M. Naeem Qureshi, 'The "Ulama" of British India and the Hijrat', *MAS*, 13, 1, 1979; and Minault, *The Khilafat Movement*, p. 106.
[71] Robert L. Hardgrave, 'The Mapilla Rebellion, 1921: Peasant Revolt in Malabar', *MAS*, 11, 1, 1977; and Minault, *The Khilafat Movement*, pp. 145–9.

1915 and revived in December 1922.[72] It was the Mahasabha's leader, Madan Mohan Malaviya, a pandit from the United Provinces and close companion of Gandhi, who had spearheaded this move. In September 1922 the Arya Samaj held its 36th anniversary meeting in Karachi. The presiding officers spoke on the spiritual, moral, and physical weakness of Hindus that had opened the door to this tyranny of the so-called mlecchas, as witnessed most recently during the Moplah rebellion.[73] In January 1923 the Arya Samaj began converting Rajput Muslims in the United Provinces. *Al-Wahid*, once an advocate of Non-cooperation but now an opponent, called upon the ulema to save these people from becoming 'kafirs'. *Bharatvasi*, a Hindu-owned paper, took exception to the term, referring sarcastically to *al-Wahid's* previous efforts to secure unity with the 'kafirs'.[74] The shuddhi campaign continued into March.[75] Arya Samajis concentrated their efforts in the urban areas of Sind, but also spent some time further afield. A shuddhi committee was formed at the end of April with the intention of working among the sheikhs of Shadadkot in the Upper Sind Frontier. This community of Muslims, which still used Hindu names and followed many Hindu customs, would, it was believed, be more open to being 'reclaimed'.[76]

The campaign led to a wave of recriminations within Muslim circles. *Al-Wahid* argued that it was religious ignorance amongst Muslims that had led to this situation. It levelled criticism against the Jamiat-ul-Ulema-i-Hind (an organization of ulema founded in 1919 by Abdul Bari) for the Aryas' shuddhi campaign, blaming maulvis for not having 'educat[ed] Muhammadans sufficiently in the tenets of their religion.'[77] Yet it was the Jamiat that took the lead in responding

[72] On the early Hindu Mahasabha, see Richard Gordon, 'The Hindu Mahasabha and the Indian National Congress, 1915 to 1926', *MAS* 9, 2, 1975; and Chetan Bhatt, *Hindu Nationalism: Origins, Ideologies and Modern Myths* (Oxford, 2001), pp. 56–62.

[73] Mleccha is a derogatory term for foreigners or non-Aryans. SAPI, Karachi, 9 September 1922.

[74] SAPI, Sind, 20 January 1923.

[75] SAPI, Sind, 17 March 1923.

[76] SAPI, Sukkur, 28 April 1923.

[77] SAPI, Karachi, 10 March 1923.

to the shuddhi campaign. In March 1923 it organized a protest meeting in Bombay with the intention of beginning a movement to revive religious knowledge 'amongst all those who called themselves Muslims'.[78] This movement, which came to be known as tanzim, sought first to counter the Arya Samaj's activities among Rajput Muslims.[79] Posters expressing outrage were plastered in idgahs everywhere. One, signed by several maulvis of the Anjuman Hidayat-i-Islam of Delhi, was found posted in many of the mosques of Karachi:

> Muslims save your flags from bending down and preserve the faith of the Malkana Rajputs. The fire of converting Malkana brethren is kindling daily. Aryas have trespassed into the Garden of Mohamed's followers and are plundering the same. Will you not save the Islamic Garden from religious robbers? God be praised that the Turks won victory by the sword and hoisted the flag of victory over the whole world. The Aryas have now started a religious battle against Musalmans, and it was the latter's duty to gain a glorious victory.[80]

Of the breach between Hindu and Muslim communities in Sind there was now no doubt. The gaping chasm that existed was echoed in the antagonistic language of the press. Newspapers that had once supported both the Khilafat and Non-cooperation movements and Hindu–Muslim unity were now increasingly partisan. In an article in *Sind Vasi* entitled 'How did Islam spread in India?', one Tirithdas Verhomal dwelt on what he believed to be the violent zeal inherent in Muslims: 'The suppressed religious zeal of the Mussalmans has now, after the Khilafat movement of the past few years, burst forth afresh, and everywhere led to bloodshed, folly, bad manners and filth. This is no new thing in the history of Islam. If one looks at the pages of history one will find that this wild brutalism is in Muslim blood.'[81] There

---

[78] SAPI, Bombay, 20 March 1923.

[79] SAPI, Sind, 31 March 1923.

[80] SAPI, Karachi, 4 August 1923.

[81] Prosecution of Mahomed Hashim, editor of the *Mussalman* newspaper of Mirpurkhas, Thar Parkar District. Prosecution of Vishindas Dayaram, editor of the *Sind Vasi* newspaper of Hyderabad (Sind), BPCP, August 1925, pp. 269–75, P/Conf/70, 1925, OIOC.

was no dearth of acrimony on the other side. An article in *al-Wahid* captures the spirit of the Muslim press in the mid-1920s. Taking the form of a prayer, it asks Allah to reproduce 'the glory of ancient times' where people had a passion for faith and there was 'no trace of idol worshippers'.

> May there only remain the garden of Muslim religion;
> May no temple bell be ever rung in the world;
> May the voice of Allaho Akbar only remain;
> May the name of Ram never be on any one's tongue;
> Nor the name of any idol, picture or image;
> Nor the name of Gokul, Gopi or Harnam;
> May the name of Islam only pervade the world;
> May the cry of Il Allah be heard throughout the East and West . . .[82]

Perhaps the most telling example of the divide was the fate of the three friends who together had organized the hartals of 1919, Sheikh Abdul Majid, Swami Govindanand and Choitram Gidwani. In 1921, Govindanand was sentenced to five years' transportation. On his release after serving three years in 1924, he emerged a Hindu nationalist. He began campaigning for the Hindu Mahasabha and Arya Samaj and also started a newspaper, *Kesari*, a local edition of Tilak's paper in Poona.[83] Gidwani also seems to have drifted away. At a Gandhi Day meeting, the Swami stated that Muslims were not striving for swaraj but for Khilafat raj. In response, Abdul Jabbar sprang up and verbally attacked Hindus, prompting an angry response from Choitram Gidwani. It was clear from this meeting that Hindu leaders, possibly Gidwani among them, had no regrets for the recent imprisonment of Sheikh Abdul Majid. The sheikh, too, had gone his own way, stating that no Hindu—not excluding Gandhi—could aspire to Heaven unless he recited the Kalma.[84] Ataturk's declaration of the Turkish Republic and the end of the khalifa in 1924 brought the Khilafat movement across India to a close. In Sind, the political alliances forged during this

---

[82] Warning given to the editor of *al-Wahid* for publishing an objectionable verse entitled 'We remember the story of Ibn Kassim' in his paper. BPCP, April 1926, P/Conf/71, 1926, OIOC.

[83] SAPI, Hyderabad, 19 January 1924.

[84] Ibid.

time reflected a belief that India's different religious communities were an integral and constitutive part of nationalism. It was in the post-Khilafat period that this idea of a federated nationalism would change.

The Post-Khilafat Period 1924–1932: Gandhi and Mohamed Ali

Mohamed Ali had been a central figure of the younger generation of Muslims at Aligarh who rejected the loyalist position of Sayyid Ahmed Khan and advocated instead a politics of protest and popular mobilization. He launched *Comrade* in January 1911 as a platform for his views and lectured students at Aligarh during the Italian invasion of Libya on the threat to Islam in Tripoli, Morocco, Persia, and Turkey.[85] From early on Mohamed Ali had maintained that there was nothing incompatible between what he called territorial and extra-territorial nationalism—between being a patriot of India and a Muslim. He had been impressed by the mobilization around the partition of Bengal, noting in an article in *Comrade* the importance of Congress as a vehicle for the 'genuine and vigorous aspirations which move educated India for a well-organized and common national life.'[86] However, he had been equally critical of Congress's 'avowedly Hindu . . . sympathies and aspirations . . . draw[ing] its energizing forces from Hindu religion and mythology'.[87] In an article entitled 'The Communal Patriot' (1912), he argued that, far from there existing a common nationalism in India, patriotisms were still exclusively Hindu or Muslim.[88]

Hindus, Mohamed Ali wrote, had taken to Western education with greater ease than Muslims. Through this they encountered ideas of democracy and began to dream of self-government. They looked to the past for inspiration but found it unable to chart a path for the future. For this they blamed the Muslims, who they claimed 'had viciously strayed into Bharat and demolished its political features and

[85] Hasan, *Mohamed Ali*, pp. 19–20.

[86] *Comrade*, 30 December 1911, quoted in ibid., p. 24.

[87] *Comrade*, 19 August 1911, p. 152, NMML.

[88] 'The Communal Patriot', *Comrade*, February 1912, reprinted in Afzal Iqbal (ed.), *Select Writings and Speeches of Maulana Mohamed Ali*, vol. I (Lahore, 1963), pp. 75–81.

land-marks.'[89] This, he argued, produced an attitude among educated Hindus 'of ignoring the one great reality of the Indian situation—the existence of 70 million Muslims.' They made Hinduism 'the rallying symbol for political unity' and the 'impulse towards liberalism' of the early generation of reformers was lost. Inevitably, nationality and patriotism became associated with Hinduism: 'The Hindu "communal patriot" sprang into existence with "swaraj" as his war cry. He refuses to give quarter to the Muslims unless the latter quietly shuffles off his individuality and becomes completely Hinduized.'[90] The Muslim communal patriot, on the other hand, originated in the burden of pride left over from generations of imperial rule. Muslims refused to avail themselves of the same material and intellectual opportunities that Hindus had benefited from and very soon were faced 'with a community vastly superior to it, in number, in wealth, in education, in political organisation and power, in a word a united community uttering new accents and pulsating with new hope.'[91] The Muslim, Mohamed Ali argued, was 'dazed' by the pace of change. He felt small, ignorant, and poor and was loath to give up the individuality his religion and history had afforded him. 'As a consequence he drew within his shell and nursed ideals of communal patriotism', propelled by the 'foolish yet powerful sentiment . . . about his vanished power.'[92]

There were what Mohamed Ali called 'communal fanatics' on both sides. In this atmosphere, all talk of a commonality of interests and shared patriotism was a fiction. The first step towards resolving the problem was not to 'use facile phrases about Indian unity' as Hindu patriots were prone to do, but to recognize the very real conditions that separated them. The central obstacle to Hindu–Muslim unity, he believed, lay in the 'philosophy of number'. Indian Muslims, 'suffer from the modern badge of inferiority which the philosophy of Number and the democratic wisdom of the age has placed on "minorities".'[93] He maintained that while the principles of merit and majority opinion were important, they were not always the most appropriate yardsticks.[94]

[89] Ibid., p. 76.
[90] Ibid., pp. 76–7.
[91] Ibid., p. 77.
[92] Ibid., p. 78.
[93] *Comrade*, 19 August 1911, NMML.
[94] *Comrade*, 18 February 1911, p. 102, NMML.

Indian Muslims were far more than a simple minority: their contribution to India's civilization was immeasurable, one that a liberal democratic framework could never reflect. He argued that the lines of cleavage in India were not territorial or racial but religious and that because of this a new form of nationalism had to be worked out. If nationalism was to be 'comprehensive', it had to be founded on the balanced coexistence of India's different religious communities: 'Divide India as you will, she is sure to part on the lines of religious cleavage . . . and if we do not close our eyes to the reality, we should regulate and not oppose denominationalism.'[95] India had to be a 'federation of faiths'; it had to legitimize the place of the community in the nation, a process that should apply as much to Sikhs, Jains, and untouchables as to Muslims.[96] Mohamed Ali saw the Hindu communal patriot as having hijacked the language of nationalism. What was purported to be Indian nationalism was exclusively Hindu in its cultural idiom and, by virtue of a democratic project that was numerically defined, one where Hindus were also politically dominant.

Mohamed Ali was drawn to Gandhi because he appeared to represent a different possibility for nationalism. For Gandhi, Hindu–Muslim unity was a prerequisite for swaraj. At the same time, he believed that 'in the proper solution of the Mahommedan question [lay] the realization of Swaraj.'[97] Gandhi wrote to Mohamed Ali in 1918 that the Khilafat issue had given Hindus and Muslims the opportunity of uniting 'as would not arise in a hundred years'. And this would be a fraternal bond for there was 'no other course open to them but to be brothers'.[98] The parity this implied seemed a way to redress the neglect of Muslims that Mohamed Ali had accused Congress nationalists of, and he came out strongly in support of Gandhi's movement: 'Non-Cooperation was to my mind the only panacea for the ills of India today.'[99] Mohamed Ali and Gandhi shared the opinion that politics had to be a moral exercise inspired by 'religion'. The former argued time and again that politics and religion could not be separate: 'Our politics must be as sacred a thing to us as Religion, and we must

---

[95] Ibid.
[96] *Comrade*, 22 April 1911, p. 289, and 11 February 1911, pp. 84–5, NMML.
[97] Gandhi to Mohamed Ali, 18 November 1918, *CWMG*, vol. XV, p. 64.
[98] Quoted in Hasan, *Mohamed Ali*, p. 29.
[99] *Comrade*, 16 October 1925, p. 186, NMML.

regard our political activities as acts of divine worship in which our souls must be purified and exalted.'[100] If religion existed only in mosques, churches, and temples it would begin 'to stagnate and to stink'.[101] Without religion, politics became simply about vying for position and petty conflicts between vested interests: 'If Indian politics is not to be a cesspool of self-concern and jobbery, it must be constantly rippled by the fresh breeze of religion. To us, as to Mahatma Gandhi, life is one indivisible synthesis'.[102] For Muslims, Mohamed Ali maintained, politics was about following God's law. As long as a Muslim was free to pursue his religious duties and prohibitions, it did not matter if he was the subject of a Muslim or a non-Muslim state.[103]

Mohamed Ali had been at the heart of Congress nationalism during the years of the Non-cooperation and Khilafat movements, culminating in his leadership of the Congress in 1923. He devoted the majority of his first speech as president to Hindu–Muslim relations. He condemned the narrowmindedness of the shuddhi and tanzim movements and maintained that rather than there being Khilafat committees and Hindu sabhas, there should be joint committees. The press should forgo the incendiary language that exacerbated tensions between the communities. And Muslims should realize that by being Muslims they did not stop being Indians.[104]

However, by 1925 the role of Mohamed Ali and his brother Shaukat in Congress had been eclipsed. Both had come under fire for their views on the relationship between religion and politics, or, more specifically, the relationship between Islam and Indian nationalism. A number of leading nationalists—Tej Bahadur Sapru of the Indian Liberal Party, Madan Mohan Malaviya of the Hindu Mahasabha, Lala Lajpat Rai and Bipin Chandra Pal of the Congress—believed that

[100] *Comrade*, 7 August 1925, p. 61, NMML.

[101] Ibid.

[102] Ibid.

[103] Mohamed Ali expressed this view on numerous occasions. See, for example, the leader to Gandhi's presidential address to the Indian National Congress session at Belgaum, June 1925, 'The Challenge to Our Love of Freedom', in Iqbal (ed.), *Select Writings*, vol. II, pp. 205–30.

[104] From the presidential address at the Indian National Congress session at Cocanada, December 1923, reprinted in ibid., pp. 107–89.

Muslims would always harbour primary loyalty to their faith and not their country. In an article entitled 'Extra-territorial Patriotism', sections of which Mohamed Ali republished in *Comrade*, Pal argued that the Ali brothers' ideal was not political but 'essentially theocratic':

> They never pretended to be nationalists in the sense in which that word is understood all the world over . . . They are Mohamedans first and Indians next. Their patriotism is not territorial but extra-territorial . . . The aim and intention of this movement of extra-territorial patriotism, otherwise called Pan-Islamism, is to protect what little remains to the Muslims of their once splendid empire against further encroachments. This is only possible by a combination of the Muslim peoples all the world over . . . The logic of this extra-territorial patriotism is distinctly anti-national.[105]

But Mohamed Ali maintained that there was no contradiction between loyalty to one's faith and one's nation: 'a Muslim Indian need not be a bad Muslim in order to be a good Indian, but . . . an Indian Muslim [can], and should, fight for the freedom of Kashi [i.e. Benares] as well as for the freedom of the Ka'ba.'[106] Muslims had been able to put their faith in Gandhi because, unlike others, he did not demand loyalty to a swaraj government before that of swadharma.[107]

At one level, Gandhi's position on the relationship between religion and the state was very close to that of Mohamed Ali. That Gandhi opposed the separation between religion and politics is now a truism, well documented from the outset of his career, beginning with his manifesto *Hind Swaraj*.[108] But the implications of this are not always self-evident. Gandhi advocated the village republic as the political form most appropriate to India and defended varna as a mode of social organization. At the same time, as Anthony Parel has suggested, he 'wholeheartedly

---

[105] *Comrade*, 4 September 1925, p. 112, NMML.

[106] Ibid.

[107] From a leader on Gandhi's presidential address to the INC at Belgaum, January 1925, in Iqbal (ed.), *Select Writings*, vol. II, p. 216.

[108] See M.K. Gandhi, *Hind Swaraj and Other Writings*, ed. Anthony J. Parel (Cambridge, 1997); Bhikhu Parekh, *Gandhi's Political Philosophy: A Critical Examination* (Basingstoke, 1989); David Hardiman, *Gandhi in His Time and Ours* (London, 2003).

embraced the modern idea of nation, albeit a non-violent nation',
claiming that the 'big thing' the British did for India was unify the
territory.[109] Throughout his political life Gandhi sought to moralize
politics. He argued that worldly activity had to be informed by a spiritual ethic, that politics without religion would be reduced to a crude
and self-serving affair. Bhikhu Parekh suggests that it was by arguing
for the potentially transcendent nature of political activity that Gandhi
sought to draw Indians into the nationalist movement.[110] Yet, towards
the end of his life, he gave his full support to secularism and a secular
state.

The positions Gandhi held were often dictated by circumstance, so
to look for consistency is an exercise in frustration. But many of the
contradictions are more apparent than real. Like many nationalists,
Gandhi recognized the need for the geographical entity of India to be
transformed into a political unit and he saw that the framework of the
colonial state had gone some way to doing this. But, like others before
him, he defended India against the accusation that its diversity in
creed, caste, and region meant that it could never be a nation, arguing
that Indians shared a civilization dating back 5000 years—they had in
this sense always been a nation. However, while he embraced the idea
of nationhood, he drew on older, indigenous ideas of political belonging.
Indians were not citizens as conceived of in European nations but all
part of a praja—a civic term referring to the subjects of a king.[111] The
idea that the wellspring of Indian nationhood originated in ancient
India pointed towards a period before Islam and Christianity and
raises the question of whether Gandhi believed there was something
essentially Hindu about India. But Gandhi refused to accept there was
any singular religious basis to India. Praja was a civic term, he argued,
and could apply equally to Hindus, Muslims, Buddhists, Christians,
Parsis, and Sikhs. Moreover, for Gandhi religion was an intensely personal affair, not one that a man-made institution such as the state had
any jurisdiction in.

[109] Anthony J. Parel, *Gandhi's Philosophy and the Quest for Harmony* (Cambridge, 2006), pp. 31–2.

[110] Parekh, *Gandhi's Political Philosophy*, chapter 4.

[111] Parel, *Gandhi's Philosophy*, p. 33.

Gandhi adhered to the idea of sarva dharma samabhava—that all religions are true. Thus, in no way could one religious doctrine provide the basis for national identity: 'In no part of the world are one nationality and one religion synonymous terms nor has it been so in India'.[112] Parel argues that Gandhi thought the value of religious pluralism was paramount for it provided the basis of tolerance and promoted dialogue between communities. And since all religions held the quintessence of divine understanding, individuals as well as institutions had a moral obligation to respect them.[113] Gandhi felt that pluralism and tolerance were especially important in India and exhorted nationalists to befriend a person of a religion other than their own.[114] Understood in this light, his political and personal relationship with Mohamed Ali went beyond a mere opportunistic alliance.

Many scholars have seen Gandhi's advocacy of religious tolerance, freedom of conscience, and non-interference by the state as evidence of his 'secularism'. But again, what this means is not self-evident. Gandhi upheld religious tolerance and felt that Hinduism was particularly well equipped for this. Hinduism was not a religion but represented a cultural system that had evolved over thousands of years, assimilating new influences throughout its history.[115] Islam and Christianity were more closed. This representation of the 'character' of Hinduism as fluid, open, and tolerant and that of Islam as doctrinal and rigid was a stereotype that had passed from European Orientalists of the late eighteenth century to upper-caste reformers in the nineteenth, and became a commonplace to nationalists such as Tilak and Gandhi by the early twentieth century. It was a representation that had been mapped onto the trajectory of Indian history: ancient India marked a Golden Age of tolerance and adherence to the dharma of the Aryas. As corruption entered Hinduism—the inequality between varnas, the proliferation of jatis and untouchability, idol worship, child marriage, and the degradation of women—so Hinduism became fractured and Hindus became weak, eventually falling before Islam and Christianity.

---

[112] Gandhi, *Hind Swaraj*, p. 53.
[113] Parel, *Gandhi's Philosophy*, p. 108.
[114] Ibid., p. 109.
[115] Ibid., p. 110.

This was a narrative that Gandhi held to. In his understanding, the civilization that emerged in ancient India provided a thread that tied modern-day Indians of all creeds to their ancestors and to each other. Moreover, Buddhism, Jainism, and Sikhism had all emerged from within Hindu traditions and thus their followers were part of the same broad cultural form. But, Gandhi argued, this was no less true of Muslims and Christians. These religions may have originated elsewhere, but those who converted to Islam were of the same cultural, ethnic, and racial stock as their Hindu brethren, and their basic culture, mores, and outlook were fundamentally the same.[116] Differences between them, specifically between Hindus and Muslims, Gandhi felt, were superficial and a result of the divisive effects of colonial rule. Conflicts around cow protection and music before mosques—which re-emerged as arenas of antagonism between Hindus and Muslims in many regions in the 1920s—were cosmetic problems easily remedied with good will on both sides.[117]

Gandhi's narrative of history resonated closely with Tilak's. To be sure, Gandhi fostered a more plural vision of India. Whereas Tilak had argued that the unique accommodative quality of Indian civilization meant that converts to other religions were still essentially Hindu, Gandhi maintained the more nuanced position that it was precisely this quality that enabled someone to be a Muslim and an Indian without any contradiction: 'Islamic culture is not the same in Arabia, Turkey, Egypt and India but is itself influenced by the conditions of the respective countries. Indian culture is therefore Indian. It is neither Hindu, Islamic nor any other, wholly. It is a fusion of all.'[118] Nevertheless, as Parekh argues, for Gandhi the nature of the cultural synthesis was a uniquely Hindu achievement.[119] In Gandhi's approach there was both the recognition of difference and its elision. On the one hand his emphasis on dialogue between communities appeared to circumvent the problems inherent in democratic formulations and provided the basis for his relationship with Mohamed Ali. On the other his understanding of a single divine truth and an all-encompassing cultural

---

[116] Parekh, *Gandhi's Political Philosophy*, pp. 178–91.

[117] Ibid., p. 185.

[118] 'The Loin Cloth', *Young India*, 30 April 1931, *CWMG*, vol. 52, pp. 8–9, quoted in Hardiman, *Gandhi*, p. 173.

[119] Parekh, *Gandhi's Political Philosophy*, p. 189.

tradition reduced difference to the level of small detail. It meant that he was unable to address the challenge to Congress nationalism that Muslim parties were beginning to formulate, or that posed by the increasing violence between Hindus and Muslims. He was able to call only for love and good will on both sides.

Moreover, Gandhi sought to represent Hindu India in what he saw as an inter-religious dialogue during the Non-Cooperation and Khilafat movements. But this position was challenged from all sides after Non-Cooperation ended, not least by prominent members of Congress and the Hindu Mahasabha angered by what they saw as his bringing religion into politics or his readiness to cede too much to Muslims. At the same time, Gandhi's attempts to speak for Hindu India and represent himself as a sanatani (orthodox) Hindu tied him to positions of the Mahasabha in ways that alienated a broad spectrum of Muslims. It was this dynamic—Gandhi's centrality to the politics of the 1920s and 1930s, his need to recognize but also diminish difference, and the challenge to his leadership in the aftermath of Khilafat and Non-cooperation—that had a profound bearing on how nationalism and communalism would come to be defined.

Nationalism and Communalism

As the Khilafat/Congress alliance unravelled in 1923, violent conflict between Hindus and Muslims erupted around the country, notably in Calcutta, Dhaka, Patna, Delhi, and throughout the United Provinces. In 1925, when Mohamed Ali and Gandhi continued to defend a spiritually informed politics, many saw the opposite to be true: that the preceding four years had awakened primordial tendencies that were now impossible to contain. Mahasabha leaders Lala Lajpat Rai and M.R. Jayakar were particularly critical. Writing to Lajpat Rai from his base in Maharashtra, Jayakar expressed his exasperation at the Bombay government's continued policy of special representation for Muslims on councils, arguing that this was part of the destructive legacy of Gandhi's leadership:

> [I]t is the deliberate policy of the Bombay Government to encourage this fissiparous tendency as much as they can, and my fear is that we are in for it now and for many, many years this is going to be our legacy. To speak quite frankly to you I regard it as the necessary reaction of Mr Gandhi's

policy during the last four years, which aimed at a most artificial and unreal unity between Hindu and Mahomedans, awakening sentiments and impulses in the latter community which, like the Frankenstein, it is now very difficult to allay. It makes me very sad to think that so great a patriot should have on this question bungled so badly. In . . . Maharashtra we feel that the whole of his effort in this direction has been a great failure . . . I feel like a drowning man. The tide of Mahomedan and Non-Brahmin feeling is surging all around.[120]

For Jayakar, separate representation was of a kind with the 'fissiparous tendencies' he saw as having been unleashed by Gandhi. And significantly, this was a position shared across a broad political spectrum from those in the Mahasabha to liberals in Congress and socialists.

Many on the Congress platform—Madan Mohan Malaviya, Lala Lajpat Rai, Muhammad Ali Jinnah, and Motilal Nehru, for instance—had been nervous about Gandhi's attempts at mass mobilization, fearing it would unleash a force that would be difficult to control. Their fears were compounded by his efforts to forge a Hindu–Muslim front, making religious identity the bedrock of nationalism. The violence after 1923 seemed to confirm their worst fears. In 1909 the politics of group representation in legislative councils had come to be seen as the politics of narrow 'communal' interests. In the aftermath of Non-cooperation and Khilafat, mobilization around religious identity was understood as a failed and misdirected nationalism. In the second half of the 1920s these two phenomena coincided: they came to be termed communalism and were posed in opposition to the goals of nationalism. It was the broad agreement on what constituted communalism and nationalism, and the importance of numbers to national unity, that was to prove crucial to the hardening of these definitions.

In 1922 the Mahasabha was revived after a period of relative dormancy. Its first session in December was called in response to the Moplah riots and those in Multan during Muharram, where it had been widely reported that Hindus were the disproportionate victims of violence. Malaviya presided over this session and set the agenda for the coming years. He emphasized sangathan, Hindu unity. Hindus

<hr>

[120] Jayakar to Lajpat Rai, Bombay, 8 September 1925, Jayakar Papers, reel 57, file 405, item 176, NAI.

were weak and degenerate, he said, as never before. There was a low birth rate, high death rate, and cowardice in the face of attack. There was a tremendous imperative to organize. Malaviya called for a sabha presence right down to the village level in order to protect Hindus from Muslim communal attacks.[121] Malaviya's organ, *Leader,* ran a number of editorials echoing the call to organize Hindus against Muslim aggression: 'The Mahomedans have . . . become more communal than ever before. Nothing is now left for the Hindus but to organise themselves, certainly not with a view to encroach upon the legitimate rights of Mussalmans, but to protect their rights from being encroached upon by others . . . Their first duty, in their own interest, in the interest of the country, and also in that of Hindu–Muslim unity, is that they should organise, organise, organise.'[122] The shuddhi and sangathan programme was clearly one of a militant Hinduism. It was a Hindu politics, just as tabligh and tanzim launched two years later were a politics of Muslim consolidation. In this sense they could be seen as opposite equals. However, it was the way that Mahasabha leaders like Malaviya sought to appropriate the legitimating language of nationalism that ensured this was not so. The Mahasabha aligned Hindu unity with national unity, and all else as a politics of communalism. While a spectrum of nationalists did not support its position of aggressive self-strengthening, when it came to the relationship between communalism and nationalism, and the importance of numbers to 'national' unity, they shared the same discursive ground. Speaking at the Mahasabha's 1924 session, Malaviya argued that the Lucknow Pact—the 1916 agreement between the Muslim League and Congress about Muslim representation in provincial councils—had intensified rather than diminished 'communal feelings'.[123] Nationalism and communalism,

---

[121] G.R. Thursby, *Hindu–Muslim Relations in British India: A Study of Controversy, Conflict and Communal Movements in Northern India, 1923–1928* (Leiden, 1975), pp. 161–2.

[122] *Leader,* 2 April 1923, quoted in ibid., p. 163.

[123] Members of the Muslim League and the Congress met at the Home Rule headquarters in Lucknow in 1916. Agreements were drawn up that in provinces such as Bihar, Bombay, Madras, and the Central Provinces, Muslims would be represented by seats in excess of their proportion in the population. In return, their seats in the Punjab would be reduced from 55 per cent to 50 per cent.

he said, 'are an impossible mixture. They cannot exist together . . . One must disappear before the other [can] come in . . . If communalism dominates the affairs of the country to the extent to which it is dominating the affairs of the land at present, . . . it would not be profitable for the country to have a full system of national government established in India.'[124] Communal—a term that had referred to the creation of electorates in councils, had become communalism—a means to understand violent sectarian conflict at the grassroots. Significantly, it was not used to describe conflict between different Muslim sects or between Hindu sects or castes. It was a term specific to conflict between Hindus and Muslims in the context of a debate around nationalism.

Taraknath Das, a Bengali socialist residing in the United States, argued similarly. In a letter to Jayakar in 1927, Das maintained that while he wanted as much as anybody else to 'enforce our National Demand of absolute swaraj', he preferred that 'the Indian Nationalists refuse to accept any concession which is mixed with communalism', which was 'a great curse' and should be opposed.[125] Hindu Mahasabha leaders should join forces with the leaders of the Non-Brahman movement: 'Hindu Maha Sabha should conquer the Non-Brahmin movement by accepting their just demands of abolition of social inequities, as soon as possible.' Das did not see this as Hindu communalism. On the contrary, forging Hindu unity would strengthen what he called the 'National Demand': 'If the Non-Brahmin Party leaders join your nationalists and stand by the Hindu Mahasabha then much is accomplished towards national unity.'[126] In contrast, communalism was an approach exemplified by Mohamed Ali: 'For God's sake see to it that the next President of All India National Congress does not do the same kind of disservice to India as . . . Mohamed Ali did when he said "I am a Moslem first and Indian afterwards." In Madras the President . . . should proclaim "I am an Indian first and I am opposed to all forms of communalism."'[127]

[124] Jayakar Papers, reel 64, file 448 II, item 24, NAI.

[125] Tarak Nath Das to Jayakar, Germany, 20 May 1927, Jayakar Papers, reel 57, file 406, item 123, NAI.

[126] Ibid.

[127] Ibid.

Mohamed Ali had been roundly criticized for maintaining that religious communities should be at the centre of Indian nationalism. It was on account of this that he became disillusioned, writing in *Comrade* in 1925 of Congress's 'barren record' in the area of Hindu–Muslim relations.[128] But it was not simply the naming of minority group demands as communal and anti-national that was of concern to him. Peasant and Non-Brahman groups, Left parties, regional groups and business elites all often held contrasting positions on what counted as a legitimate politics of nationalism. Rather, it was what seemed to be a widening consensus on what constituted communalism—and particularly the role of Gandhi in this—that was his greatest concern.

When Gandhi heard the news of the murder of the twenty-two policemen in Chauri Chaura he suspended Non-cooperation and civil disobedience and went on a five-day fast of expiation, calling the incident a warning from God against hasty action. Discipline was a central tenet of satyagraha. If this broke down, as it had in this instance, Gandhi took it to be his responsibility and something that necessitated personal cleansing. Nanda has argued that the decision to call off the Bardoli satyagraha was 'primarily a moral issue' since Gandhi 'would not countenance violence at any cost'.[129] However, others maintain that there was more to it.[130] Many who had once been ardent Non-cooperators, such as Hasrat Mohani, had begun to drift away from Gandhi's movement, entertaining the possibility of employing violence to combat British imperialism. Moreover, when Gandhi had met Malaviya in Bombay, the latter had urged Gandhi to call off Bardoli immediately. This had less to do with Chauri Chaura than with Malaviya's belief that with the settlement of the Turkish question, the loss of Muslim support for the movement was imminent. Gandhi, on questioning Chotani on this point, 'got no definite assurance from him to the contrary'.[131] A police report seemed to echo this sentiment:

[128] Minault, *The Khilafat Movement*, pp. 198–200.

[129] Nanda, *Gandhi*, p. 347.

[130] See Hasan, *Nationalism and Communal Politics*, pp. 168–70; and Minault, *Khilafat Movement*, pp. 184–6.

[131] From a Fortnightly Report, 16 February 1922 for Bombay, quoted in T.L. Sharma, *Hindu–Muslim Relations in All-India Politics, 1913–1925* (Delhi, 1987), p. 144.

'The real reasons why the Mahatma suspended civil disobedience [were because] he had come to know that Government was formulating peace terms with Turkey which could be acceptable to Muhammadans, who may then withdraw from the agitation. He knew that if Muhammadans withdrew, the whole business of keeping up mass civil disobedience would fall to the Hindus and that in the absence of the Muhammadans, Government would crush the movement.'[132]

There was considerable anger at Gandhi's abrupt abandonment of civil disobedience. But a more important concern was Gandhi's evolving relationship with members of the Hindu Mahasabha. Gandhi had been critical of the aggressive programme of the Mahasabha, especially as articulated by Swami Shraddhanand. But Hardiman argues that the Mahatma's unwillingness to criticize other Hindu nationalists such as Malaviya and Lajpat Rai made many wary.[133] Thus, while Gandhi insisted that the decision to suspend the satyagraha was his own—'I assure the public that Pandit Malaviyaji had absolutely no hand in shaping my decision. I have often yielded to Panditji . . . But so far as the decision of suspension is concerned, I arrived at it on my reading the detailed report of the Chauri Chaura tragedy in the [Bombay] Chronicle'—Mohamed Ali and Abdul Bari were not so sure.[134]

In a letter to Chotani in June 1922, Abdul Bari wrote that it was time for Muslims to look to each other and not to Hindus for support: 'Hindus will succeed in attaining Swaraj and that Swaraj will not be in any way beneficial to us. Malaviya by his cleverness is usurping the position [of Gandhi] but Muslims have no faith in him nor can they have as they had in Gandhi. Let us see whether we have still to cling to this movement [non-violent non cooperation] or some other way is found out of the difficulty. In my opinion it would be far more beneficial if the Muslims improve their own status, Indian Muslims in India, Arabs in Arabia, Afghans in Afghanistan and Turks in Turkey. They should then unite.'[135] The Jamiat-ul-Ulema shared Abdul Bari's concerns, alleging that the Central Khilafat Committee had merely

[132] SAPI, Bombay, 3 April 1922.

[133] Hardiman, *Gandhi*, p. 172.

[134] Gandhi, *CWMG*, vol. XXII, p. 449.

[135] Quoted in Bamford, *Histories of the Non-Cooperation and Khilafat Movements,* pp. 204–5, parentheses in original.

become 'a tail' of Congress, that they had been misled by the Non-cooperation movement and that Gandhi had forgotten the interests of the Muslims.[136] They maintained that the reasons this had happened were that 'Gandhi had been promised some special concessions and favours through Pandit Madan Mohan Malaviya and that he had left Muslims in the lurch at a real critical moment when he was satisfied that the Hindus would be benefited by the suspension of mass civil disobedience.'[137]

Gandhi was genuinely troubled by the loss of Hindu–Muslim unity. In a letter to Mohamed Ali from a hospital in Poona, he wrote of the differences that had arisen between Hindus and Muslims:

> My dear friend and brother . . . Though I know very little of the present situation in the country, I know sufficient to enable me to see that, perplexing as the national problems were at the time of the Bardoli resolutions, they are far more perplexing today. It is clear that, without unity between Hindus, Mahomedans, Sikhs, Parsis and Christians and other Indians, all talk of swaraj is idle. This unity which I fondly believed, in 1922, had been nearly achieved has, so far as Hindus and Mussalmans are concerned . . . suffered a severe check. Mutual trust has given place to distrust. An indissoluble bond between the various communities must be established if we are to win freedom. Will the thanksgiving of the nation over my release be turned into a solid unity between the communities? That will restore me to health far quicker than any medical treatment or rest-cure.[138]

Gandhi's continued close relationship with Malaviya was based on his ideal that no one, however contrary their views, should be forsaken. His failure to criticize the Mahasabha's position on the relationship between Hindu unity and Indian nationalism lay at the root of the perception among Muslim leaders that Gandhi had made a decision about where his priorities lay.

A series of communications that took place several years later between Jayakar and the secretary of the Mahasabha, Ganpat Rai, on

---

[136] SAPI, Bombay, 3 April 1922.
[137] Ibid.
[138] 7 February 1924, *CWMG*, vol. XXIII, p. 200.

the subject of the Communal Award—a provision that accorded separate electorates to a range of minority communities, including untouchables—seemed to indicate that this perception was not restricted to Muslims.[139] Rai urged Jayakar to dissuade Gandhi from accepting the terms of the award, arguing that it would 'sharply divide the Hindus amongst themselves'.[140] Jayakar responded that although he shared Rai's feelings, 'I have no power in the matter, as I have no influence with the Mahatma.' If he wanted help in this matter, Jayakar advised that Rai 'must turn to men like Pandit Malaviya and Dr Moonje who have influence with the Mahatma and have openly opposed the Communal Award from the very start'.[141] Thus, as late as 1934, at a time when the position of the Mahasabha was more militantly anti-Muslim than ten years earlier, there was a clear perception within the Mahasabha ranks that its leaders could sway Gandhi's opinion. This confidence stemmed from the fact that Gandhi tacitly accepted that the Mahasabha represented the body of Hindu opinion, and without them he could not act.

As early as 1924 the optimism that Mohamed Ali had had for Hindu–Muslim unity was fading rapidly. It is worth quoting at length from a letter to Nehru in which he describes his meetings with Gandhi following the latter's release from prison in the same year:

> I do not know whether my conversations with Bapu at Juhu had any effect at all in the matter of the Hindu–Muslim tension. Perhaps he would have heard next to nothing about the Muslim side of it if I had not told him what I had heard because I do not think many Mussalmans had corresponded with him. Since I could not speak with personal knowledge, all that my conversations could do was to suggest to him that there is a Muslim side too. In one respect however, I am positive that I failed to impress him at all and that is the character of his 'worshipful brother' Pandit Madan Mohan Malaviya. He comes out of it the best of us all! And yet both Shaukat and I were under the impression that Bapu thought very differently of the noble Pandit. If Bapu believes all that he says about

[139] See chapter 5 for details of the Communal Award.

[140] Ganpat Rai to Jayakar, Hindu Mahasabha Head Office, 24 April 1934, Jayakar Papers, reel 63, file 439, item 51, NAI.

[141] Jayakar to Ganpat Rai, Bombay, 26 April 1934, Jayakar Papers, reel 63, file 439, item 52, NAI.

him—and there can be little doubt of it—then I must despair of the near
future at any rate. I had discussed the matter frankly with your father and
he told me that he largely agreed with me that Malaviya was out to defeat
Gandhism and to become the leader of the Hindus only since he could
not be the leader of Muslims as well as Hindus, and that Hindu–Muslim
unity was not his ideal. My dear Jawahar, God knows that the Mussalmans
too have their Malaviyas and there is no love lost between them and me.
But thank God they have not the influence over their community . . . that
Panditji has over so many people of his community.[142]

Mohamed Ali's unease, then, had to do with the power he feared the
relationship between Gandhi and Malaviya gave the Hindu Mahasabha
to define Hindu unity as nationalism and Muslim politics as communalism. The decisions of the All-Parties Conference in 1928 and the
debate around the separation of Sind that followed this went no small
distance in consolidating these definitions.

Constitution-making 1928–1931

The constitutional changes of 1909 were reviewed in 1918. The
Montagu–Chelmsford reforms that resulted introduced the principle
of diarchy; now, control over departments such as education, health,
and agriculture was devolved to the provinces, while that over law and
order and finance was retained at the centre. These reforms again came
under review in 1927, under the auspices of Lord John Simon.[143] The
Statutory (Simon) Commission had no Indian representative. Leaders
of all parties and communities in India were outraged at this decision
and took a unified stand against the exclusion of Indians from a body
that could determine the future constitution of a self-governing India.
Congress declared that the British government had acted contrary to
the national will and urged all parties to boycott the commission.[144]
The Simon Commission arrived in India on a preliminary visit in early
1928 and was met with hartals and demonstrations at every step.[145] It

[142] Letter, 15 June 1924, Jawaharlal Nehru, *A Bunch of Old Letters* (New York,
1960 [1958]), p. 38.
[143] See S.R. Bakshi, *Simon Commission and Indian Nationalism* (Delhi, 1977).
[144] Ibid., pp. 41–3.
[145] Ibid., pp. 65–6.

returned in October, by which time Indians had embarked upon an independent effort to draft a constitution.

The All Parties Conference met in Delhi in February 1928 and then again in Bombay in May, when they appointed the Nehru Committee, named for its chairman Motilal Nehru. The central obstacle to the drafting of a constitution was the inability to resolve what was now called the 'communal question', in other words the place of minority communities, specifically Muslims, in an independent India. Prospects for unity had seemed positive at the end of 1927, when the different strands of political opinion had come together to oppose the Simon Commission. Jinnah had left Congress over differences with Gandhi's Non-Cooperation campaign. In 1927, now a representative of Muslim concerns, Jinnah persuaded other Muslim leaders to accept a compromise. In what came to be known as the Delhi Muslim Proposals, they agreed to give up separate electorates—a keystone of Muslim constitutional politics since 1909—if three things could be guaranteed: one-third Muslim representation in the central assembly, representation in proportion to population in the Muslim-majority provinces of Punjab and Bengal, and the creation of three new Muslim-majority provinces in Sind, Baluchistan, and the North West Frontier.[146]

The All India Congress Committee in May 1927 and the Madras Congress session in December accepted Jinnah's proposal, but Hindu Mahasabha members opposed it. In a letter to Lala Lajpat Rai, Jayakar wrote angrily about the proposals for the separation of Sind from the Bombay Presidency: 'The All India Congress Committee session was in reality a great fiasco . . . [with regard to settling the Hindu–Muslim question] I put forward the view which we had discussed between us at Delhi viz. (1) that Sind should not be made a scapegoat and cut out of Bombay only as a part of an all-India scheme of linguistic redistribution . . . Dr Moonje . . . agreed to the solution as regards Sind.'[147] The Mahasabha resisted the proposals to create new Muslim-majority provinces and legislative majorities in the Punjab and Bengal. The report of the Nehru Committee was finalized in Lucknow in August

[146] Sumit Sarkar, *Modern India, 1885–1947* (Delhi, 1983), p. 262.

[147] B.S. Moonje was a doctor and prominent Mahasabha leader in the Central Provinces. M.R. Jayakar to L.L. Rai, 12 June 1927, Jayakar Papers, reel 57, file 406, item 122, NAI.

1928 and reflected many concessions to Mahasabha demands. There would be joint electorates, with reservations for Muslims at the centre and in provinces where they were in a minority. It opposed proportional representation in provinces with Muslim majorities. The report argued that the overwhelming opinion in Sind was in favour of separation, but that it rejected demands for 'communal provinces'. The reorganization of states would only take place on linguistic grounds and, in the case of Sind, when it was determined to be an economically viable proposition. Any suggestions for the creation of further Muslim-majority provinces would not be entertained.[148] Thus, while Jinnah had agreed to a certain decentralization of political power, the Nehru Report had the beginnings of a blueprint for a political structure that emphasized a strong centre.

Jinnah's response to the Nehru Report has been well documented. He accused Congress of having reneged on its promises. In December 1928, at the session of the All Parties Conference in Calcutta, he proposed another solution: the immediate separation of Sind, residual powers to provinces, one-third of central assembly seats reserved for Muslims, and reserved seats in Punjab and Bengal until adult suffrage was established. When this was rejected Jinnah rejoined Mohammad Shafi of the Punjab Muslim League, who had earlier split with Jinnah over separate electorates, and announced his famous Fourteen Points. These repeated the old demands, including complete provincial autonomy, but also reintroduced the demand for separate electorates for Muslims until the Hindus were willing to reconsider the Muslim position.[149]

Jayakar and Moonje were among the most vocal in their stand against any consideration of Jinnah's proposals. On publication of the report, Moonje expressed his alarm at Gandhi's earlier declaration to 'let us agree to give all what Musalmans demand and be satisfied with the crumbs that shall remain behind.'[150] He could not agree to

[148] All Parties Conference, *The Nehru Report: An Anti-Separatist Manifesto* (Delhi, 1975 [1928]), pp. 31–3, 61–9.

[149] For Jinnah's fourteen points, announced 28 March 1929, see Anil Chandra Bannerjee (ed.), *Indian Constitutional Documents*, vol. III (Calcutta, 1961), pp. 245–8.

[150] B.S. Moonje to Gandhi, 5 August 1929, Jayakar Papers, file 437, NAI.

one-third of legislative assembly seats being reserved for Muslims, he
wrote, because nationalism, not reservations, was the answer:

> If you want to find a radical solution of the Hindu–Moslem relation, so
> far as the public administration of the country is concerned, I think there
> could be no safer position than that taken up by the Hindu Mahasabha
> which is one of pure unalloyed nationalism. Hindu Mahasabha does not
> recognize differences of creed and caste in the Government of this country.
> To [us] all Hindus, Moslems, Christians and Parsis etc. are all citizens of
> Hindusthan with perfectly equal rights. Religions and social differences
> ought not to be allowed to prevail in the public administration of the
> country . . . I would therefore suggest that you should make a firm stand
> on the present Nehru Report . . . I am sure that Musalmans will eventually
> see the justness and fairness of it . . . But . . . they must know first that no
> compromise is possible for the purpose of tempering nationalism with
> communalism . . . [I]f the Musalmans cannot trust and remain in the
> Congress and give up their separatist mentality, let us leave them alone . . .
> But the Congress must not stray away from the path of pure nationalism
> to placate this or that community.[151]

Jayakar also remained adamant. He wrote to Gandhi to acquaint him
with what he called 'the apprehensions of a very large body of Hindus
(outside the Hindu Mahasabha) that any attempt at this time to vary
the solution of the Hindu–Moslem question adopted in the Nehru
Committee Report is fraught with far-reaching consequences.'[152]
Hindus, he wrote, had accepted the Nehru Report, despite its 'conti-
nuance of communal representation' as a compromise. But this is
where it had to stop. Jinnah's five points had become fourteen and
there was no telling where they would end.

The faultlines in the debate around how far reservations for religious minorities and the creation of Muslim-majority provinces constituted a politics of communalism crystallized around the proposal to
separate Sind from Bombay Presidency. The question was first presented
before the reforms committee of 1917 as a memorandum to the secretary of state, arising out of a conference convened by the Sind branch

[151] Ibid.
[152] M.R. Jayakar to Gandhi, 23 August 1929, Jayakar Papers, reel 57, file 407,
part I, item 83, NAI.

of the Congress that year.[153] The memorandum argued that since its incorporation into British India in 1843, the administration of Sind had been almost entirely in the hands of the commissioner. This had led to an irresponsible and autocratic government: it had militated against any 'progressive liberalization' of the administration, denying Sind the benefits of government by the governor in Bombay. Whereas in other divisions of the presidency municipalities had the right to elect their councils, this was not the case in Sind. The implications of this were far-reaching—such obstacles to the proper practice of local self-government would also inhibit the growth of a 'public spirit and sense of local patriotism'. The memorialists urged that until such time as Sind could be instituted as an independent province with an executive and a high court, it should be brought under the direct administration of the government of Bombay.[154] There were four separate proposals in the reforms committee as to Sind's possible future: that it should be detached from Bombay Presidency and merged with Baluchistan; or alternatively with Punjab; that it should remain within the presidency but under the control of the governor; or that it should become an autonomous province. The sub-committee on Sind recommended autonomy on the grounds that Sindhis made up a 'distinct provincial nationality'. Those who opposed separation objected that most Sindhis were illiterate and would not be able to take advantage of local self-government. But, the committee argued, that could be soon overcome. The main objection was that if separated from the presidency, Sind would be a deficit province.[155]

The initial proposal for the creation of a separate province was raised by Sindhis themselves. It appeared to have a cross-section of support

[153] The conference was led by Harchandrai Vishindas, a Sindhi businessman and one of the Sind representatives on the imperial council of India. The memorandum was addressed to the viceroy and the secretary of state, lords Chelmsford and Montagu respectively, from the Special Sind Provincial Conference held at Hyderabad, Sind, 3–4 November 1917. Hamida Khuhro (ed.), *Documents on Separation of Sind from the Bombay Presidency, Volume I* (Islamabad, 1982), p. 2.

[154] Ibid., pp. 4–10.

[155] The four committee members were all businessmen from Sind: Durgadas B. Advani, Nihalchand U. Vaswani, R.K. Sidhwa, and Naraindas Anandji. Report of the Sind Reforms Committee on the Montagu–Chelmsford Reforms Proposals and Position of Sind, in ibid., pp. 11–22.

from leading members of the business community as well as Muslims such as Rais Ghulam Mohammad Bhurgri, editor of *al-Wahid* and *al-Amin*. There was no indication of any difference that could be attributed to either 'Hindu' or 'Muslim' opinion. When the question was raised again in 1928, however, this was no longer the case. By then Muslim politicians in Sind overwhelmingly supported the separation of the province. The Sind Muhammadan Association put its position to the Simon Commission in 1928 and then before the Round Table conferences in London in 1931–2, arguing that 'linguistically, ethnologically, culturally and even climatically Sind has nothing in common with the Presidency proper.'[156] The All Parties Conference in 1928 accepted that Sind would be separated, but only once India gained dominion status and only as part of a broader reorganization of provinces along linguistic lines; that is to say, the separation of Sind could not be part of the resolution of the communal question. Sindhi Hindus, in contrast, were resolutely opposed, arguing that Sind was a deficit province and relied heavily on Bombay to make up the fiscal shortfall. Many expressed the anxiety that autonomy would threaten their prosperity. In a letter to the viceroy before the Round Table conferences, the Sind Hindu Conference Committee argued that although they were a minority of 26 per cent, Hindus contributed a disproportionate share to the province's banking, trade, and education. They paid 40 per cent of land revenue, as well as the bulk of excise revenue and income tax. Any change that was likely to disrupt their economic and political security was of great concern.[157]

The Government of India conducted detailed studies to determine whether Sind could afford to go it alone.[158] But it was clear that the decision to separate would not rest on Sind's financial viability—that is, on internal considerations—alone. By 1930 Sind had been irreversibly drawn into a wider discussion of the communal problem, of which

[156] M.A. Khuhro, 'Sind's Separation from Bombay', in ibid., vol II, p. 820.

[157] Letter to the Viceroy, Earl of Willingdon, 27 July 1931, from Sind Hindu Conference Committee, Sukkur, para 4. Miscellaneous papers on the separation of Sind, November 1930–March 1934, L/P&J/9/49, pp. 412–18, OIOC.

[158] See, for example, the report of the Sind Financial Enquiry Committee (Simla, 1931), and the Brayne report from the Sind Conference (Simla, 1932), in ibid., pp. 292–338 and 204–40, respectively.

the reorganization of states was a part. Muhammad Iqbal, the Punjabi poet, emphasized in his presidential address to the Muslim League in 1930 the need for Indian Muslims to benefit from 'full and free development on the lines of his own culture and tradition in his own Indian homelands'. This would be 'the basis of a permanent communal settlement', and if this principle was recognized the Muslim 'will be ready to stake his all for the freedom of India.' For Iqbal this meant creating a region for Muslims within India, a corridor of Muslim states: 'I would like to see the Punjab, North-West Frontier Province, Sind and Baluchistan amalgamated into a single State. Self-government within the British empire or without the British empire, the formation of a consolidated North-West Indian Muslim state appears to me to be the final destiny of the Muslims, at least of North-West India.'[159]

Similarly, resistance to the idea of provincial autonomy came not simply from concerns about being in the red, but reflected a fear of minority status. Hindus expressed their anxiety at being left behind, culturally under siege, and used as pawns to advance a separate agenda. A pamphlet authored by the president of the Karachi Hindu Sabha argued that the linguistic issue had no bearing on the debate on the redistribution of provinces.[160] Rather, Congress Hindus had 'sacrificed Sind' in order to secure joint electorates: 'they lent Sind Hindus as a pawn in the hands of Muslims to hold us responsible for any ill-treatment whether fancied or otherwise, meted out to their brethren-in-faith anywhere in India.' The author continued that Congress had sought 'to suppress communalism' by upholding the principle of joint electorates on the one hand, but on the other had 'kept the fire of communal quarrels kindled up by creating communal provinces.'[161] He warned that the Hindus of Sind, who paid the bulk of the province's taxes, controlled more than half of the agricultural land and almost all trade, would face economic and cultural ruin if Sind were separated.

[159] Presidential address of Muhammad Iqbal, All-India Muslim League conference, December 1930, in Syed Sharifuddin Pirzada (ed.), *Foundations of Pakistan, All-India Muslim League Documents*, vol. II (1924–1947), (Karachi, 1970), p. 159.

[160] Dr G.T. Hingorani, 'Conditions under which Hindus live in Sind' (Karach Hindu Sabha, n.d.), in Jayakar Papers, reel 61, file 425, NAI.

[161] Ibid., p. 5.

Muslims would renege on their rents and loans, and, unqualified as they were, would usurp the position of Hindus in the administration. In addition, while the rest of the country was developing Hindi as a lingua franca, the Muslim influence in Sind would mean that 'we might see our children speaking and writing "Persian"'. The schools were, after all, 'being Mahomadanized fast enough . . . High schools . . . are on the brink of bankruptcy . . . whereas the Muslim Madrassahs and Mullah schools have been receiving special attention from the Government and Local Boards'.[162]

These anxieties were fuelled by the idea that the separation of Sind was communalism in action. Swami Govindanand's *Kesari* argued that 'the creation of new provinces in India will mean the uprooting of nationalism.'[163] The separation of Sind would 'mean that the Hindus shall fall a victim to the horrors of an Islamic Government and a Mahomedan policy.'[164] Even the liberal press seemed to agree. The *Times of India* deemed Iqbal's ideal of contiguous Muslim-majority provinces a coercive tactic devised 'to defy and bully the Central Government when necessary, leading ultimately to the setting up of a Muslim Kingdom in the west of India . . . It is, at any rate, a struggle to hold the "balance of Power" in Muslim hands and to obtain for that community a disproportionate amount of power and prestige at the centre and in the provinces not commensurate either with its numbers, wealth, education, public spirit and national service.'[165] Muslims within and outside Sind, in contrast, countered that separation was not about tyrannizing Hindus: 'if we cannot trust the Moslems here, the Hindus have no right to expect trust from Moslems in other provinces.'[166] Rather, it was a way for Muslims to be Muslims and Indian patriots simultaneously without having to subsume one position into

[162] Ibid., pp. 15–17. The Hindu Sabha of Sukkur sent letters to the secretary of state for India, Sir Samuel Hoare, also echoing these sentiments.

[163] *Kesari* (Sind), 27 March 1927, quoted in *Daily Gazette*, 9 October 1930, Jayakar Papers, reel 16, NAI.

[164] Ibid.

[165] *Times of India*, 21 August 1932, Jayakar Papers, reel 16, NAI.

[166] *Times of India*, 9 November 1932, quoted from the Unity Conference in Sind, Jayakar Papers, reel 16, NAI.

the other. M.A. Khuhro argued that separation of the province was central to the resolution of the communal problem.[167] Sir Muhammad Shafi maintained that the Nehru Report had relegated Muslims to the position of a permanent minority, despite the fact that if Sind were separated they would be a majority in five out of eleven provinces (Punjab, Bengal, Kashmir, Sind, and the North West Frontier). It was, then, this 'centripetal' form of government that was the problem: 'In India the centripetal form of federal constitution would be in the highest degree detrimental to the legitimate interests and rights of minorities and is calculated to bring into existence an oligarchy rather than a really representative Government.'[168]

Conclusion

The political alliance between individuals such as Gandhi and the Ali brothers at the all-India level, and that between Swami Govindanand, Sheikh Abdul Majid, and Choitram Gidwani in Sind, had seemed to represent a way for Muslims to be an integral and constitutive part of Indian nationalism, rather than subsumed by it. The mass demonstrations and gestures of goodwill among Hindus and Muslims in the early 1920s seemed further evidence of a growing fraternity. But the Khilafat and Non-cooperation movements in Sind, as in other regions, had been made up of divergent agendas throughout. After the suspension of civil disobedience in 1922 and disputes in the central and provincial leaderships, both movements lost momentum. Following the dismantling of the khalifa in 1924, they petered out completely. That an unwieldy coalition of forces came to an end should come as no surprise. The bitter exchange of accusations in the aftermath, as well as outbreaks of violence in different regions, has been understood by many as indicating a turning point in the possibilities for an understanding between Hindus and Muslims in the future. However, the end of Khilafat and Non-cooperation should not be understood as a parting of

---

[167] *Times of India*, 5 November 1932, Jayakar Papers, reel 16, NAI.

[168] Sir Muhammad Shafi, quoted from Lala Lajpat Rai's Presidential Address at the Provincial Hindu Conference of Agra, 1928, Jayakar Papers, NAI.

the ways, or as merely the natural end of an unstable coalition. Certainly, the divergent elements in both movements went their respective ways. But this tells us little about what happened to fragment the relationships of those who had shared the same 'nationalist' aspirations.

The understandings of nationalism and communalism that had emerged in the post-Khilafat and Non-cooperation period hardened around the question of the legitimate place of minority communities within Indian nationalism. The Nehru Report of 1928 was the outcome of what had been a highly contested debate. It had begun the process of determining the place of minority communities in a future independent nation and to address the relationship of the regions with the centre-to-be. The resolution of the communal question and that of the federal constitution were inextricably linked. Debate focused on whether provinces could remain relatively autonomous from the centre, and the extent to which this would undermine the integrity and unity of the nation. Sind was at the centre of the question of provincial autonomy. Its separation from Bombay Presidency had enjoyed support from a cross-section of administrative and commercial groups in the early part of the century. However, by the time the question was revisited in 1928, support had split along lines of religious community. Iqbal's and Jinnah's proposals for a corridor of Muslim states and provisions for Muslims at the centre flew in the face of models of unitary nationalism that many found so persuasive. A broad spectrum of political opinion had converged around the Nehru Report. However, while Congress had conceded the separation of Sind as part of a broader reorganization of states along linguistic lines, demands that Sind be separated as part of the resolution of the communal question was deemed evidence of communalism. Muslim leaders accused Congress of having become 'a wing of the Hindu Maha Sabha' and discouraged Muslims from participating in the civil disobedience movements of the 1930s.[169] Shaukat Ali was particularly vitriolic. He argued that the new Congress Muslim Party and Hindus of the Congress held views no different than those of the Hindu Mahasabha: 'They want that

[169] Shaukat Ali quoted in the *Times of India*, 5 April 1932, Home/Special File 355(73) B-I 1929, MSA.

Muslims should be allowed to live in the land only at their mercy and should obey laws framed by them.'[170]

The opposition over the separation of Sind, then, took place in the context of the struggle over the constitution. It was in turn closely tied to negotiations over what was to be the character and nature of Indian national identity. Were Indians to be individuals in an all-India context, or could the religious community exist as such within a national framework? Mohamed Ali had raised these questions earlier with his idea of a 'federation of faiths' for India. Although the Nehru Report and then the 1935 Government of India Act recognized the separation of Sind as legitimate, they were certainly not informed by Mohamed Ali's earlier aspirations for what he called the 'communal patriot'. Paradoxically, the separation of Sind, which took place in 1935, enshrined an emphasis on a unitary state, simultaneously hardening the meanings of nationalism and communalism.

[170] *Bombay Chronicle*, 24 July 1929, in ibid.

PART III
Secularism

5

From Untouchable to Hindu

Gandhi, Ambedkar, and the
Depressed Classes Question 1932

Muslims in India had been recognized as a minority since the early twentieth century. As the Simon Commission and Nehru Report sought to hammer out their respective blueprints for a constitution, Non-Brahmans and untouchables sought the same for themselves. Just as the Nehru Report hardened understandings of nationalism and communalism, so the campaign to secure constitutional recognition for the Depressed Classes—the term coined by the colonial state for untouchables—crystallized ideas of majority and minority. The colonial state had been concerned about their position since the early nineteenth century. Since the Depressed Classes were outside the varna system and therefore without caste, the census of 1911 had considered classifying them as non-Hindus. Upper-caste opposition resulted in their remaining within the broad category of Hindu, but the question of being considered non-Hindus would become a central pillar of untouchable politics in the coming years. Grassroots campaigns for the rights of backward castes proliferated in the second decade of the twentieth century and were contemporaneous with discussions on their representation in the reforms committee in 1917. Dr B.R. Ambedkar, a Mahar from Maharashtra who had returned to India from study in Europe and the United States in 1916, soon became a prominent advocate of untouchable rights.[1] He presented the case for separate representation of Depressed Classes to the

---

[1] Mahars are the largest caste of untouchables in Maharashtra.

reforms committee, and went on to be their representative in the constitutional debates in the late 1920s and at the Round Table Conferences
in London in 1931–2.

In 1932 Ambedkar clashed fiercely with Gandhi over the question
of separate representation. He argued that the Depressed Classes were
an interest group in their own right, whose historic oppression by
upper castes required constitutional protection. Gandhi agreed that
untouchability was a terrible wrong but argued that it was not an
inherent part of Hinduism. Separate electorates were not the answer,
he insisted. Rather, Hinduism had to be reformed. To remove untouchables from the body of Hinduism would be akin to a vivisection. When
it was announced during the Round Table conferences in London that
untouchables would be recognized as a minority in their own right,
Gandhi went on a 'fast unto death' to save the unity of Hinduism.
Under pressure from around the country, Ambedkar relented and gave
up the claim for separate representation.

Here I examine constitutional debates about the status of the Depressed Classes, revisiting the Round Table conferences in London in
1931–2, especially in order to examine Ambedkar's argument in
favour of separate electorates for untouchables in the context of the
debate around minority representation. The existing substantial
scholarly attention on this has been focused more on Gandhi's epic fast
and his position on untouchability rather than on the broader debate
over the communal question. My examination of this debate shows
that the communal and caste questions were not separate but intimately
intertwined. I therefore begin with a brief outline of the history of caste
reform, both colonial and indigenous, in the late nineteenth and early
twentieth centuries, and go on to examine Ambedkar's arguments for
untouchable representation to the constitutional reforms committee
in 1919. I then look at discussions that took place among members of
the minority committee at a crucial moment in late 1931 and again in
the aftermath of Gandhi's fast in 1932, exploring the differences between those who supported separate electorates for minorities on the
one hand and those who opposed them on the other. I argue that the
way in which the 'Depressed Classes question' was eventually resolved—
by retaining untouchables within Hinduism while simultaneously
reaffirming the minority status of Muslims—marked out majority and

minority populations. It was the relationship between 'class' and 'community', and the place they would occupy in India's emerging constitutional democracy, that would determine how Indian secularism came to be defined.

Low-caste and Untouchable Reform

The constitutional reforms of 1909 ensured that there would be seats on both provincial and imperial legislative councils for representatives of the various 'communal' interests in India: landowners, tea planters, commercial bodies, Muslims, and so on. All voted in a general electorate—except the Muslims, for whom there would be separate electorates. Communal rather than territorial elections were favoured since the latter were understood to have returned a group of largely upper-caste men who had succeeded in taking advantage of the new opportunities in education and employment brought about by the colonial regime. These tended to be an urban professional elite—mainly lawyers and journalists—and were deemed unrepresentative of Indian society. People from other classes and communities, landowners and Muslims, for example, who had little interest in or ability to avail themselves of these opportunities, were perceived to have been left behind.

The discussions on council reform had maintained that a system of political representation should be precisely that—representative. As Indian society was perceived to be inherently and timelessly divided into the watertight compartments of caste and religion, it had to have a system of representation that reflected these structural particularities. Thus, territorial representation was seen, in the most generous reading of the debate between Morley and Minto, as an essentially unfair method for India because it favoured urban professionals at the expense of the rest of society. Communal representation was seen as a way not only to ensure the representation of different interests, but also as a potential leveller, exposing communities hitherto uninitiated in the ways of liberal democracy.

After 1909 the minority question was largely synonymous with the Muslim question. The other religious communities of India—Jains, Sikhs, and Christians—were seen by the colonial government as numerically and politically insignificant, much more the concern of specific regions where they were most populous. Aside from Muslims, the communities about whose 'backwardness' the state had expressed concern were the Shudras and untouchables: it had long recognized the degradation of their existence. Officials saw this as an integral part of the 'un-Christian' values of Hinduism and, as early as the mid-nineteenth century, began a system of grants-in-aid to Christian missionaries for schools to serve these populations. In 1859 the state ordered the establishment of separate schools for 'depressed class' students in areas where they had not managed to secure admission to ordinary schools. In 1865, under pressure from Christian missionaries, the state agreed to the principle that government schools would be open to all classes and castes.[2] However, this approach was generally non-interventionist: legislation tended to support the removal of legal barriers to education and employment rather than actively promoting an anti-untouchability programme. After 1858 and the proclamation of 'non-interference', officials were reluctant to take any steps to undermine untouchability for fear of provoking the accusation that they were interfering in the essential tenets of Hinduism. While the expanding colonial economy and military service brought benefits to a small number of untouchables, most remained in a state of abject rural poverty.

The question of untouchable reform, particularly the issue of whether or not they were to be considered Hindus, first emerged during the debates that prefigured the reforms of 1909. In 1906 the Aga Khan wrote to Minto arguing that the Depressed Classes were not Hindus and should not be regarded as such in any constitutional arrangements: 'The Mahomedans of India number according to the census taken in the year 1901, over sixty two millions or between one fifth to one fourth of the total population of His Majesty's Indian dominions, and if a reduction is made for . . . those classes who are ordinarily classified as Hindus but properly speaking are not Hindus at all, the proportion of Mahomedans to the Hindu majority becomes much larger.'[3] In support of the Aga Khan's suggestion, officials proposed creating constituencies on the basis of caste.[4] This drew vociferous and outraged opposition from upper-caste liberal-minded politicians

---

[2] Trilok Nath, *Politics of the Depressed Classes* (Delhi, 1987), pp. 26–9.

[3] *Times of India,* 6 October 1906, quoted in ibid., p. 43.

[4] *Indian Social Reformer,* 3 January 1909, quoted in ibid., p. 44.

and religious reformers who argued that the caste system was already in decline and to make it the bedrock of an electoral arrangement would serve to fossilize hierarchy, not undermine it. Consequently, the proposal was withdrawn and the reforms provided only a separate electorate for Muslims. However, the census administration in 1911 again suggested that the Depressed Class population was not really Hindu. The census commissioner, E.A. Gai, wrote to his provincial superintendents that 'the complaint has often been made that the census returns of Hindus are misleading, as they include millions of people who are not really Hindus at all', and suggested that these groups should be listed in a separate table.[5] However, in the face of opposition to this suggestion officials decided not to force the issue.

State legislation that sought the 'upliftment' of untouchables was extremely limited in its ambitions. It was the Non-Brahman and Mahar movements which began in the nineteenth century, as well as the reformist movements spearheaded by upper-caste Hindus in later decades, which made the position of lower castes an integral concern of any emerging Indian political agenda.[6] Concomitant with Jotirao Phule's movement were organizations such as the Arya Samaj in northern India and the Prarthana Samaj and Poona Sarvajanik Sabha in western India, led by upper-caste men who also argued against untouchability. Spurred by the large number of conversions among these castes to Christianity, they began the work of education among low-caste Hindus. They warned that Hindus had been converted to Islam in the past and now were being lost to Christianity. It was feared that if Hinduism was not purged of untouchability and other caste indignities, Hindus would simply die out. Unlike Phule's programme, such reform movements did not challenge the caste system itself. Rather, they argued that caste, or more accurately varna—the division of society into four broad categories rather than the myriad occupational categories of jati—had

[5] Ibid., p. 46.

[6] On the history of Non-Brahman and untouchable movements in western India, see Omvedt, *Cultural Revolt*; O'Hanlon, *Caste Conflict and Ideology*; Nath, *Politics of the Depressed Classes*; Atul Chandra Pradhan, *The Emergence of the Depressed Classes* (Bhubaneswar, 1986); Zelliot, *From Untouchable to Dalit*; Gokhale, *From Concessions to Confrontation;* Omvedt, *Dalits*; Naito, 'Anti-Untouchability Ideologies.

been perverted over the centuries. It was these corruptions that had to be purged. Reformers argued that there was no sanction for untouchability in the chaturvarna (four varna) system of the Vedas. During Vedic times, the varna of a person was not fixed by birth but was determined by character, association, and good or bad sanskars (tendencies). Thus, truth, good actions, knowledge of the Vedas, and cleanliness allowed a Shudra to enter a higher varna, and in turn the opposite would lead someone of a higher varna to degrade themselves into becoming a Shudra. While this understanding of the Hindu past asserted the equal value of each varna and the possibility for mobility between them, it maintained the Brahman at the apex of Hindu society.

Congress nationalists also had an anti-untouchability platform. Liberals such as Ranade and Gokhale argued that there could be no unity or progress in India until all enjoyed the same rights: 'You cannot have a good social system', observed Ranade, 'when you find yourself low in the scale of political rights, nor can you be fit to exercise political rights and privileges unless your social system is based on reason and justice.'[7] Extremists, in contrast, built on the intellectual traditions of those such as Chiplunkar in Maharashtra and Dayanand in Punjab. They, like the moderates, argued that untouchability prevented national unity, while defining the nation not as a body of democratically equal individuals but as the unity of Hindus. Lala Lajpat Rai, for example, cautioned that without the removal of untouchability, Hindu society could not be a unified, integrated whole, and the Depressed Classes might very well develop separatist tendencies: 'There can be no unity, no solidarity, so long as [the Depressed Classes] are what they are at present. They must come up and occupy their proper place in the social hierarchy before we can, with perfect truth, call ourselves a nation.'[8] And Tilak, in a speech delivered in 1917 at an 'Untouchability relief' conference sponsored by the Gaikwad of Baroda, argued famously that caste distinctions had to be ignored during wartime.[9]

Scholars have argued that Non-Brahman politics in the early twentieth century tended to be of two kinds. The first reflected the methods

[7] Quoted in Pradhan, *Emergence of the Depressed Classes*, p. 14.
[8] Quoted in Farquar, *Modern Religious Movements*, p. 392.
[9] Omvedt, *Dalits*, p. 145.

of the early Congress with the submission of petitions emphasizing the importance of the employment of Shudras and untouchables in the military and lower ranks of government. The second was the focus on 'self-reform'—improvement through education and the elimination of those practices that marked backward class communities as 'unclean'.[10] These modes of politics challenged the institution of Brahmanism but not the social ordering of Hinduism itself. Varna and jati were accepted as principles of social organization and mobility was perceived to lie within this framework, not in opposition to it. The caste conferences that began to be held regularly after 1910 by organizations such as the Depressed Classes Mission (founded in 1906) also propagated these views, emphasizing 'the necessity of education, the abandonment of backward practices, access to government jobs, and Mahar recruitment into the Indian military forces'.[11] It was not until the 1920s that the untouchable movement in Maharashtra would formulate itself as one opposed to Hinduism. In 1916 Bhimrao Ramji Ambedkar returned from Columbia University where he had studied for a PhD. He left for London in 1920 to study for his LlM at the London School of Economics, returning in 1924.[12] He formulated a radical philosophy that was anti-caste, presenting this as part of an argument for separate representation for untouchables before the constitutional reforms committee of 1917.

Ambedkar and the Southborough Committee 1919

During the review of the 1909 reforms in 1917–19, Non-Brahman and untouchable communities were concerned with how their position would be framed, and many non-Brahman leaders from western India

[10] Ibid., chapter 3; Gokhale, *From Concessions to Confrontation*, chapter 3.

[11] Gokhale, *From Concessions to Confrontation*, p. 68. See also Omvedt, *Dalits*, pp. 142–5; and Naito, 'Anti-Untouchability Ideologies', pp. 186–90.

[12] For scholarship on Ambedkar's life and career, see G.S. Lokhande, *Bhimrao Ramji Ambedkar: A Study in Social Democracy* (Delhi, 1982); Dhananjay Keer, *Dr Ambedkar, Life and Mission* (Bombay, 1971); Zelliot, *From Untouchable to Dalit*; M.S. Gore, *The Social Context of an Ideology: Ambedkar's Political and Social Thought* (Delhi, 1993).

sent deputations and memorials to the viceroy and secretary of state demanding representation for the Depressed Classes.[13] Ambedkar presented a testimony on the position of the Depressed Classes before the Southborough Committee, which met in 1919 in order to finalize the franchise, frame constituencies, and recommend adjustments to the Montagu-Chelmsford Report. The report had undertaken to safeguard the interests of Depressed Classes, and Ambedkar argued in his memorandum that this protection should come from untouchables being defined as a minority in their own right. The Government of India was faced in 1919 with the duty of creating representative institutions, he argued. Its task lay not merely in reflecting popular opinion, but in having people represent themselves: 'popular Government is not only Government for the people but by the people. . . . [R]epresentation of opinions by itself is not sufficient to constitute popular Government. To cover its true meaning it requires personal representation as well . . . Any scheme of franchise and constituency that fails to bring this about fails to create a popular Government.'[14] The realization of such a project would be founded on an accurate understanding of the nature, structure, and composition of India, and the constitution would have to be appropriately tailored to these particularities.

Interestingly, Ambedkar's perspective on the structure of Indian society closely reflected that of colonial officials. Ambedkar argued that the views of Lord Dufferin, viceroy in 1884–8, as 'composed of a large number of distinct nationalities, professing various religions, practising diverse rites, speaking different languages' was broadly accurate. Europeans had long insisted that it was these divisions that precluded India from being a unified society and made her unfit for self-rule. However, Ambedkar maintained that all societies were full of such faultlines and that discord and fragmentation were not necessarily the outcome of such differences. It was natural that those who shared 'aims, beliefs, aspirations, knowledge, a common understanding', would form a community of like-minded people, and that each community would naturally tend to evolve its 'own distinctive type of

[13] Nath, *Politics of Depressed Classes*, p. 56.
[14] Evidence Before the Southborough Committee, *Dr. Babasaheb Ambedkar, Writings and Speeches* (Bombay, 1979), vol. 1, p. 247.

likemindedness'.[15] When these different social groups were brought together to create a political union, conflict would occur only if they remained isolated from one another: 'it is the isolation of the groups that is the chief evil.'[16] The antidote to the poison of isolation, he argued, was 'endosmosis'—a fluid interaction between and amongst members of different groups which would make possible 'a resocialization of once socialized attitudes. In place of the old, it creates a new like-mindedness, which is representative of the interests, aims and aspirations of all the various groups concerned.'[17]

In India, he argued, no such endosmosis was possible. Indian society was made up of groups—Hindus, Muslims, Christians, Parsis, Jews—that were perfectly divided from each other. Except for Hindus, members of these groups could be understood as like-minded with respect to one another. The case of the Hindus was different, since 'before they are Hindus, they are members of some caste.'[18] Caste distinctions did not breed like-mindedness, only conflict. And while this was true throughout the caste system, Ambedkar argued, in the final analysis Hindus divided themselves into 'touchables' and untouchables. He warned that it would do no good to ignore the very real divisions of caste society if representative politics had any hope of being broad based and popular, rather than narrow and exclusive. Territorial constituencies would be entirely inappropriate for they were properly representative only of material interests. The divisions of 'landlords, labourers, capitalists, free traders, protectionists' did not accurately reflect the faultlines of India. If the divisions in Indian society were along lines of material interest, there would be 'no such people as Mohammedans, Hindus, Parsees, etc.' However, the injustice that would be committed by instituting territorial elections would be that while 'it may not leave unrepresented the interests of the members of the minor groups, [it] leaves them without any chance of personal representation.'[19] A candidate may be elected to a constituency by a majority, but

[15] Ibid., pp. 247–9.
[16] Ibid.
[17] Ibid.
[18] Ibid.
[19] Ibid., p. 251.

would this ensure that he would, or could, properly represent all the interests therein: 'to be concrete, will a Hindu candidate represent Mohammedan interests?'[20]

Ambedkar's understanding was that in India this could never be so. If two people from different communities purporting to represent the same interest stood for election, 'the voters will mark their votes on the person belonging to the same community. Any group yielding a large number of electors will have its own candidate elected.'[21] Thus, a high-caste Hindu could campaign on a platform of protecting untouchable interests and, being part of a majority, the candidate would easily succeed in the election. Once elected, however, what guarantee was there that he would work against the interests of his own caste by making untouchable interests central to a programme of social reform? Likewise, what would prevent caste Hindus from electing a token untouchable, a stooge who would work not in the interests of his community but of the Hindu majority?

The premise of democratic government, Ambedkar argued, was that each member of the polity should have the opportunity to realize his or her potential. But if a government could not properly represent the needs, aspirations, and interests of all its people, then it could not function as a democracy. Territorial constituencies, he continued, in failing to guarantee that the candidate elected would represent the interests of minority communities, failed to create a genuinely representative government. The way to address this problem was either to reserve seats in the general electorate or to grant communal electorates. Ambedkar favoured proportional representation for untouchables in the different regions of India and communal electorates as a means to achieve this. Congress had accepted the principle of separate electorates for Muslims in 1916 with the Lucknow Pact. However, this would not extend to any other group on the grounds that it would only serve to perpetuate social divisions and not undermine them. Indeed, Ambedkar remarked that liberal democracies made no provision for communal representation on the grounds that they undermined the unity of

[20] Ibid., p. 250.
[21] Ibid., p. 251.

the nation. However, he maintained that the premise of this position was simplistic. It held that the social and the political could easily be separated, that untouchability could be treated as a social issue and constitutionalism as a political one. But the social and the political were inseparable and could not be 'worn one at a time as the season demands'. Open competition 'is as it should be if all were equally free to fight', but 'to educate the untouchables by Shahtras [*sic*] into pro-touchables and the touchables into anti-untouchables and then to propose that the two should fight out at an open poll is to betray signs of mental aberration or a mentality fed on cunning.'[22] Indeed, it was this approach that would tend to 'develop the personality of the few at the cost of the many.'[23]

Communal representation, on the other hand, would not entrench social divisions but would overcome them, for they would bring together people who would not ordinarily cross paths:

> While communal electorates will be co-terminous with social divisions their chief effect will be to bring together men from diverse castes who would not otherwise mix together into the Legislative Council . . . [and into] an associated life . . . A caste or religious group today is a certain attitude. So long as each caste or a group remains isolated its attitude remains fossilized. But the moment the several castes and groups begin to have contact and co-operation with one another the resocialization of the fossilized attitude is bound to be the result . . . [and] caste and divisions will vanish.[24]

In his memorandum, which had unanimous support from other Depressed Class leaders, Ambedkar recommended that they should be able to elect their own representatives. However, the Southborough Committee decided otherwise. Its report stated that the Depressed Classes were outside the pale of Hinduism and required protection. However, given their low literacy rates and general lack of political awareness, it did not appear possible to 'provide an electorate on any

[22] Ibid., p. 263.
[23] Ibid., p. 251.
[24] Ibid., p. 266.

satisfactory system of franchise'.[25] The number of representatives—
who would be nominated rather than elected—designated for each
region was also far smaller than had been hoped: two in Madras
(Ambedkar had recommended eight) and one each in Bombay, Bengal, the United Provinces, Bihar and Orissa, and the Central Provinces
and Berar. Moreover, these recommendations were to be only a guide
in their respective provinces and not a directive which would bind
officials in their framing of the regulations. It was not until the Round
Table conferences, when the question of framing a constitution for
India was far more prescient, that Ambedkar would be able to return
to these questions.

Direct Action and Constitutionalism: Untouchable Politics in the 1920s

After his proposals were rejected by the Southborough Committee,
Ambedkar decided that there should be a conference for untouchables
that provided an alternative vision of reform. The All-India Depressed
Classes Conference was held in Nagpur in May 1920 with Shahu
Chhatrapati, the maharaja of Kolhapur, as president. The conference
rejected nationalism as it had been framed by Congress and condemned
the Depressed Classes Mission, until now the most prominent advocate
of untouchable rights, and its founder Vitthal Ramji Shinde, for encouraging such classes to become more closely aligned with mainstream
nationalism. The conference took the position that upper-caste movements—including Congress—had not taken the state of untouchable
society seriously, and, as Gail Omvedt argues, maintained that 'no untouchable representative chosen by a caste Hindu majority could ever
move against *chaturvarna*.'[26] What distinguished the Depressed Classes
Conference from earlier movements for caste reform was its calling for
the complete destruction of caste. Ambedkar sought an alliance between untouchable and Non-Brahman communities, the latter led by

[25] *Southborough Report*, vol. I, p. 11, quoted in Nath, *Politics of Depressed Classes*, p. 59.
[26] Omvedt, *Dalits*, p. 147; Rosalind O'Hanlon, 'Acts of Appropriation: Non-Brahmin Radicals and the Congress in Early Twentieth-Century Maharashtra', in M. Shepperdson and C. Simmons (eds), *The Indian National Congress and the Political Economy of India 1885–1985* (Aldershot, 1988), pp. 107–9.

the maharaja of Kolhapur. But there was a world of difference in Maharashtra between the largely landless labourers that were the Mahars and those who they often perceived as their direct exploiters, the landed Maratha-kunbi peasantry. Eleanor Zelliot, in her study of the Mahar movement, argues that these differences meant that while Ambedkar continued to seek common cause with Marathas, the Non-Brahman movement in Maharashtra had little in common with untouchables.[27]

During the early 1920s Ambedkar increasingly became a focus of untouchable political aspirations, receiving letters from supporters all over western India that told of atrocities suffered and hardships endured. He gave his support to peasant and anti-landlord movements, founding the Bahishkrut Hitakarini Sabha in 1924, a forum that sought to organize meetings and conferences in the countryside. The 1920s also witnessed concerted mobilization for the opening of public places to untouchables, particularly tanks and wells. A 1927 satyagraha in Mahad, a taluka town in the Konkan, was the first mass rally of the Bahishkrut Hitakarini Sabha, the mobilization providing a focus to political grievances that had been growing for a generation. The Mahad municipality had passed a resolution to open the Chawdar tank, but this had not been implemented. On the second day of the sabha's conference, 20 March 1927, the 1,500 people attending proceeded to the tank. On drinking from it they were attacked by caste Hindus, who were afraid they would continue to the local temple. News of the attack and of the subsequent 'cleansing' of the tank by horrified Brahmans spread across Maharashtra and later came to be called 'Untouchable Independence Day'.[28] Ambedkar's support base among untouchables continued to grow as he became an advocate for industrial labour in the 1930s. He steadfastly resisted attempts by Congress politicians to absorb the movement for untouchable rights, as had been the fate of Non-Brahman, peasant, and working-class movements. By the time of the Nehru Report, when the question of representation and constitutional protection for minorities was again reopened, Ambedkar was recognized as the preeminent leader of the untouchable movement.

[27] Eleanor Zelliot, 'Learning the Use of Political Means: The Mahars of Maharashtra', in R. Kothari (ed.), *Caste in Indian Politics* (Poona, 1970), pp. 44–5.

[28] Omvedt, *Dalits*, pp. 156–91.

The Nehru Report had effectively alienated the Muslim League from joint negotiation and, like Jinnah, Ambedkar was deeply disillusioned by its recommendations. The report stated that despite the efforts of the British government and Christian missionaries to ameliorate their burden, the depressed sections of Hindu society continued to suffer gross indignities. However, its suggestions to change this did not include any provision for their representation in the legislatures. It maintained that untouchability should be abolished by untouchables being 'raised socially and economically', arguing that the 'only effective way to do this is to give them educational and other facilities for this advance and to remove all obstacles in the way of this advance'.[29] The solution to the problem of untouchability, therefore, was to be found in society and not through legislation. The report dismissed all question of separate electorates for Depressed Classes on the same grounds that it had for other minority groups: they were deemed 'bad for the growth of a national spirit' and 'were still worse for a minority community'. It stated that separate electorates 'make the majority wholly independent of the minority and its votes and usually hostile to it. Under separate electorates, therefore, the chances are that the minority will always have to face a hostile majority which can always, by sheer force of numbers, override the wishes of the minority. . . Extreme communalists flourish thereunder and the majority community, far from suffering, actually benefits by them. Separate electorates must therefore be discarded completely as a condition precedent to any rational system of representation. We can only have joint or mixed electorates.'[30] It was the opposition in the Nehru Report to any compromise on the question of separate electorates that was to have important implications for how the untouchable and communal questions would later be resolved.

The second visit of the Simon Commission, like the first, was met with widespread protests. Its report, published in May 1930, recommended the abolition of dyarchy and its replacement with responsible government in the provinces. However, the proposed constitution remained essentially autocratic in structure since the British governor

[29] All Parties Conference, *Nehru Report*, pp. 59–60.
[30] Ibid., p. 30.

would be able to override the decisions made by both executive cabinet and council on questions of law and order, communal differences, financial obligations, civil service issues, and instructions from the central government or the secretary of state.[31] A few weeks earlier, on the back of Gandhi's famous salt march, Congress had launched a mass civil disobedience movement that resulted in the imprisonment of thousands of demonstrators.[32] The British prime minister, Ramsay Macdonald, saw that any attempt to implement the proposals of the Simon Commission would be futile and called for a round table conference to be convened in London at the end of that year. The conference was to be a further attempt at formulating a constitution, and this time representatives of a range of Indian parties would be present.

The Round Table Conferences

The first Round Table Conference was held in London from 12 November 1930 to 19 January 1931. It comprised 89 members: 16 from the 3 British parties, 1 from each of 20 native states, and 53 members from the different Indian parties, including the Hindu Mahasabha (Moonje and Jayakar), the Liberals (Sir Tej Bahadur Sapru and C.Y. Chintamani), the Depressed Classes (B.R. Ambedkar and Rao Bahadur Srinivasan), the Muslims (the Aga Khan, Sir Muhammad Shafi, Muhammad Ali Jinnah, Fazl-ul-Haq, with Fazl-i-Hussain as a member of the viceroy's executive council), the Sikhs (Sardar Ujjal Singh), and the Indian Christians (K.T. Paul).[33] With demonstrations going on all around India, Congress had boycotted the event. The first session set up nine subcommittees which were to address the extent of the franchise, the future of the services, provincial autonomy, the native states, provisions for minorities, and so on.

Ambedkar spoke on behalf of the Depressed Classes in the minority committee, making many of the same arguments in 1930 that he had

[31] Bakshi, *Simon Commission*, p. 147.

[32] See Judith Brown, *Gandhi and Civil Disobedience: The Mahatma in Indian Politics, 1928–34* (Cambridge, 1977).

[33] D.C. Ahir, *Dr. Ambedkar at the Round Table Conferences London (1930–1932)* (Delhi, 1999), p. 1.

in 1919: that the Depressed Classes formed a group by themselves, separate from the Muslims, and, although seen as Hindus, 'in no sense form an integral part of that community'. Their position in society was unlike any other community in India, and was 'midway between that of the serf and the slave'.[34] But while the need to abolish untouchability was something that most now recognized, Ambedkar argued, the questions uppermost for the Depressed Classes were: 'how will Dominion India function? Where will the centre of political power be? Who will have it?' And, most importantly, 'will the Depressed Classes be heirs to it?'[35] While the intelligentsia of Indian society 'speaks in the name of the country and leads the political movement', it was drawn from the upper strata of the caste system and 'has not shed the narrow particularism of the class from which it is drawn'. Any constitution for India, therefore, 'must take account of and must have a definite relation to the psychology of the society for which it is devised. Otherwise you are likely to produce a constitution which, however symmetrical, will be [a] truncated one and a total misfit to the society for which it is designed.'[36] It was to this end that Ambedkar advocated recognition of Depressed Classes as a separate political community: 'At every successive step taken by the British Government to widen the scope of representative Government the Depressed Classes have been systematically left out. No thought has been given to their claim for political power. I protest with all the emphasis I can that we will not stand this any longer. The settlement to our problem must be a part of the general political settlement and must not be left over to the shifting sands of the sympathy and goodwill of the rulers of the future.'[37] This representation would be achieved through reservation of seats in the legislature and executive, to be filled by election and not nomination, as well as in the public services. In addition, although this was to change later, Ambedkar accepted that representation could be achieved through joint electorates provided that there was universal suffrage for Depressed

[34] Ambedkar's presentation, fifth sitting of the Minorities Committee at the plenary session, 20 November 1930, quoted in ibid., p. 5.

[35] Ibid., p. 8.

[36] Ibid., p. 9.

[37] Ibid., pp. 9–10.

Classes. If this was not the case, then they would be forced to demand separate electorates.

The second conference began in September 1931. It differed significantly from the first because of the participation of Gandhi, who came as the sole representative of Congress. Following talks in Delhi with Viceroy Irwin earlier in the year, Gandhi agreed to call off the Civil Disobedience campaign in order to pursue discussions in London on the issues of 'federation', 'Indian responsibility', and 'reservations and safeguards'.[38] It was during this second round of negotiations that the question of the representation of minorities, in particular the Depressed Classes, was fully taken up. The conference opened with a speech by Gandhi in the Federal Structure Committee in which he emphasized his unequivocal opposition to the demands put forward by Ambedkar. At the second sitting of the Minorities Committee on 1 October 1931 the Aga Khan suggested that Gandhi organize a separate smaller meeting of community representatives to address the question of minority representation. Sardar Ujjal Singh, the Sikh representative, indicated that he would be amenable to this idea. However, Ambedkar, with the memory of Gandhi's opening speech fresh in his mind, asked which communities exactly would make up this committee: 'I do not know what sort of Committee Mahatma Gandhi proposes to appoint to be formed to consider this question . . . but I suppose the Depressed Classes will be represented on [it].'[39] Gandhi responded in the affirmative, but Ambedkar continued:

Thank you. But I do not know whether . . . it would be of any use for me or my colleague to work on the proposed committee . . . Mahatma Gandhi told us on the first day . . . that as a representative of the Indian National Congress he was not prepared to give political recognition to any community other than the Muhammadans and the Sikhs. He was not prepared to recognize the Anglo-Indians, the Depressed Classes, and the Indian Christians . . . What I would like to say is that unless at the outset I know

[38] See, Sumit Sarkar, 'The Logic of Gandhian Nationalism: Civil Disobedience and the Gandhi-Irwin Pact, 1930–31', *Indian Historical Review*, 3, 1, 1976.

[39] Indian Round Table Conference (second session), 7 September 1931 to 1 December 1931, *Proceedings of Federal Structure Committee and Minorities Committee* (London, 1932), p. 528.

that the Depressed Classes are going to be recognised as a community entitled to political recognition in the future constitution of India, I do not know whether it will serve any purpose for me to join the particular committee that is proposed by Mahatma Gandhi and be constituted to go into this matter.[40]

While much of the discussion on minority safeguards had so far centred on Muslims, Ambedkar argued that the problem was a much larger one: 'Is [this committee] only going to consider the question of the Muhammadans *vis-à-vis* the Hindus? Is it going to consider the question of the Muhammadans *vis-à-vis* the Sikhs in the Punjab? Or is it going to consider the question of the Sikhs *vis-à-vis* the Hindus? Is it going to consider the question of the Christians, the Anglo-Indians, and the Depressed Classes?'[41]

The eighth sitting was adjourned and it was decided to proceed with informal discussions of this issue over the next week. The following discussion is based on a diary kept during those days by B.S. Moonje, one of the two representatives of the Hindu Mahasabha at the conference. Gandhi reiterated his position the following day. He disagreed with Ambedkar's point 'that the Depressed Classes and other communities must be recognised as separate political entities for special representation in the Federal and Provincial Legislatures.' His view, and that of the Congress, was that 'except the Sikhs and the Muslims for historical reasons no other communities should be recognised as separate political entities.'[42] Gandhi's reference was to the Lucknow Pact of 1916 that had made a commitment to separate electorates for Muslims and had recognized them as a historically important community, over and above their numerical importance. Subsequently, Gandhi had also agreed for these provisions to be extended to the Sikh minority, but insisted that recognition for minorities would not extend further than these two communities.

The difference between Gandhi and Ambedkar lay in their understandings of what exactly the Depressed Classes constituted: a minority

[40] Ibid.
[41] Ibid, p. 529.
[42] 2 October 1931, B.S. Moonje's Diaries and Letter Pads, reel 1, NMML (henceforth Moonje's Diaries).

in soon-to-be Dominion India, or a subset of Hindu society. For Ambedkar there was no question:

> If Moslems and Sikhs are to be recognised [as a separate entity for representation in the legislatures], then their case and my case are so analogous that I think it is not a question for discussion at all . . . It may be said that the Depressed Classes are Hindus and therefore need not be recognised separately as [a] separate political entity. But in answer to that I say that the customs and manners of life in India and amongst the Hindus are such that Moslems, Sikhs [and] Christians are notionally more near the Hindus than the Depressed Classes. They are all touchables to the Hindus; but we are untouchables and even unapproachables.[43]

The discussion that ensued reflected the whole spectrum of opinion on the Depressed Class question, from those who opposed the idea of separate representation (Raja Narendranath), to those who accepted the idea of a form of special representation but wanted to see something other than separate electorates (Sardar Sampusan Sing), to those who supported it (Sir Tej Bahadur Sapru, Sir Muhammad Shafi). Gandhi was openly supportive of Muslim demands: 'I will surrender to the Muslims. Hindus form the majority and as such I will laddle [*sic*] out with generous hands, I will be satisfied with what is left behind.' But in the same breath he questioned Ambedkar's legitimacy as the spokesman for his community: 'I have letters and resolutions from the Depressed Classes and the Christians that they do not want special representation.' Ambedkar's demands, he said, would result in a 'vivisection of India' of which he would have no part.[44]

Gandhi and Congress also opposed constitutional recognition for other communities such as the Indian Christians and the Anglo-Indian commercial communities. Sir Hubert Carr, the representative of the latter, expressed his surprise at Gandhi's opposition: 'The attitude of Mahatma Gandhi of not recognising anybody else except the Sikhs and the Moslems . . . has taken us by surprise. I hope my community will be similarly recognised.'[45] Carr reasoned that the

[43] Ibid.
[44] Ibid.
[45] Ibid., 3 October 1931.

community desired 'to make our own contribution to the political growth of India'. The problem, however, was that 'in a general electorate we will not be able to make a common appeal to the vast masses of voters'. The discussion turned on which communities were historically important, separate and unique enough to be *deserving* of separate representation—the argument made for Muslims and Sikhs to justify their special status. Opposition to Carr's demand was based on the idea that the Anglo-Indian commercial community was made up of mere sojourners, and was therefore not deserving of such recognition. In addition, Gandhi stated that the Minorities Committee was in fact the wrong venue for Carr's proposal because 'we are here concerned with the communal question . . . and not commerce'—a telling statement that revealed the central faultline of the debate. For Gandhi, the question of communal representation was a religious and not a political one. It was particular to confessional groups and could not extend to groups with material interests. For Ambedkar, however, Carr's claim in this forum was perfectly legitimate: 'I cannot understand how their claim can be ignored. . . . In the Belgium [*sic*] constitution there is special provision for a domiciled community.'[46]

The Christian claims for representation reflected other weaknesses in the Congress opposition to Ambedkar. Panir Selvam, a Christian representative, argued that Christians were neither being given separate recognition nor were they allowed to participate as Hindus: 'Christians as a community want separate electorates in spite of letters and resolutions received by Mahatma Gandhi to the contrary. I had a conversation with Mahatma at Tanjore on Brahman Non-Brahman controversy. I was sharply told by Mahatmaji that I being a Christian should have no concern with it. Thus, although originally Hindus, we are treated as [a] separate community.'[47] Selvam argued, therefore, that if Christians were treated as a separate community in the cultural life of India, they should likewise enjoy the legislative and electoral implications of this separateness. He maintained that while Gandhi had agreed that only Sikhs and Muslims would have separate representation, this was not, in fact, the reality: in regions where Hindus were a numerical minority,

[46] Ibid.
[47] Ibid.

in the North West Provinces, Sind, Punjab, and Bengal, they had been promised constitutional protection. And if the argument in favour of protection for Muslims was made on historical grounds, 'Christianity in India is older than Islam.' Why, he argued, 'should we alone be excluded from the scheme of protection?'[48]

Selvam's pointed criticisms highlighted the central issue: if Muslims and Sikhs were to enjoy special provisions, what made Congress deny the claims of the Depressed Classes and other communities? Gandhi's answer was the Lucknow Pact. Congress had agreed to the principle of provisions for Muslims in 1916, and now 'it was a point of honour . . . not to recede from the position.'[49] However, Jinnah knew that not all Hindus supported this position. He turned to Madan Mohan Malaviya, saying: 'we know Pandit Malaviya has a large opinion behind him. Do you recognise the claim of Muslims for special recognition?' Malaviya replied that in fact he was 'opposed on principle to recognise special claims in the National Government'.[50] The contrast Malaviya drew between 'special claims' and those of the 'national government' made the former representative of smaller, particular interests, and the latter of the general interest and the common good. However, B.S. Moonje stated that 'Hindus in Punjab and Bengal are minorities and require the same protection.'[51]

It quickly became clear to those representing minority communities that if a serious proposal for electoral provisions for Hindus in provinces where they were a numerical minority was on the table, then the defence for separate electorates only for Muslims and Sikhs stood on shaky ground. Thus, Jinnah stated that he supported separate electorates for Depressed Classes, as did the Aga Khan. Selvam, Colonel Gidney, and Sardar Ujjal Singh on behalf of the Christians, Anglo-Indians, and Sikhs respectively, also reiterated their support. Gandhi had accepted the idea of separate representation for Muslims and Sikhs by way of a concession. For him, the communal or minority question had nothing to do with nationalism but was a problem for nationalism to overcome.

[48] Ibid.
[49] Ibid.
[50] Ibid.
[51] Ibid., 5 October 1931.

For the representatives of minority communities, in contrast, it was their very place in a democratic India that was at stake. As Ambedkar argued: 'The principle [*sic*] problem is how to adjust the claims of the different communities. Punjab case cannot be settled by consulting the Moslems alone but also Hindus and Sikhs whose claims are unreasonable. First settle the general principle then try to fit in the differences.'[52] How these questions were resolved was critical for it would reflect the very nature of what it meant to be Indian.

Muslims claimed that their social and economic 'backwardness' entitled them to separate electorates with reserved seats. This was true even in provinces such as Punjab and Bengal, where they were in a numerical majority. These claims had drawn criticism and resistance from many sections. Gandhi vocalized much of this dissatisfaction: 'I hate the idea of a majority asking for statutory protection and separate electorates'.[53] Constitution-making, he continued, did not have to wait for the communal question to be resolved and should continue: 'Solution or settlement of [the] communal problem should not be a condition precedent [on] or a bar to the settlement of purely constitutional issues. If we fail utterly to come to [a] communal settlement still constitutional-making must go on and should not be impeded in any way by anybody.'[54]

The informal negotiations came to a halt the next day as the Minorities Committee reconvened. Gandhi reported to Macdonald: 'it is with deep sorrow and deeper humiliation that I have to announce utter failure on my part to secure an agreed solution of the communal question through informal conversations among and with the representatives of different groups'.[55] However, he said, the failure was temporary and should not impede progress on the hammering out of a constitution. 'I have not a shadow of a doubt', he went on, 'that the iceberg of communal differences will melt under the the warmth of the sun of freedom.' Soon enough, Congress would be recognized as the wholly representative body that it was, specifically of the 'millions among

[52] Ibid.

[53] Ibid., 7 October 1931.

[54] Ibid.

[55] Indian Round Table Conference (second session), *Proceedings*, ninth sitting, 8 October 1931, p. 530.

whom are included the numberless untouchables.'[56] Congress, as well as upper-caste Hindus, would work to bring down the evil institution of untouchability, but through social amelioration rather than political intervention '[the Depressed Classes] need protection from social and religious persecution [rather] than election to legislatures.'[57]

The Resolution of the Depressed Classes Question

Discussions had broken down on the issue of minority representation not because participants did not support the idea. On the contrary, it was significant that the participants spoke in a united voice, reiterating the importance of protection for minority communities and the need for them to feel that their interests would be safeguarded in the framework for the new nation. Rather, it was the way this protection would come about that had proved to be the stumbling block. Gandhi expressed his well-known opposition on religious grounds. Although deeply disturbed by caste hierarchy, Gandhi did not see it as an inherent problem of the chaturvarna social order. He had been developing his ideas on caste since his time in South Africa and by the mid-1920s had arrived at his own, unorthodox understanding. Gandhi's approach to caste had shifted significantly over the course of his career. In the years after his return to India (1916–21), he spoke often in its defence.[58] While he decried its inequalities, he praised the system itself, seeing it as a 'natural institution' with 'wonderful powers of organisation'.[59] The prohibitions on inter-marriage and inter-dining prescribed by the caste system were beneficial, he believed, for they fostered 'self-control'.[60] By the late 1920s, however, he had begun to argue, like many reformers before him, that caste and varna should be understood as distinct.

[56] Ibid.

[57] Moonje's Diaries, 8 October 1931.

[58] Dennis Dalton, 'The Gandhian View of Caste, and Caste after Gandhi', in P. Mason (ed.), *India and Ceylon: Unity and Diversity* (Oxford, 1967).

[59] Dennis Dalton, *Mahatma Gandhi: Nonviolent Power in Action* (New York, 1993), p. 49.

[60] Ibid., quoted from *CWMG*, vol. XIII, pp. 301–3.

Gandhi maintained that the thousands of subcastes that existed within each of the four varna categories, between which there existed a myriad of social restrictions, were 'excrescences' of Hinduism.[61] The restrictions on intermarriage and interdining, he now believed, were an 'abuse of varna'. They had come about when 'Hindus were seized with inertia' and were both 'unnecessary and harmful', a 'handicap on progress'. Gandhi despised what he called this understanding of 'caste in the modern sense' for its propagation of inequality: 'Assumption of superiority by any person over any other is a sin against God and man. Thus caste, in so far as it connotes distinctions in status, is an evil.' As far as he was concerned, 'We are all absolutely equal', and it was Gandhi's understanding of what it meant to be 'equal' that proved critical to the development of his ideas on caste. 'Equality', he wrote, 'is of souls and not bodies. Hence it is a mental state'.[62] The modern idea of caste was false precisely because it rested on ideas of superiority and inferiority, but 'the law of varna has nothing to do with these restrictions'. While Gandhi did not stand by caste, he believed in varna, maintaining that it was not hierarchical but represented an organic social order: 'The four *varnas* have been compared in the Vedas to the four members of the body, and no simile could be happier. If they are members of one body, how can one be superior or inferior to another? If the members of the body had the power of expression and each of them were to say that it was higher and better than the rest, the body would go to pieces. Even so, our body politic, the body of humanity, would go to pieces, if it were to perpetuate the canker of superiority or inferiority.'[63] Equality and democracy thus meant the dignity of all; thus, a Brahman and a Shudra may intermarry without transgressing their varna.[64] And it was these four divisions, not the innumerable castes, that Gandhi considered to be 'fundamental, natural and essential'.[65]

[61] 'On Caste and Communal Question', *Young India*, 4 June 1931, reprinted in *CWMG*, vol. XLVI, pp. 302–3.

[62] Ibid.

[63] *CWMG*, vol. LIX, pp. 65–6, quoted in Dalton, *Mahatma Gandhi*, p. 53.

[64] *CWMG*, vol. XLVI, p. 303.

[65] *CWMG*, vol. XIX, pp. 83–4, quoted in Dalton, *Mahatma Gandhi*, p. 50.

A range of representatives from other parties also expressed opposition on political grounds. Significantly, it was here that the liberal and more extreme Hindu nationalist positions dovetailed. Congress, the Indian Liberal Party, and the Hindu Mahasabha all argued that separate electorates would hinder the possibility of national unity. India was to be a liberal democracy where citizens—not groups—would be represented, with constitutional protection for minority interests. However, after negotiations in the Minorities Committee failed in October 1931, members of those communities who sought separate political representation presented Macdonald with the Minorities Pact in November. The central recommendation was that 'all communities at present enjoying representation in any Legislature through nomination or election shall have representation in all Legislatures through separate electorates'.[66] For religious minorities and interest groups this would be for at least ten years, after which time they could enter joint electorates. For the Depressed Classes this would hold for twenty years. Congress had boycotted the Franchise Committee and in light of the distinct possibility of an agreement on separate electorates for minority communities, members of its leadership as well as those in the Mahasabha such as Moonje began to organize meetings with untouchables who could challenge Ambedkar's claims to represent the community.

In early 1932 Moonje sought out M.C. Rajah, an untouchable leader from Madras, and G.A. Gavai from Nagpur in the Central Provinces, encouraging them to come out in support of joint electorates and present this to the Franchise Committee. Ambedkar's support remained strong in Maharashtra, while he had the support of the majority of existing organizations in other provinces. But the determination with which Congress and the Mahasabha sought to woo untouchable leaders had profound implications.[67] Gavai was a strong advocate of separate electorates. Moonje wrote in his diary that to bring Gavai on

[66] Resolution 9 of the Minorities Pact, Appendix III: Provisions for a Settlement of the Communal Problem put forward jointly by Muslims, Depressed Classes, Indian Christians, Anglo-Indians and Europeans, Indian Round Table Conference (second session), p. 551.

[67] Omvedt, *Dalits*, pp. 172–3.

board he had offered him a compromise of joint electorates with
reservation of seats in proportion to their population: 22 per cent according to the last census. Gavai initially consented, but when he
realized that Moonje's intention to safeguard untouchable interests 'for the sake of preserving the Hindu community intact' did
not coincide with that of orthodox Brahmans who felt that even with
joint electorates 22 per cent was too much, he reverted to his original
position.[68]

The position of orthodox Hindus, what Moonje called the assertion
of 'Brahminical greed', horrified him, for he saw it being at the cost of
Hindu unity: 'the Brahmins are digging a grave for their religion and
community.'[69] His concern was that if the Depressed Classes and Non-
Brahman communities broke away from a broad grouping of Hindus,
the constitution would be reduced to representing India as a series of
minorities—something from which Muslims would unduly benefit.
It was, he warned, an inherently volatile situation:

> What a pity these Non-Brahmin leaders have no wide vision. They are
> only obsessed with Brahmin supremacy. The question of Separate Electo-
> rates should be regarded as the vital concern of the Non-Brahmins but
> they have no insight. If the Depressed Classes are separated by Separate
> Electorates the Non-Brahmins are at once reduced from their majority
> position by no less than 7 crores . . . and become practically subservient
> to Moslems who, joining hands with the separated Depressed Classes rise
> up to 14 crores. The Brahmins are nowhere in this matter as they are
> hardly 2 crores in all India. But the Non-Brahmin does not see it being
> blinded by his hate for the Brahmins. Perhaps he may even prefer the
> supremacy of the Moslem to the Brahmin supremacy.[70]

For Moonje the imperative to subvert Depressed Class demands had
everything to do with Muslim demands for representation and provincial autonomy and the fear that the battle against Muslim claims
could easily be lost. He, as well as many Hindus within Congress, saw
the constitution as a zero-sum game. The piece that was the Depressed
Classes was not one they were willing to lose.

[68] Moonje's Diaries, reel 2, 11 February 1932.
[69] Ibid.
[70] Ibid., 26 February 1932. A crore is one hundred lakhs, or ten million.

M.C. Rajah remained a political ally of Moonje's. Rajah agreed to Depressed Class reservations in a joint electorate and together they organized public demonstrations against separate electorates.[71] They sought to present the Depressed Classes Association, denounced by Ambedkar in 1930 as existing merely on paper, as the all-India organization for untouchables, with Rajah as its leader.[72] Moonje wrote to Ambedkar indicating his willingness to compromise on everything but separate electorates.[73] But Ambedkar stood firm. In response to the Rajah-Moonje pact, Ambedkar's supporters organized a conference in Nagpur in May 1932 supporting the recommendations of the Minorities Pact. Leaders of a long list of untouchable associations around India also came out against the pact. In a joint statement to the press, the Depressed Classes Association of Bengal, the United Provinces Adi-Hindu Association, the All Assam Depressed Classes Association, and the vice president of the Ad-Dharam Mandal Punjab wrote that Rajah's All India Depressed Classes Association was not representative of their opinions.[74] By the beginning of August 1932 the Round Table Conference had come to no resolution on the question of communal representation, ending with the delegates to the Minorities Committee agreeing that Macdonald should arbitrate.

The Communal Award recommended that Muslims, Sikhs, Europeans, and Christians were all to receive separate electorates. The Depressed Classes would receive separate electorates in the provinces in which they were the most populous, but would also be allowed to vote in general constituencies. The justification for this 'double vote' was in order 'to avoid electoral arrangements which would perpetuate their segregation':

> Depressed Class voters will vote in general Hindu constituencies and the elected member in such a constituency will be influenced by his responsibility to this section of the electorate; but for the next 20 years there will also be a number of special seats filled from the special Depressed Class electorates in areas where these voters chiefly prevail. The anomaly

[71] Ibid., 29 March 1932.
[72] Omvedt, *Dalits*, p. 173.
[73] Moonje Diaries, 11 July 1932.
[74] Nath, *Politics of Depressed Classes*, p. 149.

of giving certain members of the Depressed Classes two votes is abundantly justified by the urgent need of securing that their claims should be effectively expressed and the prospects of improving their actual condition promoted.[75]

The response from India was mixed. Europeans and Indian Christians accepted the award as a fair compromise. Non-Congress Muslim associations of Bombay Presidency, including Sind, were also largely accommodative.[76] B.J. Deorukhkar, the leader of the Rajah faction in Bombay, registered his disappointment with the award, stating that separate electorates were unnecessary and that this would isolate untouchables from the Hindus. The statement issued by Ambedkar also expressed dissatisfaction, but on the grounds that it had 'ruthlessly scaled down the representation of the Depressed Classes in the Provincial Legislature to quite insignificant proportions.'[77] Thus, his objection lay not in the principle of the provisions, with which he agreed, but in their degree. Congress, however, attacked the award at its foundations, claiming that it was reactionary and that it threatened national unity in India. The retention of separate electorates would perpetuate communal differences and those for the Depressed Classes would divide Hindus. It was, in short, a sabotaging of Indian nationalism.

Gandhi also responded with dismay. He had been incarcerated in Yeravda prison in Poona soon after his return to India in December 1931 on account of his rejoining the second phase of the civil disobedience movement. In prison, he had been able to follow developments in the Minorities Committee in London and on 11 March 1932 wrote to Sir Samuel Hoare, the secretary of state for India:

> when the minorities' claim was presented, I had said that I should resist with my life the grant of a separate electorate to the Depressed Classes. This was not said in the heat of the moment or by way of rhetoric. It was meant to be a serious statement . . . I am not against their representation

[75] 'General Appreciation of the Communal Award', statement of the Prime Minister, para 7, Home/Poll file no. 41–4 & K.W. 1932, serial nos 1–37, NAI.
[76] Ibid., Appendix I.
[77] Ibid.

in the legislatures . . . But I hold that separate electorate is harmful for them and for Hinduism, whatever it may be from a purely political standpoint . . . I feel that no penance that caste Hindus may do can, in any way, compensate for the calculated degradation to which they have consigned the Depressed Classes for centuries. But I know that separate electorate is neither penance nor any remedy.[78]

The day after the announcement of the award, 18 August 1932, Gandhi wrote to Macdonald indicating his decision to undertake a 'perpetual fast unto death'. He would begin at noon on 20 September and would cease only when the government agreed to 'withdraw their scheme for communal electorates for the "depressed" classes, whose representatives should be elected by the general electorate under the common franchise.'[79]

Macdonald replied that Gandhi's proposed fast was intended to prevent a community living under 'terrible disabilities' from securing for itself 'representatives of their own choosing'. He acknowledged the concern that separate representation would fragment Hindu society, but assured him it was only a temporary measure:

Whilst in view of the numerous appeals that we have received from Depressed Class organizations and generally admitted that the social disabilities under which they labour and which you have often recognised we feel it our duty to safeguard what we believed to be the right of the Depressed Classes to a fair proportion of representation in the Legislatures. We are equally careful to do nothing that would split their community from the Hindu world . . . Under Government's scheme the 'Depressed' Classes will remain part of the Hindu community and will vote with the Hindu electorate on an equal footing, but for the first twenty years, while still remaining electorally part of the Hindu community, they will receive through a limited number of special constituencies means of safeguarding their rights and interests.[80]

[78] Gandhi to Sir Samuel Hoare, 11 March 1932, *CWMG*, vol. 49, pp. 190–1.

[79] Gandhi to Ramsay Macdonald, 18 August 1932, *CWMG*, vol. 50, pp. 383–4.

[80] Ramsay Macdonald to Gandhi, 8 September 1932, quoted in Mandal, *Poona Pact*, pp. 76–7.

The government's decision would stand, Macdonald insisted, until an alternative agreement was reached between leaders of the caste Hindus and Depressed Classes. Gandhi's reply the following day insisted that 'the mere fact of "Depressed" Classes having double votes does not protect them or Hindu society from being disrupted . . . I sense the injection of a poison that is calculated to destroy Hinduism and do no good whatsoever to [them].'[81] The separation of Depressed Classes from the Hindu fold, he insisted, would arrest the efforts of Hindu reformers who had worked so hard and so successfully for the 'uplift-ment' of their suppressed brethren. Gandhi reiterated these gravest of his fears to Sardar Vallabhbhai Patel, a conservative Congress member and prominent Gandhian from Gujarat: 'The possible consequences of separate electorates for harijans fill me with horror . . . [They] will create division among Hindus so much so that it will lead to bloodshed. Untouchable hooligans will make common cause with Muslim hooli-gans and kill caste Hindus. Has the British Government no idea of all this?'[82]

The element that drew together the spectrum of Gandhian, conser-vative Hindu, and liberal opinion was the fear that separate electorates would mean that there would not be a prevailing and identifiable majority and that this would lead to chaos. News of the proposed fast was met with general apprehension at the possibility of Gandhi's death and great pressure was put on Ambedkar from all sides to accept joint electorates. Rajah began a campaign to save Gandhi's life, telegraphing Depressed Class leaders all over India and urging them to rally the support of their constituencies.[83] Likewise, Moonje met with Ambed-kar's followers in Nagpur, hoping to persuade them to reconsider. Millworkers in Ahmedabad, most of whom were from Depressed Class communities and whose mobilization for union rights Gandhi had supported, sent delegates to Bombay to press Ambedkar to alter his position.[84]

[81] Gandhi to Macdonald, 9 September 1932, *CWMG*, vol. 51, pp. 31–2.

[82] 'Harijan', literally 'man of God', was a term coined by Gandhi for un-touchables. Gandhi to Vallabhbhai Patel, 21 August 1932, *CWMG*, vol. 50, p. 469.

[83] 'Gandhi's Fast Unto Death', article from the *Times of India*, 15 September 1932, Home/Special file 800 (40)(4) A-I, 1932, MSA.

[84] Ibid., *Times of India*, 16 September 1932.

Although the tide of opinion was behind Gandhi, there were also many dissenters. Ambedkar's own response to Gandhi's fast was deeply critical: 'I do not care for these political stunts', he declared. The 'threat of Mr. Gandhi . . . to starve himself to death is not a moral fight but only a political move.'[85] An editorial in the *Times of India* argued that Gandhi's methods for securing his principles were manipulative, unreasonable, and had potentially dangerous implications for the culture of politics in the future: 'If Mr. Gandhi's method is pushed to its logical conclusion every reasonable means of reaching decisions on state affairs goes by the board . . . all that any community would have to do to gain its ends would be for its leaders to emulate Mr. Gandhi's example. The result would be chaos and the utter impossibility of carrying on any kind of ordered government in the country.'[86] One P.N. Peter, a retired postmaster from South India and president of the Adhi-Dravida General Relief Association of Nagercoil, expressed outrage at Gandhi's methods. 'The depressed class are not Hindus', he wrote, insisting that they had been in India since before the Aryan invasion, when there were no Hindus. Indians had been 'spirit worshippers', some of whom were persuaded to join Hinduism.[87] Gandhi had declared that there was no difference between him and the Depressed Classes, that they were 'his bone of bone and his flesh of flesh'. However, Peter argued, if that were really the case, he would have marched with the untouchables from Trichendure to Madras and allowed them to make temple offerings to the gods. But he did not: 'He was afraid of the so-called caste Hindus as they would desert him.'[88] Gandhi had emphasized joint over separate electorates, he wrote,

> to keep the depressed community under depression and slavery and dance to his fiddle. These people are now included among the Hindus. If they leave his fold then Hindus would become almost a minority . . . Separate electorate would deprive his community of the oppression on

[85] Ibid., 14 September 1932.

[86] Ibid., 15 September 1932.

[87] Letter to the Editor (publication unknown) from P.N. Peter, retired Head Postmaster, Municipal Councillor and President of the Adhi-Dravida General Relief Association of Nagercoil, South India, date unknown, Home/Special file 800 (40)(4) AA, pt I, 1932, MSA.

[88] Ibid.

these voiceless people who . . . [could] elect their true representatives to the legislaters [*sic*] and leave away the persecutions and humiliations they now undergo at the hand of the caste Hindus who now at the 11th hour call the parayan 'oh my brother come and dine with me'.[89]

But Peter's was the minority opinion and the country geared up to find a way around the impasse.

A deputation of Hindus went to Poona and met Gandhi on 16 September 1932. Gandhi indicated that he would consider reservations for Depressed Classes in a joint electorate since this, although contrary to the spirit of the movement for their integration into Hindu society, was not as objectionable as separate electorates.[90] The following day, after a consultation with Malaviya, Ambedkar also announced his willingness to reconsider his position. 'Ambedkar Ready to Consider Everything', the *Times of India* announced on 17 September, reporting the untouchable leader as having said 'I am open to conviction. So far as I am concerned I am willing to consider everything though I am not willing to allow the rights of the depressed classes to be curtailed in any way.'[91] Malaviya invited Ambedkar to a conference to be held in Bombay on 19 September, the eve of the fast. Members of several political parties would be attending: Chakravarti Rajagopalachari and Rajendra Prasad of Congress, Moonje of the Hindu Mahasabha, Tej Bahadur Sapru of the Liberal Party, Rajah, P. Baloo, and B.J. Deorukhkar representing Depressed Classes associations supportive of joint electorates with reserved seats, and B.R. Ambedkar and P.G. Solanki for separate electorates.

When the conference opened, all eyes were on Ambedkar. Moonje demanded to know his position: 'if we desire to save the life of Mahatma Gandhi we must know definitely whether Dr Ambedkar will accept Joint Electorates.'[92] Ambedkar replied that Gandhi had put forward no new proposals. Moonje responded that the only way to satisfy Gandhi's conscience was if he abandoned his position on separate electorates. And so the discussion went on. The meeting reconvened

[89] Ibid.

[90] Pradhan, *Emergence of Depressed Classes*, p. 183.

[91] *Times of India*, 17 September 1932, Home/Special file 800 (40)(4) A-I, 1932.

[92] Moonje's Diaries, 19 September 1932.

the following day, as Gandhi was to begin his fast. It opened with several members pressing Ambedkar to give up his position. Then Ambedkar spoke:

> You have assigned the part of a hero to someone else and that of the villain of the piece to me. I cannot understand how the matter can be settled so quickly. We have not yet got any concrete proposals from Mahatmaji. In fairness, we should ask him to postpone his fast. Mahatma cannot point a bullet at our head and then coerce us. Let us have a fortnight's time for conversations and negotiations. I am prepared for a compromise, but I cannot surrender.[93]

The industrialist G.D. Birla, a close friend of Gandhi and leading benefactor of Congress, responded bitterly: 'Do you want the caste Hindus to surrender?' Ambedkar replied that he was not a dictator, that he had to consult his constituency and that a resolution should be passed to ask the Mahatma to postpone his fast. An outcry followed. Sir C.V. Mehta said that it was 'impossible that Mahatmaji will postpone his fast.'[94] Malaviya then addressed the conference, saying that he 'cannot ask Mahatmaji to postpone his fast. It is Mahatmaji's strength . . . that has enabled him to shake the whole of India.'[95] Any possibility of further discussion was effectively aborted.

Gandhi began his fast at noon. By three o'clock, when the conference reconvened, Ambedkar had backed down and Gandhi called off his fast. The Poona Pact that resulted ensured that untouchables were retained within a general electorate of Hindus.[96] Under the Communal Award, untouchables were accorded 78 seats in the legislature along with a double vote, that is, the right to elect their own candidates through a separate electorate as well as vote in the general electorate. Under the Poona Pact, untouchables were granted 148 seats with 18 per cent reserved for untouchable candidates in the central legislature.[97]

[93] Ibid., 20 September 1932.
[94] Ibid.
[95] Ibid.
[96] On the provisions of the Poona Pact, see Ravinder Kumar, 'Gandhi, Ambedkar and the Poona Pact, 1932', *South Asia*, 8, 1985; Mandal, *Poona Pact and Depressed Classes*.
[97] The way this would work would be for seats to be reserved for the Depressed Classes from the general electorate in the provincial legislatures. Election would

However, the key point was that elections would take place through joint electorates. These provisions were maintained in the Government of India Act of 1935, which also brought the term 'Scheduled Castes' into use—to correspond with 'Depressed Classes'. The Government of India (Scheduled Castes) Order of 1936 drew up a list or 'schedule' of castes and tribes who would be beneficiaries of special representation in local and legislative bodies.

Conclusion

Once again, constitution-making had sharpened an understanding of social categories and political concepts in India. The provisions of the Poona Pact saw their way into the Government of India Act of 1935 and then into the final constitution almost completely intact. The possibilities represented by the Minorities Pact and the Communal Award, of what they could have meant for the priorities of nationalism, died a quick death in the face of Gandhi's fast for unity. Disillusioned, Ambedkar accused Gandhi of political opportunism. In a speech entitled 'Annihilation of Caste' written for the 1936 Jat Pat Todak Mandal of Lahore, he called the Poona Pact Gandhi's 'vindication' of caste and lambasted him for 'preaching Caste under the name of Varna.'[98] Indeed, the unity gained was a paltry one. In arguing that provisions for Depressed Classes would fragment both the unity of Hinduism and the unity of the nation, Congress had effectively reinforced the idea of a majority population.

This process was intimately tied to the Muslim question. That Muslims would have constitutional protection as a minority was never

---

be by joint electorates. However, all those Depressed Classes on the electoral roll would, in a primary election, elect a panel of four candidates from the Depressed Classes for each of the reserved seats (for example, Bombay and Sind had fifteen seats). Thereafter, the general election, which would be in joint electorates, would elect one out of each of the four nominations, for each constituency of the Depressed Classes.

[98] He was ultimately prevented from delivering the speech on account of its criticism of the caste system. See 'Annihilation of Caste', in B.R. Ambedkar, *Dr. Babasaheb Ambedkar, Writings and Speeches Vol. 1.* (Bombay, 1989 [1936]), pp. 37–80.

in dispute, but the implication was that this was an unfortunate reality. Congress could not retreat from the promise of parity that they had given Muslims in the Lucknow Pact. In time, it was hoped, Muslims would see themselves as Indians, making these provisions unnecessary. But the Muslim question was perceived as a 'communal' question. The same could not be said for untouchables. After all, how could India be a nation of minorities? Where then was the unity? Where would be the nation? For the most extreme Hindu nationalist opinion, the exigencies of keeping untouchables within the fold had everything to do with the numerical advantage this would give them *vis-à-vis* Muslims. For the rest, it had to do with an acceptance of a formulation of unity that emphasized a uniform civic identity while sanctioning private difference. The process had sidelined other possibilities. It had reiterated that 'Hindus' were the democratic national majority and hardened ideas of who could legitimately count as a 'minority'.

It is to the final moment of constitution-making, where secularism and universal citizenship would be determined for India, that we now turn.

6

From Nationalism to Secularism
Defining the Secular Citizen
1946–1950

Peasant, Left, Non-Brahman and untouchable movements, Khilafat, Non-cooperation, and Civil Disobedience campaigns, Congress nationalists, Hindu nationalists, liberals, socialists and Muslim parties had all defined Indian nationalism and its priorities in myriad and often contradictory ways. It was the process of constitution-making that hardened particular meanings of nationalism and communalism. In the aftermath of the Khilafat/Non-cooperation alliance, the publication of the Nehru Report, and Gandhi's protest fast opposing Ambedkar's position in 1932, those within Congress had defined nationalism as unity in the struggle against colonial rule: independence first, with issues of caste and community to be addressed only later. Mohamed Ali had challenged this formulation when he proposed that a parity existed between Hindus and Muslims that overrode their demographic imbalance. Likewise, Ambedkar asked if there was a majority population in India at all. Resistance to these positions crystallized in the evolving constitutional avatars. By the time of the Poona Pact in 1932, national identity had come to be aligned with the idea of a democratic majority, while communalism was widely understood as the politics of religious minorities. India's independence constitution, ratified in 1950, was to provide a framework for the new state and answer the questions that were still pending—about citizenship, the protection of minorities, and the nature of the secular state.

There has been significant scholarly research on the framing of the Indian constitution. Much of it has been by legal historians or political scientists who have examined its importance for constitutional theory or as providing a foundation for a new nation.[1] Furthermore, studies on the ways in which the constitution addressed the question of secularism have focused on the relationship of the liberal state to religion.[2] An exception, by Rochana Bajpai, shows that debates in the constituent assembly on secularism had as much to do with notions of justice and group rights as with 'religion'.[3] I draw here on this scholarship, but take a different direction. This final chapter examines the constituent assembly debates (1946–50) and argues that it was in the course of these debates that a meaning for secularism in India was established. The constituent assembly can be seen to mark the end of one historical process and the beginning of another.

This meaning of secularism emerged from the issue of political safeguards for minorities. These safeguards were to take the form of reservation quotas in legislatures, as well as in a range of public institutions in order to ensure that minority communities were fairly and adequately represented. At the outset of the debates, and indeed for much of the broader history of reservations, the claims of religious and caste minorities were considered together. But by 1949 these claims were deemed qualitatively different. Scholars pointing to this moment of bifurcation have argued its significance in terms of the attenuation of the rights of

[1] See, for example, Granville Austin, *The Indian Constitution: Cornerstone of a Nation* (Oxford, 1966); Shibani Kinkar Chaube, *Constituent Assembly of India: Springboard of Revolution* (Delhi, 1973); Zoya Hasan, E. Sridharan, and R. Sudarshan (eds), *India's Living Constitution: Ideas, Practices, Controversies* (Delhi, 2002); Gary Jeffrey Jacobsohn, *The Wheel of Law: India's Secularism in Comparative Constitutional Context* (Princeton, 2003).

[2] D.E. Smith, *India as a Secular State* (Princeton, 1963); Rajeev Bhargava, 'India's Secular Constitution', and U. Baxi, 'The (Im)possibility of Constitutional Justice: Seismographic Notes on Indian Constitutionalism', in Hasan *et al.* (eds), *India's Living Constitution*.

[3] Rochana Bajpai, 'The Conceptual Vocabularies of Secularism and Minority Rights in India', *Journal of Political Ideologies* 7, 2, 2002. On the embeddedness of an idea of justice and minority rights in Indian secularism, see Chatterjee, 'Secularism and Toleration'; and Chandhoke, *Beyond Secularism*.

religious minorities.[4] I will take this point further, arguing that the point at which the rights of caste and religious minorities were considered separately determined how secularism came to be defined in 1950 and into the post-Independence period.

The process of de-linking is crucial. Until this point, the so-called communal question had been addressed through reservations and separate representation. Thus, the communal and minority questions were one and the same. After Partition, such provisions for religious minorities were seen to foster a separatist—that is, a 'communal'— outlook. Many assembly members argued that the constitutional guarantee of freedom of religion and equal treatment before the law was adequate protection. In contrast, the spokesmen for religious minorities as well as historically disenfranchised communities such as the Scheduled Castes and Tribes argued that they required a helping hand in order to ensure that the promise of equality of opportunity was made good. Reservations, in this sense, were an unfortunate necessity to be introduced for a limited period. It was in this context that 'secularism' was invoked as an argument against reservations for religious minorities. Secularism would protect fundamental religious freedoms and at the same time would be the panacea for the ills of communalism. Protection of caste minorities was articulated quite differently—as part of the responsibility of an egalitarian state.

A Context for the Constituent Assembly

Generations of historians have analysed political developments in India that preceded Independence and Partition. Overwhelmingly, scholars have paid attention to nationalism and decolonization as they took place in the regions or at the administrative centre. Many also examine the constitutional markers that precede the point when the assembly met for its first session in 1946—the Government of India Act (1935), the Cripps Offer in 1942, the negotiations at Simla in 1945,

---

[4] I. Ansari, 'Minorities and the Politics of Constitution Making in India', in D.L. Sheth and Gurpreet Mahajan (eds), *Minority Identities and the Nation-State* (Delhi, 1999); and Rochana Bajpai, 'The Legitimating Vocabulary of Group Rights in Contemporary India', DPhil, Oxford University, 2003.

and the Cabinet Mission plan of 1946.[5] It is thus not my intention to provide an analysis of these in detail. This section briefly addresses the context in which it was decided to convene a constituent assembly, and outlines its final structure.

The Round Table conferences in 1931–2 had been conducted in the belief that an ultimate transfer of power in India was inevitable. After the Communal Award and the collapse of civil disobedience, the Congress Working Committee began to advocate an end to the boycott of positions in provincial government councils. They instead demanded, for the first time, a constituent assembly 'representative of all sections of the Indian people' as the only way that the principle of self-government could be applied in India.[6] The review that began in 1928 with the Simon Commission ended in the Government of India Act in 1935. Like all such negotiations to that point, the act came about with negligible Indian participation and was debated in the British parliament alone. It introduced a large measure of provincial autonomy and devolved power. It also widened the franchise from 6.5 to nearly 35 million. Yet Britain continued its control of the key departments of state at the centre: finance, law and order, and defence. The act allowed the viceroy to intervene during an 'emergency', the executive was not responsible to the legislature, and there was no mention of Dominion Status for India, let alone full independence. Furthermore, the act proposed a federal structure, but one that would only come into effect once half the princely states had acceded to it. In retaining a strong centre and making an all-India federation reliant on loyalist princes, the framework it provided was designed for Britain to retain control of its Indian empire rather than establish a trajectory to full independence.[7]

[5] See, for example, V.P. Menon, *The Transfer of Power in India* (Delhi, 1957); Ayesha Jalal, *The Sole Spokesman: Jinnah, the Muslim League and the Demand for Pakistan* (Cambridge, 1985); Ian Copland, *The Princes of India in the Endgame of Empire, 1917–1947* (Cambridge, 1997); D.A. Low, *Britain and Indian Nationalism: The Imprint of Ambiguity, 1929–1942* (Cambridge, 1997).

[6] Indian Annual Register, 1934, vol. I, quoted in Chaube, *Constituent Assembly*, p. 26. Unless otherwise indicated, this account, and that of the following section, draw from Austin, *Indian Constitution*, and Chaube, *Constituent Assembly*.

[7] See David Washbrook, 'The Rhetoric of Democracy and Development in

The formulation of a constitution had always foundered on the issue of communal representation. In a resolution on 18 September 1939, following the outbreak of the Second World War, the Muslim League Working Committee demanded a review of constitutional issues, securing an agreement from the British government that no constitutional advance would be made without its approval. In October 1939 the Congress ministers resigned in protest at the unilateral announcement by the British that India would be fully involved in the war effort. In November Gandhi came out in full support of a constituent assembly. He wrote in *Harijan*: 'the constituent assembly provides the easiest method of arriving at a just solution of the communal problem. Today we are unable to say with mathematical precision who represents whom . . . But the constituent assembly will represent all communities in their exact proportion.'[8]

The year 1940 marked a watershed. The Congress Working Committee announced only one resolution in the Ramgarh session in March: it called for complete independence and a constituent assembly. Jinnah, however, had told Gandhi that in the existing situation a constituent assembly would simply mean 'a second and larger edition of the Congress' and was out of the question.[9] Soon after the Congress resolution, on 23 March 1940, Jinnah called on Indian Muslims to adopt the demand for the 'independent states of Pakistan' at the League's session in Lahore. In response to these divergent positions, Viceroy Linlithgow made his 'August Offer': Dominion Status with a date still unnamed; a post-war body to devise a constitution, but one that would still be subject to the views of the British parliament; and expansion of the viceroy's executive council to include more Indians who would, for the first time, be in a majority—although again, British officials would control the defence, finance, and home portfolios.[10] Perhaps the most significant aspect of the offer was that it made clear the British would

---

Late Colonial India', in Bose and Jalal (eds), *Nationalism, Democracy and Development*; Jalal, *Sole Spokesman*, 17; and Sarkar, *Modern India*, pp. 336–7.

[8] Chaube, *Constituent Assembly*, p. 31.

[9] Muhammad Ali Jinnah on the Constituent Assembly, reply to Mahatma Gandhi, 14 December 1939, in Anil Chandra Bannerjee (ed.), *Indian Constitutional Documents*, vol. IV (Calcutta, 1961), pp. 140–2.

[10] Sarkar, *Modern India*, p. 377.

not transfer 'their present responsibilities to any system of government whose authority is directly denied by large and powerful elements in India's national life'—a concession to Jinnah's central demand.[11]

As Japanese forces reached Burma in 1942, threatening India as well, the British were again forced to respond to demands for Dominion Status and a national government. In March 1942 Stafford Cripps went to India and promised that steps would 'be taken for the earliest possible realisation of self-government.' Significantly, Cripps's offer included the clear promise of a constituent assembly, but also a federation with the right of non-accession for any province or state.[12] The Cripps plan was rejected by Congress for not going far enough on issues such as the establishment of a national cabinet. The Muslim League's objection was that a constituent assembly would be convened with the object of framing an Indian union when they were arguing that there was no such unity: 'So far as the Muslim League is concerned, it has finally decided that the only solution of India's constitutional problem is the partition of India into independent zones; and it will, therefore, be unfair to the Mussalmans to compel them to enter such a constitution-making body, whose main object is the creation of a new Indian union.'[13] Minority groups had argued in 1931 that constitutional and communal questions were inextricably intertwined, and Jinnah maintained the same position a decade later. He argued that Congress was not a national but a Hindu party and a constituent assembly could not proceed without the agreement of India's Muslims. It was the League's insistence that they alone supplied the Muslim representatives to a constituent assembly that caused the negotiations at Simla to break down in July 1945.

The 1946 Cabinet Mission plan recognized the problems posed by a unitary centre 'in which the Hindus with the greatly superior numbers must be a dominating element.'[14] It therefore proposed a three-tiered all-India federation with a relatively weak centre. The central

[11] Statement of Linlithgow, 8 August 1940, in Bannerjee, *Indian Constitutional Documents*, vol. IV, pp. 150–1.

[12] Chaube, *Constituent Assembly*, p. 34.

[13] Resolution of the Muslim League Working Committee, 2 April 1942, in Bannerjee, *Indian Constitutional Documents*, vol. IV, pp. 171–2.

[14] Cabinet Mission's Statement, 16 May 1946 para 3, in N. Mansergh (ed.), *Transfer of Power Documents*, vol. VII (London, 1977), p. 583.

government would have the powers to raise its own revenue, but would control only foreign affairs, defence, and communication. The provinces, grouped into three sections, would have autonomy over all other areas. Section A comprised provinces with a predominantly Hindu population—Madras, Bombay, the United Provinces, Bihar, the Central Provinces and Orissa; Section B the Muslim-majority provinces of Punjab, the North West Frontier, and Sind; and Section C Bengal and Assam, where Hindus and Muslims were approximately equal in number. The Cabinet Mission recommended that representatives to a constituent assembly should be chosen by the provincial legislative assemblies that had been elected in 1946. Each province would be allotted seats according to its population, approximately 1 to a million. These seats would be divided between communities in proportion to their population. The plan, however, proposed only three communities: Muslim, Sikh, and 'General', the latter incorporating Hindus and all others: Jains, Parsis, Anglo-Indians and Indian Christians, as well as the Scheduled Castes and Tribes. The princely states would have ninety-three members, although how they would be selected was left to a decision between the assembly and the various princes.[15] This was a long-term plan: grouping of provinces was to be compulsory at first with the possibility of opting out later.

The Cabinet Mission plan came closest to answering Jinnah's objections and it was a plan he ultimately accepted. Congress also initially accepted the proposed framework, but soon scuppered the potential for a long-term agreement when Nehru announced in July 1946 that their only commitment was to participate in the election of a constituent assembly.[16] Seeing this as reneging on their agreement, the League withdrew its acceptance of the plan on 29 July and called for Direct Action. Jinnah announced that Direct Action Day would be held on 16 August 1946, reiterating his call for the creation of a separate Muslim state of Pakistan. Direct Action was to be a peaceful mass campaign, but was followed by the massacres in Calcutta, marking some of the most brutal communal violence witnessed in this period.

Despite their rejection of the Cabinet Mission plan, the Muslim League joined the interim government—brought into being to continue

[15] Ibid., para 18, pp. 587–8.
[16] Sarkar, *Modern India*, p. 430.

the administration of the country until a constitution was decided—on 22 October 1946. But participation in an interim government was different to a constituent assembly. When the government announced in November that the preliminary meeting of the assembly would be held on 9 December 1946, the League was warned that it would only be allowed to join if it accepted the long-term plan. But Congress, although accepting of the regional groupings, opposed the mandatory listing of a province in any group if this meant that provincial representatives considered such an arrangement contrary to their province's interests.[17] The government pushed forward with the constituent assembly, which was ultimately convened in the absence of the Muslim League.

Composition of the Constituent Assembly

Elections to the constituent assembly were held in July 1946 in accordance with the schedule laid out by the Cabinet Mission and while it still had the tentative support of both the main parties. Congress had been hugely successful in the provincial elections held earlier that year and thus gained a large majority in the constituent assembly, filling 203 of the 212 places in the General category. They also elected 4 Muslims and 1 Sikh, giving them 208 seats out of the 296 allotted to the provinces. Out of the 80 seats reserved for Muslims, the League won all but 7. The 16 remaining seats went to five smaller parties: the Akali Sikhs and the minorities from Punjab, who took 3 each; the Communists and the Scheduled Caste Federation, who took 1 each; and 8 independents. There had been three sittings of the assembly prior to Mountbatten's announcement on 3 June 1947 that the British would transfer power to two independent states, India and Pakistan, on 15 August. After Partition, the League's 73 representatives fell to 28 and Congress's share of the constituent assembly seats rose to 82 per cent.

There were no separate provisions within the General category for the representation of minority interests, but the Congress Working Committee recommended that provincial Congress committees should ensure the selection of candidates from a range of communities. For instance, it recommended that the Congress committee in Madras

[17] Chaube, *Constituent Assembly*, p. 57.

nominate two Christians, Bihar and Orissa should nominate at least one member of a Scheduled Tribe, and all provinces should nominate members of Scheduled Castes in proportion to their population. The working committee also ensured the selection of Congress leaders such as Jawaharlal Nehru and Pandit Govind Ballabh Pant from the United Provinces, Sarojini Naidu and Rajendra Prasad from Bihar, and Pattabhi Sitaramayya, C. Rajagopalachari, and B. Shiva Rao from Madras. There was an imperative to bring in those experienced in constitutional law and administration, even though they were not Congress members. These included H.N. Kunzru, B.R. Ambedkar, and K.M. Munshi.[18] The parties that remained without representation were the communists, the socialists and the Hindu Mahasabha. The communists had lost their only seat after Partition. The Socialist Party had mistrusted the Cabinet Mission plan and decided not to join the assembly, maintaining this position after Independence. The absence of the Mahasabha was of little consequence. As Granville Austin has argued, their more virulently communal positions would have been given short shrift and their positions on the institutional aspects of the constitution were very close to those of Congress. Moreover, a number of prominent Mahasabha members and three ex-presidents had seats in the assembly. And Congress had its own conservatives in the form of Sardar Vallabhbhai Patel and Purushottam Das Tandon.[19]

The constituent assembly had eight major committees: Rules, Steering, Advisory, States, Drafting, Union Constitution, Union Powers, and Provincial Constitution. The Advisory Committee in turn had four sub-committees: Fundamental Rights, Minorities, Tribal and Excluded Areas including Assam, and Excluded and Partially Excluded Areas outside Assam.[20] Nehru, Patel, Prasad, and Maulana Abul Kalam Azad chaired the committees or had a presence on them. They,

---

[18] Ambedkar had been elected as the representative for the Scheduled Caste Federation, but lost his seat with the partition of Bengal. He was re-elected by the Bombay Congress at the request of the working committee. Austin, *Indian Constitution*, pp. 12–13.

[19] Ibid., p. 15.

[20] For details of the membership of these committees, see ibid., Appendix II, pp. 333–6.

along with 16 others, comprised the most influential members of the assembly.[21] Of these, all were university-educated and 12 were lawyers. There were 2 Muslims and 1 Christian—the rest were Hindus. Of the Hindus, 9 were Brahmans, Ambedkar being the only Scheduled Caste member; 9 of the 20 had been in the Congress Working Committee— indeed, 14 of the 18 Working Committee members sat in the assembly— and 6 had been Congress presidents; 5 had never been Congress members and only 2 had been its opponents—Ambedkar and Mohammed Saadulla of the Muslim League.

The deliberations in the constituent assembly can be broadly divided into two phases. The first, from December 1946 to the end of August 1947, involved the setting up of committees, each preparing reports on constitutional provisions which were debated and adopted by the assembly. Most committees functioned as standing committees, and many others continued to meet long after the submission of their reports. The Advisory Committee for instance, was set up on 24 January 1947 and dissolved only on 11 May 1949, after it had made its final decisions on reservations for minorities. The assembly was adjourned on 29 August until February 1948. In this time the constitutional adviser B.N. Rau prepared a draft that the Drafting Committee, with Ambedkar as chairman, reworked between the end of October 1947 and February the following year. Hundreds of memoranda were submitted by assembly members, as well as individuals and organizations, with suggestions for amendments. The assembly reconvened after the publication of the draft constitution in February 1948. It spent the second phase, the period between February 1948 and December 1949, deliberating the draft constitution, which was finally ratified in 1950.

[21] These were: B.R. Ambedkar, M.A. Ayyangar, N.G. Ayyangar, A.K. Ayyar, Jairamdas Daulatram, Shankarrao Deo, Mrs Durgabai, Acharya Kripalani, T.T. Krishnamachari, H.C. Mookerjee, K.M. Munshi, N.M. Rau, B.N. Rau, Mohammed Saadulla, Satyanarayan Sinha and Pattabhi Sitaramayya. B.N. Rau was the constitutional adviser and was not a member of the assembly. Azad was a Congress member but came under the Muslim category. Saadulla was a Muslim League member. All others were Congress members and came under the General category. See ibid., Appendix III, pp. 337–46.

Minority Protection: Equality through Reservation

India's constitution enshrined the values of liberalism. The freedoms it promised reflected those of the liberal democracies it sought to emulate. The Objectives Resolution adopted by the constituent assembly in January 1947 envisioned a constitution that: 'guaranteed and secured to all people equality of status, of opportunity, and before the law, freedom of thought, expression, belief, faith, worship, vocation, association and action, subject to law and public morality; and wherein adequate safeguards shall be provided for minorities, backward and tribal areas, and depressed and other backward classes.'[22] The rights relating to religion had to do with the guarantee of the freedom of conscience, religious worship, and the freedom to profess religion subject to public order and morality. That the rights of minorities—linguistic, cultural, religious, educational, and political—should be protected was never at issue. The most pressing questions regarding the promise of safeguards for minorities were—who constituted a minority? What was the nature and scope of safeguards required? What measures could ensure this protection? The Minorities sub-committee met for two days in February and then again in April and July to prepare its report. The Muslim League participated only in the last session.

Since 1909, separate electorates and reservation of seats in government had been seen by self-defined minorities and also by the British government as the best method to ensure the proper representation of minority interests. Opposition had come primarily from Congress, whose members argued that such provisions were an obstacle to national unity and institutionalized the community as the basic unit of democracy at the expense of the individual. Pandit Govind Ballabh Pant recognized that 'a satisfactory solution of questions pertaining to minorities will ensure the health, vitality and strength of the free State of India.' But, he argued, Indians had 'an unwholesome habit of thinking in communities'. The individual had become lost in the 'indiscriminate' community and, he maintained, Indians must now begin to

[22] From B. Shiva Rao (ed.), *The Framing of India's Constitution, Select Documents* (Delhi: Indian Institute of Public Administration, 1967), vol. II, p. 61. Taken from Pandit Govind Ballabh Pant's speech in the constituent assembly moving the Resolution.

think in terms of individual citizenship.[23] Likewise, B. Das, a Congress member from Orissa, felt it 'very unfortunate that minority communities do not demand justice and fair play, but claim safeguards and weightage . . . the minority problem should not overshadow the main issue which was the independence of India.[24] The interests of communities were pitched against the unity of the nation, and presented as inherently contradictory. This remained the prevailing opinion.

The Minorities sub-committee met again in April 1947 to examine the report of the Fundamental Rights sub-committee from the vantage point of minorities. The committee considered a number of memoranda and questionnaires submitted by its members. Some, such as Rajkumari Amrit Kaur, argued against reservations. 'Safeguards for minorities are wholly undesirable', she wrote. Women 'may be said technically to be the largest single minority in India. Not only have custom and usage dealt harshly with us, but even the law has militated and still continues to militate against us. But we do not and must never look upon ourselves as anything but an integral part of the whole, nor must we claim any privileges.'[25] Others such as M. Ruthnaswamy and P.K. Salve, neither of whom were assembly members but sat on the Minorities committee, argued that such measures were not ideal, but that safeguards should be phased out only after political unity reached a stage where no minority felt that their community was prevented from enjoying the rights that were granted as a matter of course to the majority. This was a position supported by Jagjivan Ram with specific reference to Scheduled Castes.[26]

Sikh respondents, Sardars Ujjal Singh and Harnam Singh, argued that the contribution of Sikhs was disproportionate to their numbers and entitled them to a full set of provisions. They demanded reservation of 6 per cent of all seats in the central legislature, in upper and lower houses, a seat for at least one Sikh in the cabinet of the Union, 5 per cent reservations in the central services, and recognition of their historic presence in the army in recruiting to the defence forces. Sikhs

[23] *Constituent Assembly Debates* (henceforth *CAD*), vol. II, 24 January 1947, pp. 310–12.

[24] Ibid., p. 323.

[25] From 'Memorandum on Minorities', Rajkumari Amrit Kaur, 20 March 1947, in Shiva Rao, *Framing*, vol. II, p. 311.

[26] From questionnaires dated 31 March, 13 April and 3 April 1947, in ibid.,

should also be represented on various statutory bodies of the union government and recognized in the provinces as a minority except in Punjab, which should have a separate legislature.[27] The All-India Adi-Hindu Depressed Classes Association submitted that the constitution should provide for representation for Scheduled Castes in proportion to their population in central and provincial legislatures and executives, in municipalities and statutory bodies, and in public services. This should be by separate electorates or by reservation of seats in joint electorates, provided in the latter case that, for a candidate to be considered elected, she or he must have received 40 per cent of the total number of votes cast by Scheduled Castes.[28]

The committee considered these as well as memoranda from organizations and individuals of other communities. To determine the relative claims of each, minorities were divided into three groups. Group A comprised those who made up less than half a per cent of India's population, omitting the princely states. These were the Anglo-Indians, Parsis, and plains tribesmen of Assam. Group B were those whose population was below 1.5 per cent: Indian Christians and Sikhs. Group C comprised those who exceeded this: Muslims and Scheduled Castes. The committee recommended that Anglo-Indians and Parsis be given the right of reserved representation at the centre, while discussion of the plains tribesmen was deferred. For Indian Christians the committee recommended reservations in provincial legislatures without weightage. The decision for Sikhs was also deferred because the position of East Punjab remained uncertain. Significantly, the committee agreed by 9 to 4 votes that separate electorates be abolished and no weightage be given to any minority in Groups B or C.[29] Instead, there would be joint electorates with reservations in proportion to the population for Muslims and Scheduled Castes for ten years.

By the time the recommendations of the Minorities sub-committee were considered in the constituent assembly at the end of August 1947,

---

pp. 312, 328, and 330 respectively. Jagjivan Ram was a Scheduled Caste person from Bihar, a Congress member, and part of the General category.

[27] Memorandum on Minorities, March/April 1947, in ibid., pp. 362–8.

[28] Ibid., 15 April 1947, pp. 381–3.

[29] Ibid., pp. 393–4.

Partition had become a reality. This cast a long shadow over proceedings, shifting the dynamic in two ways. First, the departure of 55 Muslim League members left behind what came to be called the League 'rump'—a mere 28 individuals who were now under enormous pressure to demonstrate their loyalty to India. The League's ability to demand accountability in constitutional provisions was now practically dead. Second, Partition was seen by an overwhelming number in the assembly as the result of the secessionist politics of a minority. Nehru and Patel adamantly stated that such politics would never again be entertained. When announcing the recommendations of the sub-committee to the assembly on 27 August, Patel congratulated those who had surrendered their right to reservations, saying 'they wanted neither weightage nor separate electorates but . . . they want to merge themselves in the nation and stand on their own legs.'[30] Such measures undermined the unity of the nation, he said, and many others reiterated the same point. P.S. Deshmukh, a Congress member from the Central Provinces, maintained that the interests of minorities and their protection had been an obstacle to the progress of the country. Minorities tyrannized the majority and Muslims had enjoyed privileges 'far in excess of what may be called just or fair'.[31] Many deemed reservations a generous concession. F.R. Anthony, for instance, thanked the majority community for what he called its 'magnanimity'. Every wise minority, he stated, would look forward to the time when 'it will take its place not under any communal designation but as part and parcel of the whole Indian community.'[32]

That there were minorities who supported this position was presented as a consensus against the continuation of separate electorates. But it was clear that this was not so. Two League members, B. Pocker Sahib Bahadur from Madras and Chaudhury Khaliquzzaman from the United Provinces, launched a passionate defence of separate electorates, arguing that they would satisfy the needs of all communities. But the tide of opinion was against them. Pandit Pant continued that while the success of a democracy could be measured by the confidence it

[30] *CAD*, vol. v, 27 August 1947, p. 199.
[31] Ibid., p. 201.
[32] Ibid., p. 204.

generated among minority communities, and there should be a real sense of sympathy with them, it would be 'suicidal' for minorities themselves if separate electorates were upheld: 'Do the minorities always want to remain as minorities or do they ever expect to form an integral part of a great nation and as such to guide and control its destinies?'[33] Isolation and segregation would never allow them this. He saw what he called 'the upsurge of communal passions' of recent times as closely linked to the division arising from separate electorates. They were an anachronism, an obstacle to freedom. The review of the committee's report confirmed that, in terms of political safeguards, separate electorates should be abolished in favour of joint electorates.

But the criteria for what constituted minority status were far from evident. Was this an ethical category or did it simply represent the numerical proportion of different groups? The elasticity of this concept made many uneasy. Jaipal Singh, an adivasi advocate from Bihar, questioned that adivasis were a 'minority'.[34] He maintained that as the aboriginal people of India, their place could not be dismissed in this way. Their position was of particular significance in India and could not be subsumed under a politics of numbers: 'a group of people who are the original owners of this country, even if they are only a few, can never be considered a minority. They have prescriptive rights which no one can deny.'[35] However, for Sri Nagappa, a Scheduled Caste Congress representative from Madras, it was imperative that Scheduled Castes were recognized as a minority. Hindus and Muslims were working to expand their numbers and wanted to lay claim to the Scheduled Castes, he said. Recognition as a minority was crucial if they were to resist appropriation into one or other community. Their numbers should be protected, he argued, because it was only this that would ensure their proper visibility in institutions.[36]

But the opposition to their separate categorization that had been evident during the Round Table conferences remained—often for precisely the reasons that Nagappa argued. Professor Shibban Lal Saksena

[33] Ibid., pp. 222–4.
[34] Jaipal Singh was an independent candidate and came in the General category.
[35] Ibid., p. 209.
[36] Ibid., pp. 206–7.

from the United Provinces stated that 'Mr. Jinnah has always tried to include the Scheduled Castes as a minority, but, so far as we are concerned, we consider the Scheduled Castes as belonging to Hindus, they are not a minority, they have always formed part of us.'[37] While there was much to argue over in terms of the proportions of reservations that Muslims, Anglo-Indians, Jains, Sikhs, and Christians were entitled to, that they were minorities was not contested. It was the Scheduled Caste question around which the discussion turned. K.M. Munshi sought to clarify the position of Scheduled Castes. 'Minority', he said, was defined in international treaties and international law along racial, religious, and linguistic lines, but the Scheduled Castes were none of these. The use of the term 'minority' to refer to them as such was, he felt, 'a very mischievous extension'. Munshi argued that Harijans were 'part and parcel of [the] Hindu community, and the safeguards are given to them to protect their rights only till [*sic*] they are completely absorbed in the Hindu community.'[38]

The debate around minority representation revealed a profound set of differences about the nature of democracy. The central constitutional question had always been how to reconcile the political recognition of communities with the priority of national unity. How far were those who agitated for separate electorates fomenting an isolationist attitude and segregating themselves from the nation? The balance of numbers in this democratic endeavour remained as important as it had been in 1931. Debi Prosad Khaitan, a Congress member from West Bengal, articulating the fears of many, argued that if Scheduled Castes were made a category in their own right, then together with Muslims they would form close to half the total population, after which there would be reservations for Christians, Sikhs, Buddhists, and others, rendering Hindus a minority. Independent India could not be composed of a series of minorities, he warned, this was not democracy as people knew it.[39] The Scheduled Castes were key in this understanding of democracy. It is significant and perhaps surprising that the issue of minority representation turned on the Scheduled Castes and not Muslims. But

[37] Ibid., p. 235.
[38] Ibid., p. 227.
[39] *CAD*, vol. VI, 28 August 1947, p. 255.

the former were so central because the question of whether they were to be recognized as a community separate from Hindus forced a consideration of what precisely the purpose of reservations was. Should a representative structure ensure that all communities—however defined—found a public presence to reflect the diversity of India? Or was reservation to be justified as a leveller and distributed on the basis of a community's 'backwardness'? How the disenfranchised castes were to be categorized—as communities in their own right, something Ambedkar had fought for; or as historically backward people in need of a temporary leg up—would ultimately determine what place 'community' would have in the future nation.

Secularism

During the first phase of the constituent assembly, separate electorates had been entertained as a possible solution to allay apprehensions that minority concerns would be overlooked in the emerging democratic framework. Partition changed the landscape of what seemed possible, putting huge pressure on representatives to forgo these demands, to favour 'national unity' over 'communalism'. This debate around reservations and the protection of fundamental rights for minorities was therefore closely woven into the fabric of the discussion in the assembly on secularism and what constituted a secular state. Although 'secular' was not part of the formal description of the Indian state until 1976, it was universally accepted at Independence that this would be so. The protection of minorities—cultural, linguistic, and religious—was assured in the resolutions on fundamental rights and was central to the discussion of how India should be constituted as a secular state. In this discussion, religion and caste were considered together.

Many assembly members argued that protection through reservations was defensible only to uplift the historically disenfranchised so that they could eventually take their place as citizens in a modern nation. For Nehru, reservations were part of the 'duty and responsibility of the majority', necessary to win the confidence of minorities.[40] These measures would be temporary and their intended effects were seen as undermining the need for the measures themselves. There were many others

[40] *CAD*, vol. VII, 8 November 1948, p. 323.

who took a more exacting position, insisting that protection for a group violated the principles of a secular state. Mahavir Tyagi, a Congress member from the United Provinces, argued that no one—not Scheduled Castes, Sikhs, Muslims or Hindus—should ask for any kind of reservations because 'we are a secular state . . . we cannot give recognition or weightage to any religious group of individuals'.[41] Krishnaswamy Bharati from Madras made a similar point: 'community should not be made the basis of civic rights . . . In a secular State the right to representation is only the right to represent a territory in which all communities live.'[42] The idea that the Indian state should be secular was universally accepted. But what precisely constituted secularism was taken up by a number of contradictory and often opposing political agendas. Tyagi's point was that, as a secular state, India should not recognize religious communities in its institutional framework. However, by placing Hindus alongside other communities, he effectively levelled their differences. In implying that they were simply one community among many and equally entitled to protection, he failed to acknowledge that reservations emerged from an imperative to address the relationship between what were considered to be numerically and politically unequal populations. K.T. Shah, a Congress member from Bihar, argued that the state should be secular not simply to counter the danger of sectarian violence, but to emphasize the equality of citizens before the law. Material realities and not religious affiliations should preside in the consideration of all matters.[43]

Muslim members who defended the right to follow personal law mobilized the promise of a secular state to ensure freedom of religion. Muhammad Ismail Sahib, a League member from Madras, argued thus:

> The right of a group or community of people to follow and adhere to its own personal law is among the fundamental rights . . . Now the right to follow personal law is part of the way of life of those people who are following such laws; it is part of their religion and part of their culture. If anything is done affecting the personal laws, it will be tantamount to

[41] Ibid., 9 November 1948, p. 362.
[42] Ibid., p. 366.
[43] Ibid., 15 November 1948, pp. 399–400.

interference with the way of life of those people who have been observing these laws for generations and ages. This secular State which we are trying to create should not do anything to interfere with the way of life and religion of the people.[44]

This position was echoed by other Muslim representatives. Mehboob Ali Baig Sahib Bahadur maintained that those who believed 'that under a secular State, there must be a common law observed by its citizens in all matters, including matters of their daily life, their language, their culture, their personal laws', were misguided. Rather, 'in a secular State, citizens belonging to different communities must have the freedom to practice their own religion, observe their own life and their personal laws should be applied to them.'[45]

But many opposed protection of personal law precisely on the grounds that this violated the rights of minorities and the principles of a secular state. 'Religion', K.M. Munshi stated in his defence of a uniform civil code, 'must be restricted to spheres which legitimately appertain to religion, and the rest of life must be regulated, unified and modified in such a manner that we may evolve . . . a strong and consolidated nation.' There were Hindus who defended the retention of personal law for many of the same reasons as Muslims—they saw a civil law as an illegitimate interference in the practise of their religion. But there were many aspects of these laws that were discriminatory. The Hindu laws of inheritance and succession, for instance, were particularly unjust towards women. Similarly, when sharia law was introduced for Muslims, Khojas, and Kacchi Memons were unhappy. By introducing religiously neutral laws, the civil code would serve as a just and unifying force.[46]

The debate on what the priorities of the secular state in India would be, rested on the importance of delineating domestic and civic spheres. The practise of religion would be a private concern and thus outside the jurisdiction of the state. Further, religious institutions would not receive state patronage. However, the state retained the right to regulate the 'secular' activities of religious institutions. Thus, the plethora

[44] Ibid., 23 November 1948, pp. 540–1.
[45] Ibid., p. 544.
[46] Ibid., pp. 547–8.

of questions: whether a secular state should be able to tax religious buildings; whether it had the jurisdiction to order that a temple serving high-caste communities should be open to all; whether Muslims in a sabil (a public drinking fountain) could be allowed to restrict water to non-Muslims; whether state-funded schools should include religious instruction in their curricula. All these questions featured in the consideration of the nature and structure of the Indian secular state.[47]

Independence had a significant bearing on the debate over secularism. The transition to a secular democracy marked a disjuncture with the past in important ways. First, secularism now embodied the values of unity and tolerance that nationalism had before. Whereas 'communal reservations' and 'communalism' had challenged nationalism before 1947, now they were seen to pose a threat to secularism. Second, in the constitutional provisions before Independence, the communal and minority questions were the same. Independence and Partition seemed to answer the communal problem—Partition created the state of Pakistan, the ostensible home for India's Muslims, and Independence created a democratic secular republic for India where minorities would be protected. Thus, after 1947, specifically when the constituent assembly returned to consider the draft constitution, the debate around how to protect religious and caste minorities became quite separate issues. Provisions for ensuring freedom of religion and the protection of religious minorities were now addressed in the discussions on secularism, while those to do with ensuring justice for the Scheduled Castes turned on the issue of 'backwardness'.

This de-linking of secularism from minority protection shifted what had thus far been the perceived purpose of reservations. The assembly's first phase of deliberations emphasized the purpose of reservations as levelling the playing field—to bring historically disenfranchised communities up to speed. But there was also an element that carried over from many of the earliest debates on reservations and separate electorates—of representation, in a sense, for the sake of it. Since the late nineteenth century, the role of representation had been to reflect the 'communal' character of India—Muslims, landowners, tea planters, jute farmers, commercial interests, and so on—and to ensure their

[47] See the debate on secularism in *CAD*, vol. VII, 24 November 1948.

participation in public life. Such an approach implied the inherent value of group representation and that minor groups be able to represent themselves. But India was in the process of framing a democracy that guaranteed the protection of fundamental rights, among which the rights of minorities featured prominently. The necessity of retaining group identity through separate categories thus came to be seen as unnecessary and also undesirable. Reservations were not rejected altogether, but their purpose became solely to protect the 'educationally and culturally backward'.[48]

Backwardness

The issue of whether the term 'classes' or 'minorities' should be used was raised first in the Advisory committee in April 1947 in the context of a discussion on fundamental rights. The committee agreed on the principle that there should be no discrimination against any citizen on grounds of 'religion, race, caste, language or sex', but that it must not preclude the provision of political safeguards for particular groups *vis-à-vis* their adequate representation in the services, even though this could be deemed discriminatory.[49] Munshi raised a cautionary point that the beneficiaries of such provisions would not necessarily be 'the backward classes, but . . . certain minorities'.[50] The danger was, many agreed, that if 'minority' was too narrowly understood, then a range of others, equally deserving, would be excluded. K.M. Panniker, for instance, argued that in India, 'minority' had come to acquire a particular meaning, referring to religious or political minorities—Sikh, Muslim, or Scheduled Castes. But, he said, there 'may be among the majority, among the Hindus for example, many classes who have not adequate representation in the services. . . . It may be desirable to make some kind of provision . . . for certain classes which we have to encourage to come forward.'[51]

[48] Ibid., 30 November 1948, p. 682.
[49] Shiva Rao, Advisory Committee Proceedings, 21–22 April 1947, *Framing*, vol. II, p. 222.
[50] Ibid. See also Ansari, 'Minorities and the Politics of Constitution Making in India', pp. 123–6.
[51] Shiva Rao, *Framing*, vol. II, p. 259.

Some raised the concern that by forgoing 'minority' for 'class', the majority would be able to extend its position. But this was dismissed on the grounds that only those communities that were not adequately represented would have places reserved for them. It was considered whether both terms should be used, but the chairman, Sardar Patel, insisted that 'classes' was a broader term that included 'minorities', a point with which a number of others concurred.[52] The Advisory committee recommended that such reservations would be in force for ten years only and the clause that went into the report for consideration by the Drafting committee read as follows: 'There shall be equality of opportunity for all citizens in matters of public employment and in the exercise of carrying on of any occupation, trade, business or profession. Nothing herein contained shall prevent the State from making provision for reservations in favour of classes who, in the opinion of the State, are not adequately represented in the public services.'[53] However, in a significant departure, the draft constitution substituted 'classes' with 'any backward classes'. The insertion of the term 'backward' proved important on two counts. First, it was left undefined, and second, its introduction marked the effective exclusion of 'minorities' from such provisions.

Thus, backward classes were to be the beneficiaries of reservations in the services as outlined in clause 3 article 10 of the draft constitution. But, because it was left undefined, what constituted backwardness inevitably became the focus of a range of competing positions. Dharam Prakash from the United Provinces highlighted the fundamental problem—that claims to backwardness would be almost impossible to contain, for every community had a section of its population that could be defined as either socially, economically, or educationally backward. Thus, before provisions were made for reservations in the services for an entire community, its present and future position needed careful consideration. One thing he was sure of was that, at this point in history, 'in a country which is being framed with full freedom' there was no need of reservations for minorities. The constitution guaranteed the right to freedom of conscience and it was 'not proper'

[52] Ibid., p. 262.
[53] Ibid., p. 296.

for there to be reservations over and above this.[54] Reservations had to be limited to the backward classes and the Scheduled Castes and Tribes who otherwise would not be able to overcome the barriers they encountered. Chandrika Ram took this point further. He argued that simply to promise equality of opportunity was not enough, for by failing to ensure this the state effectively denied the majority of the people their rights. It was not a population's relative size but its relative 'backwardness' that should determine entitlement.

Muhammad Ismail Sahib, a Muslim League member from Madras, claimed a stake in this term, arguing that Muslims and Christians were also 'backward'.[55] They had been excluded from this classification as reservations for their communities were deemed communal. But, he said, people charged with communalism were simply asking for their rights: 'communalism does not come in because people want their rights. When people find that they are not adequately represented, they rightly feel that they must have due representation and then such a demand [for reservations] comes up'. On the other hand, 'when people . . . find that they are given as good an opportunity as others', that is, when the conditions of backwardness are removed, 'harmony will be there and the so-called communalism will not come in at all'.[56]

Underlying these discussions was the question of what the relationship was between community and class. An article had been introduced into the draft constitution that seemed to do for minorities what article 10(3) did for backward classes. Article 296 provided that the claims of minority communities would be taken into consideration in the making of appointments to services and posts. But the relationship between the two was not clear. H.N. Kunzru pointed to the basic fault-line. The only difference between the two articles, he said, was that one used the word minority and the other backward classes. But whatever the terminology, protection was only granted to a group 'on the ground that it is backward and if left to itself, would be unable to protect its interests.'[57] Munshi agreed. He pointed out that in Bombay and Madras there had been a definition of backward classes for some time which

[54] Ibid., p. 687.
[55] Ibid., p. 693.
[56] Ibid.
[57] *CAD*, vol. VII, 30 November 1948, pp. 680–1.

included the Scheduled Castes and Scheduled Tribes but also other communities that were economically, educationally, and socially backward. The term need not be so circumscribed, but should cover all who were deemed backward.[58] Ambedkar, as chairman of the Drafting committee, explained the insertion of the term. The constitution had to ensure two potentially contradictory goals: equality of opportunity and provisions for certain communities to enter an administration which, for historical reasons, was controlled by a narrow range of castes and classes. The term 'backward' signalled a condition of social, economic, and political marginalization. Its addition had been necessary in order to prevent a whole host of other communities from attempting to stake a claim. Reservations were to be the exception, not the rule. As for minorities, article 296 would provide for the safeguarding of their interests.[59] It was with the insertion of 'backward' that class and community were separated.

Minority Protection Revisited: Equality *versus* Reservations

The report of the Minorities sub-committee prepared in August 1947 determined to abolish separate electorates but to retain reservations for Muslims and Scheduled Castes in joint electorates for ten years. Many in the assembly had opposed the principle of reservations. Those who defended them stressed their potential to dismantle political inequalities. However, by 1949 the faith that many had held in what reservations could achieve was beginning to wane. Scheduled Caste, Muslim, and Sikh representatives warned that representation should not be a substitute for equality—it should be a means to an end, not the end in itself. Sardar Hukam Singh, for instance, argued that if separate electorates perpetuated communalism, then reservations were no different. Reservations did not safeguard the interests of minorities. On the contrary, they guaranteed the dominance of the majority. If 30 per cent of posts were reserved for a minority, this still meant that 'indirectly you are reserving 70 per cent for the majority.'[60] What many pointed to was that reservations had taken the form of a concession and

[58] Ibid., p. 697.
[59] Ibid., pp. 701–2.
[60] Ibid., 4 January 1949, p. 1249.

did not address the problem of political and economic inequality. Rather, they fixed majority and minority populations in perpetuity. Hasrat Mohani was similarly resistant to being locked into the position of a permanent minority. It was this, not the demand for separate electorates, that was communalism. To assert that Muslims constituted a minority population of 14 per cent meant that 'you still consider yourselves 86 per cent. . . . Why do you say that Muslims are a minority? So long as you depict Muslims in communal colours they will remain a minority'.[61] Similarly, consigning Muslims to minority status would force them to behave as a communal body. Thus, Mohani argued for the elimination of the notion of a majority altogether.

On 11 May 1949 Patel submitted to the Advisory committee the report of a special sub-committee that had met in December 1948 to consider the problems facing minority populations in East Punjab and West Bengal. The committee comprised Nehru, Prasad, Munshi, and Ambedkar. In their opinion the conditions in the country had changed to such an extent that 'it was no longer appropriate in the context of free India and of present conditions that there should be reservations of seats for Muslims, Christians, Sikhs or any other religious minority.'[62] The abolition of separate electorates had 'removed much of the poison from the body politic.' Nevertheless, reservations for religious communities 'did lead to a certain degree of separatism and was to that extent contrary to the conception of a secular democratic state.' The Advisory committee voted overwhelmingly to support this, recognizing that 'the peculiar position of the Scheduled Castes would make it necessary to give them reservations for a period of ten years as originally decided.'[63] In his presentation to the committee, Patel outlined a concern of many Sikhs that recent converts to Sikhism from Scheduled Castes continued to live under the same disabilities as prior to their conversion. Although Sikhism did not recognize untouchability, it was important that Scheduled Caste Sikhs receive the same protection as other Scheduled Castes or there would be the danger of their reconversion to

[61] Ibid., 4 November 1948, p. 46.
[62] In a letter from Sardar Patel, chairman, Advisory committee on Minorities, Fundamental Rights etc to the President, Constituent Assembly of India, 11 May 1949, *CAD*, vol. VIII, appendix A, p. 311.
[63] Ibid.

Hinduism. The committee accepted this argument and agreed that four sections of the Sikhs in East Punjab—the Mazhabis, Ramdasis, Kabirpanthis, and Sikligars—would be listed among the Scheduled Castes.

The withdrawal of reservations for minorities was a dramatic reversal of fortune that prompted a bitter response. Muslim League members seemed to go into a tailspin, many abandoning their support of reservations. Tajamul Husain argued that reservations restricted the growth of political opinion: 'Do not make us a minority community', he demanded. 'Make us your equal partners, then there will be no majority or minority communities in India.'[64] Sri Nagappa challenged the reservation formulation for its failure to address material inequality: 'I am prepared for the abolition of the reservation, provided every Harijan family gets ten acres of wet land, twenty acres of dry land and all the children of Harijans are educated, free of cost, up to the University course and given one-fifth of key posts either in the civilian departments or in the military departments. I throw a challenge to the majority community that if they are prepared to give this much, I will forgo the whole reservation.'[65] However, opinion was behind Nehru, who argued that barriers that prevented minorities from integrating into politics and society must be removed—but not through reservations. The Scheduled Castes were the exception, because they were a way of 'helping backward groups in the country'. This was not an issue of religion or caste, but of backwardness. Removing reservation was good for minorities, but also good psychologically for the nation and the world, for 'it shows that we are really sincere about this business of having a secular democracy.'[66]

For Nehru, Patel, and Munshi, doing away with reservations was central to creating universal citizenship and a unified nation. For Sri Nagappa, Hasrat Mohani, and Sardar Hukam Singh, this was not nationalism but exclusion. Ambedkar had earlier argued that Indians had taken the wrong path on the question of minority protection: 'It is wrong for the majority to deny the existence of minorities. It is equally wrong for the minorities to perpetuate themselves.' A new solution

[64] *CAD*, vol. VIII, 25–26 May 1949, p. 337.
[65] Ibid., pp. 292–3.
[66] Ibid., pp. 331–2.

must be found that 'will enable majorities and minorities to merge someday into one.' But, he warned, the diehards among the majority had developed a fanaticism against reservations. In India, minorities had put their faith in the rule of the majority and it was the duty of the latter not to discriminate against them. The moment discrimination ceased, 'the minorities can have no ground to exist. They will vanish.' However, Ambedkar continued, the problem lay in the fact that the majority in India was 'a communal . . . and not a political majority.'[67] Herein lay the problem of liberal nationalism and it was one that minorities were acutely aware of—it presented itself as a position that was universal and secular when it was, in fact, particular and communal.

Sardar Hukam Singh reiterated this point with considerable force almost a year later, when the assembly was considering the question of the national language, attacking what he saw as the oppressive position of the majority. Singh argued that now Hindi was to be a national language it was important to safeguard the position of Punjabi as a regional language. But, he continued bitterly, the Hindu majority in Punjab denied that Punjabi was their mother tongue and so it was left to the Sikh minority to advocate it. But, unlike in the rest of India where linguistic issues were seen to be territorial questions, in Punjab the agitation for the demarcation of linguistic boundaries was deemed a communal one. Communalism, he said, had never been correctly defined, but 'a convenient definition may be that whatever is said and done by the majority community in a democratic country or at least in India is pure nationalism and whatever is said by a minority community is communalism.'[68] Hukam Singh saw the imbalance in the position between minority and majority as inherently undemocratic. Minorities had put their faith in the goodwill of the majority, but that meant that they now had to look to it for everything—'for favours, for rights or for concessions.' The opposition to the safeguarding of Punjabi was, he felt, an abuse of the power of the majority. Singh echoed Ambedkar's and Hasrat Mohani's earlier points that minorities were forced to adopt a corporate identity. But if the majority stopped behaving as such and started behaving truly democratically, minorities

[67] From Ambedkar's motion on the draft constitution, *CAD*, vol. VII, 4 November 1948, p. 39.
[68] *CAD*, vol. IX, 14 September 1949, p. 1438.

would cease to exist. It was not the democracy of the majority that was the problem, but 'the communalism of the majority'.[69] Hukam Singh argued that, with Independence, everyone was a nationalist. The conflict that had existed before 1947 between nationalism and communalism was now the question of majorities and minorities. Contrary to the accusations launched at them, minorities wanted 'pure democracy' and not the aggressive politics of the majority that currently passed for nationalism but which in fact was a politics of vested interests.[70]

In October 1949, article 296 came up for consideration by the assembly. This had provided for reservations for religious minorities in services, but the Advisory committee had voted in May 1949 to abolish this provision. Ambedkar proposed that where article 296 had read 'minorities', it should be substituted with 'members of the Scheduled Castes and Scheduled Tribes', to read thus: 'The claims of members of the Scheduled Castes and Scheduled Tribes shall be taken into consideration consistently with the maintenance of efficiency of administration, in the making of appointments to services and posts in connection with the affairs of the Union or of a State.'[71] Sardars Hukam Singh and Bhopinder Singh Man were outraged—what had once been wholly supported was now being rolled back, not just in part but in its entirety. This was a farce of a democracy, they argued, and made an equal mockery of secularism. If reservations were given to backward castes but denied to religious minorities, what was to happen to those who were equally backward but denied safeguards and reservations because they professed a religion like Sikhism?, Hukam Singh asked. 'What kind of secularism is this?'[72]

Conclusion

In its early deliberations the constituent assembly endorsed a recommendation for the recognition of minorities—a category that in 1947 incorporated both religion and caste—by reservations through joint electorates. In November 1949, as the review of the draft constitution

[69] Ibid., p. 1439.
[70] Ibid.
[71] *CAD*, vol. x, 14 October 1949, p. 229.
[72] Ibid., p. 235.

drew to a close, the assembly decided to limit this entitlement to Scheduled Castes and Tribes as well as to the more loosely defined category of 'other backward classes'. There would be no such provision for religious minorities. It was deemed the role of the secular state to ensure freedom of conscience and equal treatment before the law. The result, it was hoped, would be integration and the consolidation of national identity. Reservations on the grounds of religion were seen to foster the same political, social, and psychological isolation that had led to Partition and the creation of Pakistan.

By 1949 the consensus that had existed among Muslim representatives on the issue of reservations had fractured. Hasrat Mohani, once among the most vocal in the defence of reservations for Muslims, distanced himself from this position, arguing that it would consign Muslims to the status of a permanent minority from which they would be unable to emerge. His position was startlingly close to those such as Pandit Pant whom he had long opposed on the issue. Some scholars have seen this as a retreat and as evidence of a lack of political direction among Muslims.[73] However, while there was certainly a fragmentation of Muslim opinion in the assembly, questioning the commitment to separate representation was not a simple concession of defeat. Mohani argued that in delineating the size of the Muslim minority the assembly had reinscribed the contours of the majority. His point was significant because it showed that majority and minority were defined together and that reservations would serve to confirm, rather than undermine, their respective dominance and subordination. Similarly, Sri Nagappa's assertion that he would be willing to forgo reservations in return for specific measures to address the economic, social, and educational backwardness of Scheduled Castes also highlighted the desire to confront inequality rather than reaffirm identity.

Sikh representatives were bitterly disillusioned. In the last days of November 1949 Bhopinder Singh Man observed that the initial commitment to protect the interests of minorities had been very easily set aside: 'The impression has gone around . . . that towards the latter days of the framing of this Constitution, the minority question which was such a sacred trust with the majority, was brushed aside and lightly

[73] Chaube, *Constituent Assembly*, p. 152.

brushed aside and . . . without the consent and wishes of the representatives of the minority communities. I feel that it is a deviation from the earlier trends which evinced anxiety to give full satisfaction to the different minority groups.'[74] However, the most astute interpretation of what Man saw as a dismissal of minority interests came from Mohammad Tahir, a Muslim League member from Bihar, who argued that the constitution did not 'reflect the condition of the country'. You would not know from looking at it, he said, that Sikhs and Muslims exist. Only Anglo-Indians, Tribals, Scheduled Castes, and Hindus were visible: 'It seems as if in this Constitution the Muslims as a community have no place in politics.'[75] For Mohammad Tahir this represented a fundamental failure of the constitution. For the constitution's framers, in contrast, it was one of its core principles. The formal recognition of Muslims as a political category was beyond what a liberal democracy could accommodate. Communalism had always been the term attributed to political mobilization around a non-national identity. In this sense, its politics were particular, where nationalist politics were represented as universal. But Hukam Singh, Mohani and Ambedkar had all shown that the universal position was itself particular. Hukam Singh's outrage at what he called the 'communalism of the majority' held a mirror up to precisely this.

Reservations for the Scheduled Castes and Tribes and the so-called 'other backward classes' were justified as a protective measure. They were devised to create equality of opportunity in politically and educationally nascent populations with the aim of their integration into the new nation. Yet, the dynamic created by the recognition of religious communities was seen to be one of inequality and isolation. Representatives of religious minorities had argued their case for reservation on the grounds of their inequality. But the legitimacy that a language of liberalism had attained by 1949 meant that this lay outside the realm of the possible. It was between equality and identity that the faultline of Indian liberalism emerged. The state intervention represented by protective discrimination could only be justified on the grounds that it would go some way towards dissolving caste boundaries

[74] *CAD*, vol. XI, 21 November 1949, p. 722.
[75] Ibid., 24 November 1949, p. 877.

and inequality. The same grounds, ironically, did not exist for religious minorities because consideration of their future came within the purview of the secular state, and the premise of state secularism was precisely *non*-intervention. The goal of a secular state was also one of integration, but through containing difference within its own sphere. The challenge of difference that religion posed to the secular state lay in its identity, not its inequality. The transition from nationalism to a secular democracy required religious minorities to forgo any claim to inequality.

Studies on Indian nationalism and secularism have tended to treat constitutional politics on the one hand, and popular politics on the other, as analytically separate arenas. What I have attempted to show in this book is that, far from being distinct, they were in fact mutually constitutive. Anti-colonial mobilization had a profound impact on the course of negotiations around how Indians would eventually share power. Likewise, constitutional negotiations evolved a language of liberalism that crystallized meanings for nationalism and communalism, majority and minority. These categories framed understandings of particular historical events and also demarcated the contours of what was politically possible. The idea of secular democracy defined these possibilities as well as their limits. Such democracy in India emerged out of nationalism and the form it would take was therefore inflected by the same contradictions. Patriotism, as it had been defined in late-nineteenth- and early-twentieth-century Maharashtra, was deeply inflected with an upper-caste idiom. The Khilafat and Non-Cooperation campaigns had held out the possibility of defining nationalism as a partnership between India's 'communities'. However, between 1928 and 1931 a broad spectrum of political opinion reinforced a meaning for nationalism as the unity of the (Hindu) majority. Challenges to this by non-Hindu and untouchable communities were assigned to the realm of the 'communal'.

In India's current political climate, where Christian communities are being forcibly 'reclaimed' into the fold of Hinduism, where violence against Muslims has been legitimized by state authorities and their loyalty to the nation repeatedly made suspect, and where caste politics has proliferated since the 'other backward classes' were instituted as a formal reservation category with the Mandal Commission in 1989, it is imperative that the notion of secularism be subjected to historical re-examination. For too long, scholars have approached religion and secularism as predetermined categories locked in a mutually exclusive binary embrace. The historical approach to understanding the emergence and consolidation of these terms has allowed us to pry apart this opposition. It has shown that it was at the nexus of nationalism, communalism, and an emergent liberal democracy that the category of secularism was defined in India. Retracing how meanings for these categories evolved historically elucidates the relationships between religion and caste, identity and inequality.

The relationship between identity and inequality lies at the heart of secularism and democracy in India. It will be through a properly historical understanding of this that the potentially destructive formulations which have underpinned ideologies of belonging in India can be discarded in order to allow a more democratic and plural society to emerge.

Bibliography

Primary Sources

ORIENTAL AND INDIA OFFICE COLLECTION, LONDON

Proceedings, etc. of Government Records

Bombay (Home) Confidential Proceedings
Bombay Confidential Proceedings
Bombay Education (Confidential) Proceedings
Bombay Judicial Proceedings
Bombay Judicial (Confidential) Proceedings
Bombay Political Proceedings
Miscellaneous Papers on the Separation of Sind, November 1930–March 1934, L/P&J/9/49
Public and Judicial Records L/P&J/3, L/P&J/6, L/P&J/12

Private Papers

Montague Papers
Morley Papers
Willingdon Papers

Memoirs of Sir Maurice Henry Weston Hayward, ICS Bombay, 1889–1926
Papers of Dr William Bernard Manley, IPS Bombay, 1905–1926, including official diaries as District Superintendent of Police, Dharwar, West Khandesh, Satara and on Cattle-lifting
Address presented to Simon by the All-India Dravidian Mahajana Sabha on behalf of the Depressed Classes, 1929

Papers of Sir Arthur Hirtzel, Permanent Under Secretary of State 1924–1930 on the Political Situation in India

NATIONAL ARCHIVES OF INDIA, NEW DELHI

Proceedings, etc. of Government Records

Home (Public) Proceedings (including Ecclesiastical, Educational, Judicial, and Police Departments)
Home (Political) Proceedings

Private Papers

Gokhale Papers
Jayakar Papers
N.C. Kelkar Papers
Tyabji Papers

NEHRU MEMORIAL MUSEUM AND LIBRARY, NEW DELHI

Private Papers

Ambedkar Papers
Mohamed Ali Papers
Moonje Papers
All-India Congress Committee Papers
Servants of India Society Papers
Deccan Sabha Papers
All-India Hindu Mahasabha Papers
Mahar Movement Papers

MAHARASHTRA STATE ARCHIVES, BOMBAY

Proceedings, etc. of Government Records

Education Department Records
General Department Records
Home Department Records
Home Department (Special) Records

Home Department (Political) Records
Judicial Department Records

DEPUTY INSPECTOR GENERAL'S OFFICE,
BOMBAY

Secret Abstracts of Police Intelligence for the Bombay Presidency,
1890–1924

Official Publications

Annual Police Administration Reports of the Province of Bombay
Census of India, 1891–1911
Constituent Assembly Debates, 12 volumes (1946–1950)
Deccan Riots Commission Report (1875)
Gazetteer of the Bombay Presidency, Volumes I–III
Gazetteer of the Bombay Presidency, Nasik, Volume XVI
Gazetteer of the Bombay Presidency, Poona, Volume XVIII
Indian Round Table Conference (second session) (London, 1932)
Reports on Native Papers published in the Bombay Presidency
Reports on Publications in the Bombay Presidency
Settlement Reports (V/27) for the Collectorates of Ahmednagar,
    Dharwar, Hyderabad, Khandesh, Nasik, Poona, Satara, Yeola,
    1889–1899

Aitken, E.H., *Gazetteer of the Province of Sind* (Karachi, 1907)
Al-Hassan, Syed Siraj, *Castes and Tribes in HEH the Nizam's Dominions*
    (Haryana, 1990 [1920])
Enthovan, R.E., *Tribes and Castes of Bombay*, Vols 1–3 (Bombay, 1920)
Mansergh, N., *The Transfer of Power, 1942–47*, Vol. VII: The Cabinet
    Mission (London, 1977)

Tract and Pamphlet Literature

Aiyangar, P. Rangaswami, *Analysis of Lee-Warner's* Citizen of India
    (Madras, 1903)
Ali, Mohamed, *Proposed Mohamedan University* (Bombay, 1904)
Chatterjee, P.N., *The Higher Nationality* (Calcutta, 1906)
Malaviya, M.M., *The Hindu University of Benares, Why and What*
    Aims (1911)
Mitra, *Moslem-Hindu Entente Cordiale* (Woking, 1909)

Mujadid, Pir Ghulam of Matiari, *Facts about the Khalifate*, translated from Sindhi dissertation of Moulana Faizul Karim and authenticated by the principal Pirs and Ulemas of Sind (Karachi, 1919)

Pal, B.C., *Speeches of Sri Bepin Chandra Pal delivered at Madras* (Madras, 1907)

————, *Hindus, Mohamedans and Swaraj in India* (Madras, 1907)

Rai, Lala Lajpat, *Speech on Uplift of the Depressed Classes at Karachi* (n.d.)

Ranade, M.G., *Mr. Justice Ranade on Revival and Reform* (Bombay, 1898)

Soleman, Shaikh Abdul Aziz Mahomed, *Anti-Khalif Intrigues in Sind* (n.d.)

Tilak, B.G., *Speeches of Srj. B.G. Tilak delivered at Bellary* (Bellary, n.d.)

————, *Two Remarkable Speeches by the Great Nationalist Leader, Srijut Bal Gangadhar Tilak, on the Tenets of the New Party, and Our Present Situation* (Sylhet, 1907)

————, *Verbatim Report of His Address to the Jury* (Surat, 1908).

Bombay Riots, 1874 (Bombay, 1874)

Bombay Riots of August 1893, reprinted from the *Times of India* (Bombay, 1894)

Cow Question in India, With Hints on the Management of Cattle (Madras, 1894)

Lala Lajpat Rai, A Study (Madras, 1907)

Nationalism (Lahore, 1895)

National Social Conference (Poona, 1897 and 1900)

Pan-Islamic Society, London (London, 1903)

Pandit M.M. Malaviya: A Sketch of His Life (Madras, 1909)

Paramount Importance of Moral and Religious Education (Madras, 1896)

Reason and Religion (Trichinopoly, 1913)

Report of the Deccan Education Society for 1885 (Poona, 1885)

Revival of Religion or Love of God in the Reign of Lord Curzon (Bhowanipore, 1904)

Solutions of Controversial Hindu Problems (Allahabad, 1900)

Newspapers

Bombay Chronicle
Comrade

Harijan
Mahratta
Quarterly Journal of the Poona Sarvajanik Sabha
Times of India
Young India

Books and Articles

Abbott, J. 1924. *Sind: A Reinterpretation of the Unhappy Valley* London: Oxford University Press

Ahir, D.C. 1999. *Dr. Ambedkar at the Round Table Conferences London (1930–1932)* New Delhi: Blumoon Books

Ahmad, Aziz. 1967. *Islamic Modernism in India and Pakistan, 1857–1964* London: Oxford University Press

Ahmad, Imtiaz (ed.). 1973. *Caste and Social Stratification among the Muslims* Delhi: Manohar

Ahmed, Rafiuddin. 1981. *The Bengal Muslims, 1871–1906—A Quest for Identity* New Delhi: Oxford University Press

Alam, Javed. 1999. 'The Composite Culture and its Historiography'. In A. Roy and H. Brasted (eds). *Islam in History and Politics: A South Asian Perspective*, special issue *South Asia*, 22

All Parties Conference. 1975 [1928]. *The Nehru Report: An Anti-Separatist Manifesto* New Delhi: Michiko & Panjathan

Ambedkar, B.R. 1989. *Dr. Babasaheb Ambedkar, Writings and Speeches*, Vols 1–8 Bombay: Education Dept, Govt. of Maharashtra

Amin, Shahid. 1984. 'Gandhi as Mahatma, Gorakhpur District, Eastern UP, 1921–22'. In R. Guha (ed.). *Subaltern Studies III* New Delhi: Oxford University Press

———. 1995. *Event, Metaphor, Memory: Chauri Chaura, 1922–1992* Berkeley: University of California Press

Anderson, Benedict. 1991. *Imagined Communities: Reflections on the Origin and Spread of Nationalism* London: Verso

Ansari, I. 1999. 'Minorities and the Politics of Constitution Making in India'. In D.L. Sheth and G. Mahajan (eds). *Minority Identities and the Nation-State* New Delhi: Oxford University Press

Ansari, Sara. 1992. *Sufi Saints and State Power: The Pirs of Sind* Cambridge: Cambridge University Press

Apte, M.L. 1973. 'Lokahitavadi and V.K. Chiplunkar: Spokesmen of Change in Nineteenth-Century Maharashtra', *MAS*, 7, 2

Armitage, David. 2000. *The Ideological Origins of the British Empire* Cambridge: Cambridge University Press

Asad, Talal. 1983. 'Anthropological Definitions of Religion: Reflections on Geertz', *Man*, 18

———. 1992. 'Religion and Politics: An Introduction', *Social Research*, 59, 1

———. 1993. *Genealogies of Religion: Discipline and Reasons of Power in Christianity and Islam* Baltimore: Johns Hopkins University Press

———. 1999. 'Religion, Nation-State, Secularism'. In P. van der Veer (ed.). *Nation and Religion: Perspectives on Europe and Asia* Princeton: Princeton University Press

———. 2000. 'Muslims and European Identity: Can Europe Represent Islam?'. In E. Hallam and B.V. Street (eds). *Cultural Encounters: Representing 'Otherness'* London: Routledge

———. 2001. 'Reading a Modern Classic: W.C. Smith's *The Meaning and End of Religion'*, *History of Religions*, 40, 3

———. 2003. *Formations of the Secular: Christianity, Islam, Modernity* Stanford: Stanford University Press

Attwood, D.W., M. Israel and N.K. Wagle (eds). 1988. *City, Countryside and Society in Maharashtra* Toronto: University of Toronto Press

Austin, Granville. 1966. *The Indian Constitution: Cornerstone of a Nation* Oxford: Clarendon Press

Aziz, K.K. (ed.). 1993. *Public Life in Muslim India, 1850–1947* Delhi: Renaissance Publishing House

Bahl, Vinay. 1995. *The Making of the Indian Working Class: A Case of the Tata Iron and Steel Company 1880–1946* New Delhi: Sage

Bajpai, Rochana. 2002. 'The Conceptual Vocabularies of Secularism and Minority Rights in India', *Journal of Political Ideologies* 7, 2

Bakhle, Janaki. 2005. *Two Men and Music: Nationalism in the Making of an Indian Classical Tradition* New York: Oxford University Press

Bakshi, S.R. 1977. *Simon Commission and Indian Nationalism* New Delhi: Munshiram Manoharlal Publishers

———. 1990. *Congress, Muslim League and the Partition of India* New Delhi: Deep & Deep Publications

Ballhatchet, Kenneth. 1957. *Social Policy and Social Change in Western India, 1817–1830* London: Oxford University Press

Bamford, P.C. 1974 [1925]. *Histories of the Non-Cooperation and Khilafat Movements* New Delhi: Deep & Deep Publications

Banaji, Jairus. 1977. 'Capitalist Domination and the Small Peasantry: Deccan Districts in the Late Nineteenth Century', *EPW*, 12, 33–4.

Bannerjee, Anil Chandra (ed.). 1961. *Indian Constitutional Documents, Vol. IV 1935–1947* Calcutta: A. Mukherjee & Co.

Bari, Moin. 1994. *Saints of Sindh* Lahore: Jang Publishers

Barrier, N.G. (ed.). 1981. *The Census in British India: New Perspectives* New Delhi: Manohar

Basu, Subho. 1998. 'Strikes and Communal Riots in Calcutta in the 1890s: Industrial Workers, Bhadralok Nationalist Leadership and the Colonial State', *MAS*, 32, 4

Bates, C.N. 1981. 'The Nature of Social Change in Rural Gujarat, 1818–1918', *MAS*, 15, 4

Bayly, C.A. 1975. *Local Roots of Indian Politics: Allahabad 1880–1920* Oxford: Clarendon Press

———. 1983. *Rulers, Townsmen and Bazaars, North Indian Society in the Age of British Expansion, 1770–1870* Cambridge: Cambridge University Press

———. 1985. 'The Pre-history of "Communalism"? Religious Conflict in India, 1700–1860', *MAS*, 19, 2

———. 1996. *Empire and Information: Intelligence Gathering and Social Communication in India, 1780–1870* Cambridge: Cambridge University Press

———. 1998. *Origins of Nationality in South Asia: Patriotism and Ethical Government in the Making of Modern India* New Delhi: Oxford University Press

Bayly, Susan. 1999. *Caste, Society and Politics in India from the Eighteenth Century to the Modern Age* Cambridge: Cambridge University Press

Baxi, Upendra, Alice Jacob and Tarlok Singh (eds). 1999. *Reconstructing the Republic* New Delhi: Har-Anand

Berman, David. 1998. *A History of Atheism in Britain: From Hobbes to Russell* London: Croom Helm

Béteille, André. 1994. 'Secularism and Intellectuals', *EPW*, 29, 10

Bhargava, Rajeev. 1995. 'Religious and Secular Identities', in U. Baxi, and B. Parekh (eds). *Crisis and Change in Contemporary India* New Delhi: Sage

————— (ed.). 1998. *Secularism and its Critics* New Delhi: Oxford University Press

Bhargava, Rajeev, Amiya Kumar Bagchi, and R. Sudarshan (eds). 1999. *Multiculturalism, Liberalism and Democracy* New Delhi: Oxford University Press

Bhatt, Chetan. 2001. *Hindu Nationalism: Origins, Ideologies and Modern Myths* Oxford: Berg

—————. 2004. 'Democracy and Hindu Nationalism', *Democratization*, 11, 4

Bidwai, Praful, Harbans Mukhia, and Achin Vanaik (eds). 1996. *Religion, Religiosity and Communalism* New Delhi: Manohar

Blank, Jonah. 2001. *Mullahs on the Mainframe: Islam and Modernity Among the Daudi Bohras* Chicago: University of Chicago Press

Blom Hansen, Thomas. 1999. *The Saffron Wave: Democracy and Hindu Nationalism in Modern India* Princeton: Princeton University Press

Brass, Paul R. 1997. *Theft of an Idol: Text and Context in the Representation of Collective Violence* Princeton: Princeton University Press

Breckenridge, Carol, and Peter van der Veer (eds). 1993. *Orientalism and the Post-Colonial Predicament: Perspectives on South Asia* Philadelphia: University of Pennsylvania Press

Broomfield, J.H. 1968. *Elite Conflict in a Plural Society: Twentieth Century Bengal* Berkeley: University of California Press

Brown, Judith. 1973. *Gandhi's Rise to Power: Indian Politics, 1915– 1922* Cambridge: Cambridge University Press

—————. 1977. *Gandhi and Civil Disobedience: The Mahatma in Indian Politics, 1928–34* Cambridge: Cambridge University Press

Bruce, Steve (ed.). 1992. *Religion and Modernization: Sociologists and Historians Debate the Secularization Thesis* Oxford: Clarendon Press

Calhoun, Craig. 1995. *Critical Social Theory: Culture, History and the Challenge of Difference* Oxford: Blackwell

Casanova, Jose. 1994. *Public Religions in the Modern World* Chicago: University of Chicago Press

Cashman, Richard I. 1975. *Myth of the Lokamanya: Tilak and Mass Politics in Maharashtra* Berkeley: University of California Press

Catanach, Ian J. 1970. *Rural Credit in Western India 1875–1930* Berkeley: University of California Press

Chadwick, Owen. 1975. *The Secularization of the European Mind in the Nineteenth Century* Cambridge: Cambridge University Press

Chakrabarty, Bidyut. 1989. 'The Communal Award of 1932 and its Implications in Bengal', *MAS*, 23, 3

———— (ed.). 1990. *Secularism and Indian Polity* New Delhi: Segment Book Distributors

Chakrabarty, Dipesh. 1981. 'Communal Riots and Labour: Bengal's Jute Millhands in the 1890s', *Past and Present*, 91

Chakravarti, Uma. 1998. *Rewriting History: The Life and Times of Pandita Ramabai* New Delhi: Kali for Women

Chandavarkar, Rajnarayan. 1994. *The Origins of Industrial Capitalism in India: Business Strategies and the Working Classes in Bombay, 1900–1940* Cambridge: Cambridge University Press

————. 1998. *Imperial Power and Popular Politics: Class, Resistance and the State in India, c. 1850–1950* Cambridge: Cambridge University Press

Chandhoke, Neera. 1999. *Beyond Secularism: The Rights of Religious Minorities* New Delhi: Oxford University Press

Chandra, Bipan. 1984. *Communalism in Modern India* New Delhi: Vikas Publishing House

Charlesworth, Neil. 1985. *Peasants and Imperial Rule: Agriculture and Agrarian Society in the Bombay Presidency, 1850–1935* Cambridge: Cambridge University Press

Chatterjee, Partha. 1986. *Nationalist Thought and the Colonial World: A Derivative Discourse?* London: Zed Books

————. 1992. 'History and the Nationalization of Hinduism', *Social Research*, 59, 1

————. 1993. *The Nation and its Fragments: Colonial and Postcolonial Histories* Princeton: Princeton University Press

————. 1994. 'Secularism and Toleration', *EPW*, 29, 28

————. 1994. 'Was there a Hegemonic Project of the Colonial State?' in D. Engels and S. Marks (eds). *Contesting Colonial Hegemony: State and Society in Africa and India* London: I.B. Tauris

————. 1995. 'A Modern Science of Politics for the Colonized'. In P. Chatterjee (ed.). *Texts of Power: Emerging Disciplines in Colonial Bengal* Minneapolis, MN: University of Minnesota Press

————. 2000. 'Two Poets and Death: On Civil and Political Society in the Non-Christian World'. In T. Mitchell (ed.). *Questions of Modernity* Minneapolis, MN: University of Minnesota Press

————. 2001. 'The Nation in Heterogeneous Time', *IESHR*, 38, 4

Chatterji, Joya. 1994. *Bengal Divided: Hindu Communalism and Partition, 1932–1947* Cambridge: Cambridge University Press

Chatterji, P.C. 1984. *Secular Values for Secular India* New Delhi: Lola Chatterji

Chaube, Shibani Kinkar. 1973. *Constituent Assembly of India: Springboard of Revolution* New Delhi: People's Publishing House

Chaudhry, K.C. 1978. *Role of Religion in Indian Politics* Delhi: Sundeep Prakashan

Cheesman, David. 1997. *Landlord Power and Rural Indebtedness in Colonial Sind, 1865–1901* Richmond, Surrey: Curzon Press

Choksey, R.D. 1983. *The Story of Sind: An Economic Survey, 1843–1933* Pune: Dastane

Chowdhury-Sengupta, I. 1996. 'Reconstructing Spiritual Heroism: The Evolution of the Swadeshi Sannyasi in Bengal'. In J. Leslie (ed.). *Myth and Myth-Making* Richmond, Surrey: Curzon

Clark, Elizabeth. 2004. *History, Theory, Text: Historians and the Linguistic Turn* Cambridge, MA: Harvard University Press

Cohn, Bernard. 1983. 'Representing Authority in Victorian India'. In E. Hobsbawm and T. Ranger (eds). *The Invention of Tradition* Cambridge: Cambridge University Press

———. 1987. 'The Census, Social Structure and Objectification in South Asia', in *An Anthropologist Among the Historians and Other Essays* New Delhi: Oxford University Press

———. 1996. 'Cloth, Clothes and Colonialism', in *Colonialism and its Forms of Knowledge: The British in India* Princeton: Princeton University Press

Conlon, Frank. 1999. 'Vishnubawa Brahmachari: A Champion of Hinduism in Nineteenth Century Maharashtra', in A.R. Kulkarni and N.K. Wagle (eds). *Region, Nationality and Religion* Mumbai: Popular Prakashan

Connolly, William. 1999. *Why I Am Not a Secularist* Minneapolis, MN.: University of Minnesota Press

Cooper, Frederick and Anne L. Stoler (eds). 1997. *Tensions of Empire, Colonial Cultures in a Bourgeois World* Berkeley: University of California Press

Copland, Ian. 1997. *The Princes of India in the Endgame of Empire, 1917–1947* Cambridge: Cambridge University Press

———. 2005. *State, Community and Neighbourhood in Princely North India, c. 1900–1950* Basingstoke: Palgrave Macmillan

Courtright, Paul. 1985. *Ganesa, Lord of Obstacles* Oxford: Oxford University Press

Crook, Nigel (ed.). 1996. *The Transmission of Knowledge in South Asia: Essays on Education, Religion, History and Politics* New Delhi: Oxford University Press

Crimmins, J. (ed.). 1989. *Religion, Secularization and Political Thought: Thomas Hobbes to J.S. Mill* London: Routledge

Dalmia, Vasudha and Heinrich von Stietencron (eds). 1995. *Representing Hinduism: The Construction of Religious Traditions and National Identity* New Delhi: Sage

Dalton, Dennis. 1967. 'The Gandhian View of Caste, and Caste after Gandhi'. In P. Mason (ed.). *India and Ceylon: Unity and Diversity* London: Oxford University Press

———. 1993. *Mahatma Gandhi: Nonviolent Power in Action* New York: Columbia University Press

Das, M.N. 1964. *India Under Morley and Minto: Politics Behind Revolution, Repression and Reforms* London: Allen & Unwin

Das, Suranjan. 1991. *Communal Riots in Bengal 1905–1947* New Delhi: Oxford University Press

Das Gupta, Ashin. 1979. *Indian Merchants and the Decline of Surat, c. 1700–1750* Weisbaden: Steiner

Datta, Nonica. 1999. *Forming an Identity: A Social History of the Jats* New Delhi: Oxford University Press

Datta, Pradeep K. 2000. 'Dying Hindus: The Production of Hindu Communal Common-sense in Early Twentieth Century Bengal'. In B. Pati (ed.). *Issues in Modern Indian History* Mumbai: Popular Prakashan

Deshpande, Kusumawati, and M.V. Rajadhyaksha. 1988. *A History of Marathi Literature* New Delhi: Sahitiya Akademi

Deshpande, Prachi. 2004. 'Caste as Maratha: Social Categories, Colonial Policy and Identity in Early Twentieth Century Maharashtra', *IESHR*, 41, 1

———. 2007. *Creative Pasts: Historical Memory and Identity in Western India, 1700–1960* New Delhi: Permanent Black

Devji, Faisal Fatehali. 2005. 'A Practice of Prejudice: Gandhi's Politics of Friendship'. In S. Mayaram, M.S.S. Pandian, and A. Skaria (eds). *Subaltern Studies XII: Muslims, Dalits and the Fabrications of History* New Delhi: Permanent Black

Dirks, Nicholas. 1987. *The Hollow Crown: The Ethnohistory of an Indian Kingdom* Cambridge: Cambridge University Press

————. 2001. *Castes of Mind: Colonialism and the Making of Modern India* Princeton: Princeton University Press

Divekar, V.D. 1982. 'The Emergence of An Indigenous Business Class in Maharashtra in the Eighteenth Century,' *MAS*, 16, 3

———— (ed.). 1991. *Social Reform Movements in India: A Historical Perspective* Mumbai: Popular Prakashan

Dobbin, Christine. 1972. *Urban Leadership in Western India: Politics and Communities in Bombay City, 1840–1885* Oxford: Oxford University Press

Douglas, Ian Henderson. 1988. *Abul Kalam Azad: An Intellectual and Religious Biography* New Delhi: Oxford University Press

Dube, Saurabh. 1998. *Untouchable Pasts: Religion, Identity and Power among a Central Indian Community, 1780–1950* Albany, NY: State University of New York Press

Eaton, Richard. 1978. *The Sufis of Bijapur, 1300–1700: The Social Roles of Sufis in Medieval India* Princeton: Princeton University Press

Engineer, Asghar Ali. 2003. *Communal Challenge and Secular Response* Delhi: Shipra

———— and M. Shakir (eds). 1985. *Communalism in India* New Delhi: Ajanta

Esteves, Sarto. 1996. *Nationalism, Secularism and Communalism* Delhi: South Asia Publications

Farquar, J.N. 1915. *Modern Religious Movements in India* New York: Macmillan

Foucault, Michel. 1972. *The Archaeology of Knowledge* London: Tavistock

Fox, Richard. 1985. *Lions of the Punjab: Culture in the Making* Berkeley: University of California Press

Freitag, Sandria. 1978. '"Natural Leaders", Administrators and Social Control: Communal Riots, 1870–1925', *South Asia*, 1, 2

———. 1980. 'Sacred Symbol as Mobilising Ideology: The North Indian Search for a "Hindu" Community', *CSSH*, 22, 4

———. 1989. *Collective Action and Community: Public Arenas and the Emergence of Communalism in North India* Berkeley: University of California Press

——— (ed.). 1991. *Aspects of the 'Public' in Colonial South Asia*, special issue, *South Asia*, 14, 1

Fukazawa, Hiroshi. 1991. *The Medieval Deccan: Peasants, Social Systems and States, Sixteenth to Eighteenth Centuries* Delhi: Oxford University Press

Fuller, C.J. 1992. *The Camphor Flame: Popular Hinduism and Society in India* Princeton: Princeton University Press

Gallagher, John, Gordon Johnson, and Anil Seal (eds). 1973. *Locality, Province and Nation: Essays on Indian Politics, 1870–1940* Cambridge: Cambridge University Press

Gandhi, M.K. 1967. *The Collected Works of Mahatma Gandhi* Ahmedabad: Ministry of Information and Broadcasting

———. 1997 [1910]. *Hind Swaraj and Other Writings,* ed. Anthony J. Parel Cambridge: Cambridge University Press

Gay, Peter. 1966. *The Enlightenment: An Interpretation* New York: Norton

Gellner, Ernest. 1997. *Nationalism* London: Weidenfeld & Nicolson

Ghodke, H.M. 1990. *Revolutionary Nationalism in Western India* New Delhi: Classical Publishing Co.

Ghosh, Aurobindo. 1948. *Doctrine of Passive Resistance* Calcutta: Arya Publishing House

Ghugare, Shivaprabha. 1983. *Renaissance in Western India: Karmaveer V.R. Shinde 1873–1944* Bombay: Himalaya

Gilmartin, David. 1988. *Empire and Islam: Punjab and the Making of Pakistan* Berkeley: University of California Press

Gokhale, B.G. 1970. 'Shivram Mahadeo Paranjpe: Nationalism and the Uses of the Past', *Journal of Indian History*, 48, 143

———. 1988. *Poona in the Eighteenth Century: An Urban History* New Delhi: Oxford University Press

———. 1998. *The Fiery Quill: Nationalism and Literature in Maharashtra* Mumbai: Popular Prakashan

Gokhale, Jayashree. 1975. 'The Mahratta and Nationalism in Maharashtra', *Indian Political Science Review*, 9, 1

————. 1993. *From Concessions to Confrontation: The Politics of an Indian Untouchable Community* Bombay: Popular Prakashan

Gooptu, Nandini. 2001. *The Politics of the Urban Poor in Early Twentieth-Century India* Cambridge: Cambridge University Press

Gopal, Ram. 1956. *Lokamanya Tilak. A Biography* Bombay: Asia Publishing House

————. 1959. *Indian Muslims: A Political History (1858–1947)* Bombay: Asia Publishing House

Gopal, Sarvepalli. 1975. *Jawaharlal Nehru: A Biography* London: Cape

Gordon, Richard. 1975. 'The Hindu Mahasabha and the Indian National Congress, 1915 to 1926', *MAS*, 9, 2

Gordon, Stewart. 1993. *The Marathas, 1600–1818*. The New Cambridge History of India, II.4 Cambridge: Cambridge University Press

Gore, M.S. 1989. *Non-Brahman Movement in Maharashtra* New Delhi: Segment Books

————. 1993. *The Social Context of an Ideology: Ambedkar's Political and Social Thought* New Delhi: Sage

Gossman, Patricia. 1999. *Riots and Victims* Boulder, CO: Westview

Goswami, Manu. 2004. *Producing India: From Colonial Economy to National Space* Chicago: University of Chicago Press

Gould, William. 2004. *Hindu Nationalism and the Language of Politics in Late Colonial India* Cambridge: Cambridge University Press

Grell, Ole Peter, Jonathan I. Israel, and Nicholas Tyacke (eds). 1991. *From Persecution to Toleration: The Glorious Revolution and Religion in England* Oxford: Clarendon

Guha, Ranajit. 1983. *Elementary Aspects of Peasant Insurgency in Colonial India* Delhi: Oxford University Press

————. 1988. 'The Prose of Counter-Insurgency'. In R. Guha and G. Chakravorty Spivak (eds). *Selected Subaltern Studies* New York: Oxford University Press

————. 1989. 'Dominance Without Hegemony and its Historiography'. In R. Guha (ed.), *Subaltern Studies VI* New Delhi: Oxford University Press

Guha, Sumit. 1985. *The Agrarian Economy of the Bombay Deccan, 1818–1941* New Delhi: Oxford University Press

————. 1987. 'Commodity and Credit in Upland Maharashtra, 1800–1950', *EPW*, 32, 52

Hardgrave, Robert. 1977. 'The Mappilla Rebellion, 1921: Peasant Revolt in Malabar', *MAS*, 11, 1

Hardiman, David. 1987. *The Coming of the Devi: Adivasi Assertion in Western India* New Delhi: Oxford University Press

———. 1996. *Feeding the Baniya: Peasants and Usurers in Western India* New Delhi: Oxford University Press

———. 2003. *Gandhi: In His Time and Ours* London: Hurst

Hardy, Peter. 1972. *The Muslims of British India* Cambridge: Cambridge University Press

Hasan, Mushirul. 1979. *Nationalism and Communal Politics in India, 1916–1928* Columbia, MO: South Asia Books

———. 1981. *Mohamed Ali: Ideology and Politics* New Delhi: Manohar

———. 1981. 'Religion and Politics in India: The *Ulama* and the Khilafat Movement'. In M. Hasan (ed.). *Communal and Pan-Islamic Trends in Colonial India* New Delhi: Manohar

——— (ed.). 1981. *Communal and Pan-Islamic Trends in Colonial India* New Delhi: Manohar

———. 1982. *Mohamed Ali in Indian Politics: Select Writings*, Vols 1–3 New Delhi: Atlantic

———. 1991. *Nationalism and Communal Politics in India, 1885–1930* New Delhi: Manohar

——— (ed.). 1993. *India's Partition: Process, Strategy and Mobilization* New Delhi: Oxford University Press

——— and Margrit Pernau (eds). 2005. *Regionalizing Pan-Islamism: Documents on the Khilafat Movement* New Delhi: Manohar

Hasan, Zoya, E. Sridharan, and R. Sudarshan (eds). 2002. *India's Living Constitution: Ideas, Practices, Controversies* New Delhi: Permanent Black

Hauser, Walter. 1991–2. 'Swami Sahajanand and the Politics of Social Reform', *Indian Historical Review*, 18, 1–2

Hay, Stephen (ed.). 1988. *Sources of Indian Tradition*, Vol. II, New York: Columbia University Press

Haynes, Douglas. 1986. 'The Dynamics of Continuity in Indian Domestic Industry', *IESHR*, 23, 2

———. 1991. *Rhetoric and Ritual in Colonial India: The Shaping of a Public Culture in Surat City, 1852–1928* Berkeley: University of California Press

————. 1999. 'Market Formation in Khandesh, c. 1820–1930', *IESHR*, 36, 3

———— and Tirthankar Roy. 1999. 'Conceiving Mobility: Weavers' Migrations in Pre-colonial and Colonial India', *IESHR*, 36, 1

Heimsath, Charles. 1964. *Indian Nationalism and Hindu Social Reform* Princeton: Princeton University Press

Hobsbawm, E.J. 1992. *Nations and Nationalism since 1780: Programme, Myth, Reality* Cambridge: Cambridge University Press

Hunter, Michael and David Wootton (eds). 1992. *Atheism from the Reformation to the Enlightenment* Oxford: Clarendon

Huttenback, R.A. 1962. *British Relations with Sind: 1799–1843* Berkeley: University of California Press

Ilaiah, Kancha. 1996. *Why I am not a Hindu: A Sudra Critique of Hindutva, Philosophy, Culture, Political Economy* Calcutta: Samya

————. 1998. 'Towards the Dalitization of the Nation', in P. Chatterjee (ed.). *Wages of Freedom: Fifty Years of the Indian Nation-State* New Delhi: Oxford University Press

Iqbal, Afzal (ed.). 1963. *Select Writings and Speeches of Maulana Mohamed Ali*, Vols I and II Lahore: Sh. Muhammad Ashraf

———— (ed.). 1966. *My Life, A Fragment: An Autobiographical Sketch of Maulana Mohamed Ali* Lahore: Sh. Muhammad Ashraf

————. 1974. *The Life and Times of Mohamed Ali: An Analysis of the Hopes, Fears and Aspirations of Muslim India from 1778–1931* Lahore: Institute of Islamic Culture

Israel, Milton, and Wagle, N.K. (eds). 1983. *Islamic Society and Culture* New Delhi: Manohar

Israel, Milton. 1994. *Communications and Power: Propaganda and the Press in the Indian Nationalist Struggle, 1920–1947* Cambridge: Cambridge University Press

Jacob, Margaret. 1981. *The Radical Enlightenment: Pantheists, Freemasons and Republicans* London: Allen Unwin

Jacobsohn, Gary Jeffrey. 2003. *The Wheel of Law: India's Secularism in Comparative Constitutional Context* Princeton: Princeton University Press

Jaffrelot, Christophe. 2005. *Dr. Ambedkar and Untouchability: Fighting the Indian Caste System* New York: Columbia University Press

Jakobsen, J.R. and A. Pellegrini. 2000. 'World Secularisms at the Millennium', *Social Text*, 64, 18, 3

Jalal, Ayesha. 1985. *The Sole Spokesman: Jinnah, the Muslim League and the Demand for Pakistan* Cambridge: Cambridge University Press

———. 1996. 'Secularists, Subalterns and the Stigma of "Communalism": Partition Historiography Revisited', *IESHR*, 33, 1

———. 1997. 'Exploding Communalism: The Politics of Muslim Identity in South Asia', in S. Bose and A. Jalal (eds). *Nationalism, Democracy and Development: State and Politics in India* New Delhi: Oxford University Press

———. 2000. *Self and Sovereignty: Individual and Community in South Asian Islam since 1850* London: Routledge

Jayaram, N. and Satish Saberwal (eds). 1996. *Social Conflict* New Delhi: Oxford University Press

Johnson, Gordon. 1970. 'Chitpavan Brahmins and Politics in Western India in the Late Nineteenth and Early Twentieth Centuries'. In E. Leach and S.N. Mukherjee (eds). *Elites in South Asia* Cambridge: Cambridge University Press

Jones, Kenneth. 1976. *Arya Dharm: Hindu Consciousness in 19th Century Punjab* Berkeley: University of California Press

——— (ed.). 1992. *Religious Controversy in British India: Dialogues in South Asian Languages* Albany, NY: State University of New York Press

Joshi, Barbara. 1982. *Democracy in Search of Equality: Untouchable Politics and Indian Social Change* Delhi: Hindustan Publishing Co.

Joshi, Chitra 1985. 'Bonds of Community, Ties of Religion: Kanpur Textile Workers in the Early Twentieth Century', *IESHR*, 22, 3

Kakar, Sudhir. 1996. *The Colors of Violence: Cultural Identities, Religion and Conflict* Chicago: University of Chicago Press

Kamble, B.R. (ed.). 1968. *Studies in Shivaji and His Times* Kolhapur: Shivaji University, 1982

Kannangara, A.P. 1968. 'Indian Millowners and Indian Nationalism before 1914', *Past and Present*, 40

Kashyap, Anirban. 1988. *Communalism and Constitution* New Delhi: Lancers

Kaur, Raminder. 2003. *Performative Politics and the Cultures of Hinduism: Public Uses of Religion in Western India* New Delhi: Permanent Black

Kaviraj, Sudipta. 1993. 'The Imaginary Institution of India'. In P. Chatterjee and G. Pandey (eds). *Subaltern Studies VII* New Delhi: Oxford University Press

———. 1994. 'On the Construction of Colonial Power: Structure, Discourse, Hegemony'. In D. Engels and S. Marks (eds). *Contesting Colonial Hegemony: State and Society in Africa and India* London: I.B. Tauris

Keer, Dhananjay. 1971. *Dr. Ambedkar: Life and Mission* Bombay: Popular Prakashan

———. 1976. *Shahu Chhatrapati: A Royal Revolutionary* Bombay: Popular Prakashan

Khare, Ravindra. 1970. *The Changing Brahmans: Associations and Elites among the Kanya-Kubjas of North India* Chicago: University of Chicago Press

———. 1984. *The Untouchable as Himself: Ideology, Identity and Pragmatism Among the Lucknow Chamars* Cambridge: Cambridge University Press

Khilnani, Sunil. 1997. *The Idea of India* London: Hamish Hamilton

Khuhro, Hamida. 1978. *The Making of Modern Sind: British Policy and Social Change in the Nineteenth Century* Karachi: Indus Publications

——— (ed.). 1982. *Documents on Separation of Sind from the Bombay Presidency*, Vols I–II Islamabad: Institute of Islamic History, Culture and Civilization

Kooiman, Dick. 2002. *Communalism and Indian Princely States: Travancore, Baroda and Hyderbad in the 1930s* New Delhi: Manohar

Koss, Stephen. 1969. *John Morley at the India Office, 1905–1910* New Haven, CT: Yale University Press

Krishna, Gopal. 1967–68. 'The Khilafat Movement in India: The First Phase', *Journal of the Royal Asiatic Society*

Krishna Iyer, V.R. 1976. *India's Wobbling Voyage to Secularism* Ahmedabad: Gujarat University

Kshirsagar, R.K. 1994. *Dalit Movement in India and its Leaders, 1857–1956* New Delhi: M.D. Publications

Kulkarnee, N.H. 1979. 'Hindu Religious Reform Movements in Nineteenth and Twentieth Century Maharashtra'. In S.P. Sen (ed.). *Social and Religious Reform Movements in the Nineteenth and Twentieth Centuries* Calcutta: Institute of Historical Studies

Kulkarni, A. 1996. *Marathas and the Maratha Country* New Delhi: Books & Books

Kulkarni, A.R. and N.K. Wagle (eds). 1999. *Region, Nationality and Religion* Mumbai: Popular Prakashan

Kumar, Ravinder. 1968. *Western India in the Nineteenth Century: A Study in the Social History of Maharashtra* London: Routledge & Kegan Paul

———. 1985. 'Gandhi, Ambedkar and the Poona Pact, 1932', *South Asia*, 8

LaCapra, Dominic. 1989. *Soundings in Critical Theory* Ithaca: Cornell University Press

Laidlaw, James. 1995. *Riches and Renunciation: Religion, Economy and Society Among the Jains* Oxford: Clarendon

Lajpat Rai, Lala. 1965. *Autobiographical Writings*, ed. V.C. Joshi. Delhi: University Publishers

———. 1980. *Shivaji: The Great Patriot* New Delhi: Metropolitan

Lambrick, H.T. 1964. *Sind: A General Introduction* Hyderabad: Sindhi Adabi Board

Leadbeater, S.R.B. 1993. *The Politics of Textiles: The Indian Cotton Mill Industry and the Legacy of Swadeshi, 1900–1985* New Delhi: Sage

Lele, Jayant. 1982. *Elite Pluralism and Class Rule: Political Development in Maharashtra* Bombay: Popular Prakashan

Lelyveld, David. 1978. *Aligarh's First Generation: Muslim Solidarity in British India* Princeton: Princeton University Press

Limaye, P.M. 1935. *The History of the Deccan Education Society* Poona: Deccan Educational Society

Lodrick, D.O. 1981. *Sacred Cows, Sacred Places: The Origin and Survival of Animal Homes in India* Berkeley: University of California Press

Lokhande, G.S. 1982. *Bhimrao Ramji Ambedkar: A Study in Social Democracy* New Delhi: Intellectual Pub. House

Low, D.A. 1965–6. 'The Government of India and the First Non-Cooperation Movement—1920–1922', *JAS*, 25, 1

—— (ed.). 1995. *North India: Partition and Independence in South Asia*, special issue, *South Asia*, 18

——. 1997. *Britain and Indian Nationalism: The Imprint of Ambiguity, 1929–1942* Cambridge: Cambridge University Press

Ludden, David (ed.). 1996. *Contesting the Nation: Religion, Community and the Politics of Democracy in India* Philadelphia: University of Pennsylvania Press

Luthera, Ved Prakash. 1964. *The Concept of the Secular State and India* London: Oxford University Press

McCaskie, T.C. 2000. *Asante Identities: History and Modernity in an African Village, 1850–1950* Edinburgh: Edinburgh University Press

McLane, John R. 1977. *Indian Nationalism and the Early Congress* Princeton: Princeton University Press

Madan, T.N. 1987. 'Secularism in its Place', *JAS*, 46, 4

Mahajan, Gurpreet. 1992. *Explanation and Understanding in the Human Sciences* New Delhi: Oxford University Press

—— and D.L. Sheth (eds). 1999. *Minority Identities and the Nation State* New Delhi: Oxford University Press

Mandala, Jagadis Chandra. 1999. *Poona Pact and Depressed Classes* Calcutta: Sujan

Markovits, Claude. 2000. *The Global World of Indian Merchants, 1750–1947: Traders of Sind from Bukhara to Panama* Cambridge: Cambridge University Press

Marshall, P.J. (ed.). 1970. *The British Discovery of Hinduism in the Nineteenth Century* Cambridge: Cambridge University Press

Martin, David. 2005. *On Secularization: Towards a Revised General Theory* Aldershot: Ashgate

Masselos, J.C. 1974. *Towards Nationalism: Group Affiliations and the Politics of Public Associations in Nineteenth Century Western India* Bombay: Popular Prakashan

——. 1978. 'The Khojas of Bombay: The Defining of Formal Membership Criteria During the Nineteenth Century'. In Imtiaz Ahmad (ed.). *Caste and Social Stratification Among Muslims in India* New Delhi: Manohar

——. 1982. 'Change and Custom in the Format of the Bombay

Muharram During the Nineteenth and Twentieth Centuries', *South Asia* N.S., 5, 2

Mehrotra, S.R. 1969. 'The Poona Sarvajanik Sabha: The Early Phase (1870–1880)', *IESHR*, 6, 3

Mehta, Makrand (ed.). 1990. *Regional Roots of Indian Nationalism: Gujarat, Maharashtra, Rajasthan* New Delhi: Criterion

Mehta, Uday Singh. 1999. *Liberalism and Empire: A Study in Nineteenth Century British Liberal Thought* Chicago: University of Chicago Press

Mendus, Susan (ed.). 1988. *Justifying Toleration: Conceptual and Historical Perspectives* Cambridge: Cambridge University Press

Menon, Dilip. 2006. *The Blindness of Insight: Essays on Caste in Modern India* Chennai: Navayana Publications

Menon, V.P. 1957. *The Transfer of Power in India* New Delhi: Orient Longman

Metcalf, Barbara. 1982. *Islamic Revival in British India: Deoband, 1860–1900* Princeton: Princeton University Press

Mills, Sara. 1997. *Discourse* London: Routledge

Minault, Gail. 1982. *The Khilafat Movement: Religious Symbolism and Political Mobilization in India* New York: Columbia University Press

———. 1998. *Secluded Scholars: Women's Education and Muslim Social Reform in Colonial India* New Delhi: Oxford University Press

Mitchell, Timothy. 2000. 'The Stage of Modernity'. In T. Mitchell (ed.). *Questions of Modernity* Minneapolis, MN: University of Minnesota Press

Momin, A.R. 1978. 'Muslim Caste in an Industrial Township of Maharashtra'. In I. Ahmad (ed.). *Caste and Social Stratification Among Muslims in India* Delhi: Manohar

Mondal, Anshuman. 2003. *Nationalism and Post-Colonial Identity: Culture and Ideology in India and Egypt* London: Routledge

Moore, R.J. 1966. *Liberalism and Indian Politics, 1872–1922* London: Edward Arnold

———. 1967. 'The Twilight of the Whigs and the Reform of the Indian Councils, 1886–1892', *Historical Journal*, 10, 4

Mufti, Amir. 2000. 'The Aura of Authenticity', *Social Text*, 64, 18, 3

——— (ed.). 2004. *Critical Secularism* Durham, NC: Duke University Press

Muhammad, Shan. 1979. *Freedom Movement in India—The Role of the Ali Brothers* New Delhi: Associated

Mujeeb, M. 1985. *The Indian Muslims* New Delhi: Munshiram Manoharlal

Nag, Jamuna. 1988. *Social Reform Movements in Nineteenth Century India* Jaipur: RBSA Publications

Nair, Sankaran. 1985. *Swadeshi Movement: The Beginning of Student Unrest in South India* New Delhi: Mittal

Naito, Masao. 1997. 'Anti-Untouchability Ideologies and Movements in Maharashtra from the Late Nineteenth Century to the 1930s'. In H. Kotani (ed.). *Caste System, Untouchability and the Depressed* New Delhi: Manohar

Nanda, B.R. 1989. *Gandhi, Pan-Islamism, Imperialism and Nationalism in India* Bombay: Oxford University Press

Nandy, Ashis. 1983. *The Intimate Enemy: Loss and Recovery of Self Under Colonialism* New Delhi: Oxford University Press

———. 1988. 'The Politics of Secularism and the Recovery of Religious Tolerance', *Alternatives*, XII

———. 2007. 'Closing the Debate on Secularism: A Personal Statement'. In A. Dingwaney Needham and R. Sunder Rajan (eds). *The Crisis of Secularism in India* Durham, NC: Duke University Press

Nath, Trilok. 1987. *Politics of the Depressed Classes* New Delhi: Deputy

Navaro-Yashin, Yael. 2002. *Faces of the State: Secularism and Public Life in Turkey* Princeton: Princeton University Press

Nehru, Jawaharlal. 1946. *The Discovery of India* New York: John Day

———. 1949. *Jawaharlal Nehru's Speeches, Volume One, September 1946–May 1949* Calcutta: no publisher listed

———. 1960. *A Bunch of Old Letters* Bombay: Asia Publishing House

Neimeijier, A.C. 1972. *The Khilafat Movement in India, 1919–1924* The Hague: Nijhoff

Nigam, Aditya. 2000. 'Secularism, Modernity, Nation: Epistemology of the Dalit Critique', *EPW*, 35, 48

———. 2006. *The Insurrection of Little Selves: The Crisis of Secular-Nationalism in India* New Delhi: Oxford University Press

Nugent, Helen M. 1979. 'The Communal Award: the Process of Decision-Making', *South Asia*, N.S. 2

O'Hanlon, Rosalind. 1983. 'Maratha History as Polemic: Low Caste

Ideology and Political Debate in Late Nineteenth-Century Western India', *MAS,* 17, 1

———. 1985. *Caste, Conflict and Ideology, Mahatma Jotirao Phule and Low Caste Protest in Nineteenth Century Western India* Cambridge: Cambridge University Press

———. 1988. 'Acts of Appropriation: Non-Brahman Radicals and the Congress in Early Twentieth-Century Maharashtra'. In M. Shepperdson and C. Simmons (eds). *The Indian National Congress and the Political Economy of India 1885–1985* Aldershot: Avebury

———. 1993. 'Historical Approaches to Communalism: Perspectives from Western India'. In P. Robb (ed.). *Society and Ideology, Essays in South Asian History* New Delhi: Oxford University Press

Oberoi, Harjot. 1995. *The Construction of Religious Boundaries: Cultures, Identity and Diversity in the Sikh Tradition* New Delhi: Oxford University Press

Omvedt, Gail. 1976. *Cultural Revolt in a Colonial Society: The Non Brahman Movement in Western India, 1873–1930* Bombay: Scientific Socialist Education Trust

———. 1994. *Dalits and the Democratic Revolution: Dr. Ambedkar and the Dalit Movement in Colonial India* New Delhi: Sage

Page, David. 1982. *Prelude to Partition: The Indian Muslims and the Imperial System of Control, 1920–1932* New Delhi: Oxford University Press

Pal, Bipin Chandra. 1911. *The Soul of India: A Constructive Study of Indian Thoughts and Ideals* Calcutta: Choudhury & Choudhury

———. 1954. *Swadeshi and Swaraj: The Rise of the New Patriotism* Calcutta: Yugayatri Prakashak

Pandey, Gyanendra. 1982. 'Peasant Revolt and Indian Nationalism: The Peasant Movement in Awadh'. In R. Guha (ed.). *Subaltern Studies I* New Delhi: Oxford University Press

———. 1983. 'Rallying Around the Cow: Sectarian Strife in the Bhojpuri Region, c. 1888–1917'. In R. Guha (ed.). *Subaltern Studies II* New Delhi: Oxford University Press

———. 1992. *The Construction of Communalism in Colonial North India* New Delhi: Oxford University Press

——— (ed.). 1993. *Hindus and Others: The Question of Identity in India Today* New Delhi: Viking

———. 1999. *Memory, History and the Question of Violence: Reflections on the Reconstruction of Partition* Calcutta: K.P. Bagchi & Co.

———. 2001. *Remembering Partition: Violence, Nationalism and History in India* Cambridge: Cambridge University Press

Panhwar, Khan Mohammad (ed.). 1984. *Shaikh Abdul Majeed Sindhi: Life and Achievements* Karachi: Royal Book Co.

Panikkar, K.N. (ed.). 1991. *Communalism in India: History, Politics and Culture* New Delhi: Manohar

———. 1997. *Communal Threat, Secular Challenge* Madras: Earthworm Books

Parekh, Bhikhu. 1989. *Gandhi's Political Philosophy: A Critical Examination* Basingstoke: Macmillan

Parel, Anthony, J. 2006. *Gandhi's Philosophy and the Quest for Harmony* Cambridge: Cambridge University Press

Pati, Biswamoy (ed.). 2000. *Issues in Modern Indian History* Bombay: Popular Prakashan

Patterson, M.L.P. 1970. 'Changing Patterns of Occupations Among Chitpavan Brahmans', *IESHR*, 7, 3

Pirzada, Syed Sharifuddin (ed.). 1969. *Foundations of Pakistan: All-India Muslim League Documents, 1906–1947* Karachi: National Publishing House

Pecora, Vincent P. (ed.). 2001. *Nations and Identities: Classic Readings* Malden, MA: Blackwell

Pirzada, D.A. 1995. *Growth of Muslim Nationalism in Sindh: Parting of the Ways to Pakistan* Karachi: Mehran

Postans, Thomas. 1973 [1843]. *Personal Observations on Sindh* Karachi: Indus

Pradhan, Atul Chandra. 1986. *The Emergence of the Depressed Classes* Bhubaneswar: Bookland International

Prior, Katherine. 1993. 'Making History: The State's Intervention in Urban Religious Disputes in the North-Western Provinces in the Early Nineteenth Century', *MAS*, 27, 1

Qureshi, M. Naeem, 1974. 'The "Ulama" of British India and the Hijrat of 1920', *MAS*, 13, 1

———. 1999. *Pan-Islam in British Indian Politics: A Study of the Khilafat Movement, 1918–1924* Leiden: Brill

Rai, Mridu. 2003. *Hindu Rulers, Muslim Subjects: Islam, Community and the History of Kashmir* London: Hurst

Rajagopal, Indhu. 1985. *The Tyranny of Caste: The Non-Brahman Movement and Political Development in South India* New Delhi: Vikas

Rajappa, Padmini. 1988. 'Provincial Politics and Non-Cooperation in Maharashtra, 1920–22', *Indica*, 25, 2

Ranade, M.G. 1900 [1891]. *The Rise of the Maratha Power* Bombay: Punalekar

Rao, B. Shiva, 1966. *The Framing of India's Constitution, Vols 1–IV: Select Documents, Vol. V: A Study* New Delhi: Indian Institute of Public Administration

Ray, Rajat Kanta. 1974. 'Masses in Politics: The Non-Cooperation Movement in Bengal, 1920–1922', *IESHR*, 11, 4

———. 1981. 'Revolutionaries, Pan-Islamists and Bolsheviks: Maulana Abul Kalam Azad and the Political Underworld in Calcutta, 1905–1925', in M. Hasan (ed.). *Communal and Pan-Islamic Trends in Colonial India* New Delhi: Manohar

———. 1984. *Social Conflict and Political Unrest in Bengal 1875–1927* New Delhi: Oxford University Press

Reisner, I.M and N.M Goldberg (eds). 1966. *Tilak and the Struggle for Indian Freedom* New Delhi: People's Publishing House

Robb, Peter and Avril Powell (eds). 1993. *Society and Ideology: Essays in South Asian History Presented to Professor K.A. Ballhatchet* New Delhi: Oxford University Press

Robinson, Francis. 1993 [1974]. *Separatism Among Indian Muslims: The Politics of the United Provinces Muslims, 1860–1923* New Delhi: Oxford University Press

———. 1999. 'Religious Change and the Self in Muslim South Asia since 1800'. In A. Roy and H. Brasted (eds). *Islam in History and Politics: A South Asian Perspective*, special issue *South Asia*, 22

Rosanvallon, Pierre. 2001. 'Towards a Philosophical History of the Political', in D. Castiglione and I. Hampsher-Monk (eds). *The History of Political Thought in National Context* Cambridge: Cambridge University Press

———. 2006. *Democracy, Past and Future*, ed. Samuel Moyn New York: Columbia University Press

Rothermund, Dietmar. 1968. 'Emancipation or Re-Integration: The Politics of Gopal Krishna Gokhale and Herbert Hope Risley'. In D.A. Low (ed.). *Soundings in Modern South Asian History* Berkeley: University of California Press

Roy, Anuradha. 1995. 'Foreign Tyrants or Foster Brothers? Muslims in the Eyes of the Hindu Nationalists in 19th Century Bengal', *Calcutta Historical Journal*, 17, 1

Roy, Asim. 1999. 'Impact of Islamic Revival and Reform in Colonial Bengal and Bengal Muslim Identity: A Revisit'. In A. Roy and H. Brasted (eds). *Islam in History and Politics: A South Asian Perspective*, special issue *South Asia*, 22

Roy, Beth. 1994. *Some Trouble with Cows: Making Sense of Social Conflict* Berkeley: University of California Press

Rudner, David. 1994. *Caste and Capitalism in Colonial India: The Nattukottai Chettiars* Berkeley: University of California Press

Rudolph Lloyd I. and Susanne H. Rudolph. 1965. 'Barristers and Brahmans in India: Legal Cultures and Social Change', *CSSH*, 8

Sadiq, Mohammad. 1983. *The Turkish Revolution and the Indian Freedom Movement* Delhi: Macmillan

Sanyal, Usha. 1996. *Devotional Islam and Politics in British India: Ahmad Riza Khan Barelwi and his Movement, 1870–1920* Delhi: Oxford University Press

Sarkar, Jadunath. 1978. *House of Shivaji: Studies and Documents on Maratha History* Calcutta: Orient Longman

Sarkar, Sumit. 1973. *The Swadeshi Movement in Bengal: 1903–1908* New Delhi: People's Publishing House

———. 1976. 'The Logic of Gandhian Nationalism: Civil Disobedience and the Gandhi-Irwin Pact, 1930–31', *Indian Historical Review*, 3, 1

———. 1982. *'Popular' Movements and 'Middle Class' Leadership in Late Colonial India: Perspectives and Problems of a 'History from Below'* Calcutta: K.P. Bagchi. Delhi: Macmillan

———. 1983. *Modern India, 1885–1947* Delhi: Macmillan

———. 1994. 'The Anti-Secularist Critique of Hindutva: Problems of a Shared Discursive Space', *Germinal*, 1

———. 1997. *Writing Social History* New Delhi: Oxford University Press

————. 2001. 'Indian Democracy: The Historical Inheritance'. In Atul Kohli (ed.). *The Success of India's Democracy* Cambridge: Cambridge University Press

————. 2005. *Beyond Nationalist Frames: Postmodernism, Hindu Fundamentalism, History* New Delhi: Permanent Black

Sarkar, Tanika. 2001. *Hindu Wife, Hindu Nation: Community, Religion and Cultural Nationalism* New Delhi: Permanent Black

Schaebler, Birgit and Stenberg, Leif (eds). 2004. *Globalization and the Muslim World: Culture, Religion and Modernity* Syracuse: Syracuse University Press

Sen, Amartya. 1996. 'Secularism and its Discontents'. In K. Basu and S. Subrahmanyam (eds). *Unravelling the Nation: Sectarian Conflict in India* New Delhi: Penguin

Sen, Amiya. 1993. *Hindu Revivalism in Bengal, 1872–1905: Some Essays in Interpretation* New Delhi: Oxford University Press

————. 2000. 'Sri Ramakrishna and Middle Class Religion in Late Nineteenth Century Bengal: Exploring Some New Paradigms of Understanding'. In B. Pati, *Issues in Modern Indian History* Bombay: Popular Prakashan

Sen, S.P. (ed.). 1979. *Social and Religious Reform Movements in the Nineteenth and Twentieth Centuries* Calcutta: Institute of Historical Studies

Shaikh, Farzana. 1989. *Community and Consensus in Islam: Muslim Representation in Colonial India, 1860–1947* Cambridge: Cambridge University Press

Shakir, Moin. 1983. *Khilafat to Partition: A Survey of Major Political Trends Among Indian Muslims During 1919–1947* New Delhi: Ajanta

Sharma, T.L. 1987. *Hindu-Muslim Relations in All-India Politics, 1913–1925* Delhi: B.R. Publishing Corp.

Shay, Theodore L. 1956. *The Legacy of the Lokamanya: The Political Philosophy of Bal Gangadhar Tilak* Bombay: Oxford University Press

Shodhan, Amrita. 2001. *A Question of Community: Religious Groups and Colonial Law* Calcutta: Samya

Siddiqi, Asiya. 1995. 'The Business World of Jamsetjee Jejeebhoy'. In

A. Siddiqi (ed.). *Trade and Finance in Colonial India, 1750–1860* New Delhi: Oxford University Press

Singh, Pardaman. 1976. *Lord Minto and Indian Nationalism (1905–1910)* Allahabad: Chugh Publications

Skinner, Quentin. 1989. 'Introduction'. In T. Ball, J. Farr and R.L. Hanson (eds). *Political Innovation and Conceptual Change* Cambridge: Cambridge University Press

———. 2002. *Visions of Politics, Volume I: Regarding Method* Cambridge: Cambridge University Press

Smith, D.E. 1963. *India as a Secular State* Princeton: Princeton University Press

Smith, W.C. 1943. *Modern Islam in India* Lahore: Minerva

Sommerville, John C. 1992. *The Secularization of Early Modern England: From Religious Culture to Religious Faith* New York: Oxford University Press

Soomro, Mohammad Qasim. 1989. *Muslim Politics in Sindh, 1938–1947* Jamshoro: Pakistan Study Centre

Source Material of the History of the Freedom Movement in India, II. 1957. Bombay: Gazeteers Dept, Govt. of Maharashtra

Source Material for a History of the Freedom Movement, Vol. X, The Khilafat Movement, 1920–21. 1982. Bombay: Gazeteers Dept, Govt of Maharashtra

Srinivas, M.N. 1989. *The Cohesive Role of Sanskritization and Other Essays* New Delhi: Oxford University Press

Stokes, Eric. 1959. *The English Utilitarians and India* Oxford: Clarendon Press

Subramanian, Lakshmi. 1987. 'Banias and the British: The Role of Indigenous Credit in the Process of Imperial Expansion in Western India in the Second Half of the Eighteenth Century,' *MAS*, 21, 3

———. 1996. *Indigenous Capital and Imperial Expansion: Bombay, Surat and the West Coast* New Delhi: Oxford University Press

Suthankar, B.R. 1988. *Maharashtra, 1858–1920* Bombay: no publisher listed

Talreja, Kajnayalal M. 1996. *Pseudo-secularism in India* Mumbai: Rashtriya Chetana Prakashan

Thapar, Romila. 1989. 'Imagined Religious Communities? Ancient

History and the Modern Search for a Hindu Identity', *MAS*, 23, 2

Thursby, G.R. 1975. *Hindu-Muslim Relations in British India: A Study of Controversy, Conflict and Communal Movements in Northern India, 1923–1928* Leiden: Brill

Tilak, Bal Gangadhar. 1903. *The Arctic Home in the Vedas: Being Also a New Key to the Interpretation of Many Vedic Texts and Legends* Poona: no publisher listed

———. 1919. *Bal Gangadhar Tilak, His Writings and Speeches* Madras: Ganesh

Timberg, T.A. 1978. *The Marwaris: From Traders to Industrialists* New Delhi: Vikas

Tripathi, Amales. 1967. *The Extremist Challenge: India Between 1890 and 1910* Bombay: Orient Longman

Tripathi Dwijendra, and M.J. Mehta. 1984. 'Class Character of the Gujarati Business Community'. In D. Tripathi (ed.). *Business Communities of India: A Historical Perspective* New Delhi: Manohar

Tripathi, Dwijendra (ed.). 1991. *Business and Politics in India: A Historical Perspective* New Delhi: Manohar

Tucker, Richard. 1970. 'From Dharmashastra to Politics: Aspects of Social Authority in Nineteenth Century Maharashtra', *IESHR*, 7, 3

Tucker, Richard. 1976. 'Hindu Traditionalism and Nationalist Ideologies in Nineteenth-Century Maharashtra,' *MAS*, 10, 3

Tully, James (ed.). 1988. *Meaning and Context: Quentin Skinner and His Critics* Princeton: Princeton University Press

Upadhyaya, Prakash Chandra. 1992. 'The Politics of Indian Secularism', *MAS*, 26, 4

van der Veer, Peter. 1994. *Religious Nationalism. Hindus and Muslims in India* Berkeley: University of California Press

———. 2001. *Imperial Encounters: Religion and Modernity in India and Britain* Princeton: Princeton University Press

———, and Hartmut Lehmann (eds). 1999. *Nation and Religion: Perspectives on Europe and Asia* Princeton: Princeton University Press

Varshney, Ashutosh. 1993. 'Contested Meanings: India's National Identity, Hindu Nationalism and the Politics of Anxiety', *Daedalus*, 122

Verma, H.S. 1990. 'Secularism: Reflections on Meaning, Substance and Contemporary Practice'. In B. Chakrabarty (ed.). *Secularism and Indian Polity* New Delhi: Segment Books

Viswanathan, Gauri. 1989. *Masks of Conquest: Literary Study and British Rule in India* New York: Columbia University Press

———. 1998. *Outside the Fold: Conversion, Modernity and Belief* Princeton: Princeton University Press

Wagle, N.K. (ed.). 1999. *Writers, Editors and Reformers: Social and Political Transformations of Maharashtra, 1830–1930* New Delhi: Manohar

Washbrook, David. 1981. 'Law, State and Agrarian Society in Colonial India', *MAS*, 15, 3

Wasti, Syed Reza. 1964. *Lord Minto and the Indian Nationalist Movement, 1905–1910* Oxford: Clarendon Press

Waterhouse, E. 1959. 'Secularism'. In J. Hastings (ed.). *Encyclopaedia of Religion and Ethics, 11* Edinburgh: T. & T. Clark

White, David. 1995. *Competition and Collaboration: Parsi Merchants and the English East India Company* New Delhi: Munshiram Manoharlal

Wolpert, Stanley. 1962. *Tilak and Gokhale: Revolution and Reform in the Making of Modern India* Berkeley: University of California Press

———. 1967. *Morley and India, 1906–1910* Berkeley: University of California Press

Yaduvansh, U. 1967. 'Decline of the Qazis, 1793–1875', *Indian Journal of Political Science*

Yang, Anand. 1980. 'Sacred Symbol and Social Space', *CSSH*, 22, 4

Yusufi, Allah Bakhsh. 1984. *Maulana Mohamed Ali Jauhar: The Khilafat Movement* Karachi: Mohamedali Educational Society

Zakaria, Rafiq. 1970. *Rise of Muslims in Indian Politics: An Analysis of Developments from 1885–1906* Bombay: Somaiya Publ.

Zavos, John. 2000. *The Emergence of Hindu Nationalism in India* Delhi: Oxford University Press

Zelliot, Eleanor. 1970. 'Learning the Use of Political Means: The Mahars of Maharashtra'. In R. Kothari (ed.). *Caste in Indian Politics* New Delhi: Orient Longman

———. 1992. *From Untouchable to Dalit, Essays on the Ambedkar Movement* New Delhi: Manohar

Doctoral Dissertations

Bajpai, Rochana, 'The Legitimating Vocabulary of Group Rights in Contemporary India', Oxford University, 2003

Deshpande, Prachi, 'Narratives of Pride: History and Regional Identity in Maharashtra c. 1870–1960', Tufts University, 2002

Krishnaswamy, S., 'A Riot in Bombay, August 11, 1893: A Study in Hindu-Muslim Relations in Western India During the Late Nineteenth Century', University of Chicago, 1966.

Lochan, Rajiv, 'The Communal Social Process, with special reference to Maulana Mohamed Ali and Mahatma Gandhi, 1910s and 1920s', Jawaharlal Nehru University, 1987

Mufti, Aamir, 'Enlightenment in the Colony: The Jewish Question and Dilemmas in Postcolonial Modernity', Columbia University, 1997

Shodhan, Amrita, 'Legal Representations of Khojas and Pushtimarga Vaishnava Polities as Communities: The Aga Khan Case and the Maharaj Libel Case in Mid-Nineteenth Century Bombay', University of Chicago, 1995

Index

SHABNUM TEJANI is Lecturer in Modern South Asian History, School of Oriental and African Studies, University of London.

Printed and bound by CPI Group (UK) Ltd, Croydon, CR0 4YY

13/04/2025

14656547-0001